CW00428149

THE ART OF
SUPPRESSION

PLEASURE, PANIC AND PROHIBITION
SINCE 1800

CHRISTOPHER SNOWDON

Published in Great Britain in 2011
by Little Dice

Copyright 2011 © Christopher Snowdon

ISBN 978-0-9562265-3-2

Little Dice
Trinity Farm, Middleton Quernhow
Ripon, North Yorkshire
HG4 5HX
United Kingdom

Cover by Devil's Kitchen Design

Introduction

Prohibition doesn't work, most dinner party companions will agree. In their attempts to suppress popular pleasures, prohibitionists unleash a greater evil than that which they set out to destroy; fueling crime, feeding corruption and filling prisons, but conspicuously failing to prohibit. Few fiascos are more notorious than America's 'Noble Experiment' with alcohol suppression in the 1920s, and if anyone is winning the modern War on Drugs, it is the drug dealers.

And yet the world still brims with prohibitionists, as it always has. The Bible takes fewer than fifty verses to introduce the first prohibition to the Garden of Eden. After a perfunctory description of the creation of the Universe, the creator gets down to business on the second page:

"You are free to eat from any tree in the garden; but you must not eat from the tree of the knowledge of good and evil, for when you eat from it you will certainly die."[1]

If this was the world's first prohibition, it set an appropriate precedent. Eating the apple seems to be a victimless crime created for no other reason than to test the willpower of the two protagonists. No one benefits from the rule and no one will be harmed if it is breached. Here is a ban so arbitrary that it cannot fail to encourage experimentation with the literal forbidden fruit while the consequences of flouting it ("you will certainly die") are exaggerated and ultimately not enforced. The actual punishment falls short of certain death, but remains grossly disproportionate to the severity of the crime: Adam and Eve eat the apple, their eyes are opened, and they are stricken with everlasting hardship and the pains of childbirth. Not for the last time, the consequences of prohibition create more harm than the illegal act.

One rule was enough in the Garden of Eden but as the world's population expanded, a more structured list of bans was required. Only three of the Ten Commandments are still enshrined in law in modern democracies—murder, theft and perjury remain *verboten*, while adultery, blasphemy and coveting one's neighbour's wife and ass are merely frowned upon. But say what you like about the Ten Commandments, at least there were only ten of them. The next few books of the Old Testament offer a long, unfathomable list of bizarre decrees to be enforced under threat of gruesome execution. Most have since been dropped by the various denominations of the Jewish and Christian faiths for being too draconian, homophobic, sexist or plain odd. Biblical laws against wearing clothes of more than one fabric and allowing different breeds of cattle to graze in the same field are only enforced by the most orthodox sects, if at all.

As religion waned, the age of the totalitarian despot provided new ways for whim to become law. The bans and diktats of half-crazed tyrants could fill a fatter book than this but, to take one example, Saparmurat Niyazov, the ruler of Turkmenistan from 1985 until his death in 2006, banned opera, ballet, circuses, smoking in public, lip-synching, video games, recorded music and car radios. In 2004, he prohibited young men from growing their hair and outlawed the wearing of beards. He then banned gold teeth while offering citizens an alternative method of dental hygiene: "I watched young dogs when I was young. They were given bones to gnaw. Those of you whose teeth have fallen out did not gnaw on bones. This is my advice."[2]

President Niyazov was, as you might have guessed, a communist dictator (amongst his other prohibitions was a ban on opposition parties and library books not written by himself), but the belief that one's *bête noire* can be erased at the stroke of a pen remains no less tantalising in liberal democracies today. The allure of the quick ban teases politicians with the prestige that comes with taking 'tough' and 'decisive' action, just as the cudgel of coercion offers greater progress to the single-issue campaigner than the chocolate of persuasion. The phrase *something must be done*—that great clarion call of our times—can usually be translated as *someone who is not me must stop doing the things I do not like*.

The number of illegal activities in the average Western democracy has long since become incalculable, but it is a rare day that passes without fresh prohibitions being demanded by ardent pressure groups and grandstanding politicians. So fashionable have bans become that they are now a matter of national pride. In 2008, for example, Australia's Preventative Health Taskforce urged politicians to outlaw branded cigarette packaging by dangling the carrot of international bragging rights. "If we act quickly," they said, "Australia can overtake the British Government and become the first country in the world to mandate that cigarettes be sold in plain packaging."[3] Or take the case of Edward Burke, the Chicago politician who proposed a ban on trans-fats only to watch in horror as New York got there first. "I'm disappointed we're losing bragging rights to be the first city in the nation to do this," he lamented.[4] (Perhaps he took consolation when Chicago was later ranked number one in *Reason* magazine's list of America's most illiberal cities.)

The pioneers of prohibition have amassed an eclectic mix of world-firsts, including, but by no means limited to, bans on the burqa (Belgium), shale gas extraction (France), chewing gum (Singapore), miniskirts (Tunisia), plastic bags (Italy), smoking in pubs (Ireland), possession of tobacco (Bhutan), video consoles (China), minarets (Switzerland), amalgam fillings (Norway), boxing (Sweden), Dire Straits' 'Money for Nothing' (Canada), incandescent light bulbs (Australia) and *Marmite* (Denmark). Britain's nonappearance on that list is not for want of trying. It has been estimated that Tony Blair's government created an average of twenty-seven new offences every month, a rate of "legislative diarrhoea"[5] that has only been exceeded by his successor Gordon Brown.[6]

Such an orgy of lawmaking is more befitting a new republic emerging from the ashes of anarchy and civil war than a country that has enjoyed prosperity and parliamentary democracy for several centuries. Politicians in the most ban-happy parts of the world can hardly claim to have an underworked police force and yet law is piled upon law with the urgency of a nation teetering on the brink of savagery. Ministers might argue that the public welcomes, nay demands, a continuance of the legislative onslaught, and they might be right. As the philosopher Jamie Whyte ruefully observed: "Despite its manifest failings, prohibiting voluntary transactions remains popular not only with politicians but also with the voting public. If you doubt it, just spend an afternoon listening to talk radio. You will come away feeling fortunate to have any remaining liberties; if the government took the punters' advice, it would 'put a stop' to everything."[7]

An illustration of the man in the street's apparent hunger for prohibitions came in 2010, when Britain's coalition government promised to "clear the statute books of unnecessary laws and scrap excessive legislation".[8] In the spirit of mass repeal, the government invited the public to tell them which laws to cast on the bonfire, but the resulting website was soon flooded with suggestions for still more bans. Amongst a high volume of entries of the hang 'em and flog 'em variety came demands for horses and caravans to be banned from the roads, for the government to "make it illegal to be fat" and for people to be limited to the ownership of "one large or two small dogs." The government was urged to ban bank holidays, online gambling, the killing of all animals, alcohol, tobacco, all firearms, abortion and circumcision. Others were intent on repealing laws that did not actually exist, including some who wanted the "freedom to speak Welsh", the "right to marry at 18" and, as a result of an unfortunate typographical error, "the right to bare arms".

No less telling than the public's misuse of the website was the coalition's treatment of the results. When the responses were counted and it was found that repealing drug prohibition, relaxing the smoking ban and restoring the death penalty were amongst the most popular ideas, the government's experiment in direct democracy was quietly shelved. Some ideas, it seemed, were off-limits.

Just as every action has an equal and opposite reaction, every prohibition has a negative unintended consequence, although these are sometimes so negligible—or limited to such a small segment of the population—as to go unnoticed. The ban on *Scrabble* in Romania, for example, was never likely to give rise to a criminal empire that bore comparison with those of Al Capone and Pablo Escobar. The unintended consequences of banning *Marmite* or trans-fats are clearly not commensurate with the unintended consequences of banning alcohol, abortion or free speech. It is no surprise that laws against impersonating a traffic warden or selling a grey squirrel (both enacted under Blair) are rarely breached. The public desire to do so is clearly limited. Likewise, few people have the means to flout bans on entering the hull of the Titanic or causing a nuclear explosion (ditto).

The laws that are most widely respected are those which are obeyed without thought, for they do no more than underline the beliefs of all decent people. "The law that makes larceny, arson or murder a crime," wrote Fabian Franklin, one of

Prohibition's disgruntled drinkers, "merely registers, and emphasizes, and makes effective through the power of the Government, the dictates of the moral sense of practically all mankind."[9] America's attempt to use manmade laws to defeat the laws of fermentation manifestly did not meet this level of public support, nor do bans on marijuana, gambling or tobacco today, though many would still support them.

When the law stands in direct opposition to a large body of opinion—even though it may be a minority opinion—trouble is inevitable. In non-totalitarian countries, laws require the consent of the people. If a prohibition does not reflect the will of the overwhelming majority, it is doomed to failure, as Franklin explained:

> However desirable it may be that the sudden transformation of an innocent act into a crime by mere governmental edict should carry with it the same degree of respect as is paid to laws against crimes which all normal men hold in abhorrence, it is idle to expect any such thing... A nation which could instantly get itself into the frame of mind necessary for such supine submission would be a nation fit for servitude, not freedom.[10]

It is only when a significant number of people have the inclination and opportunity to break the law that prohibition is seriously tested. The temptation to disobey is never stronger than when the prohibition involves substances which stimulate, intoxicate or otherwise provide interludes from reality. Some call them pleasures, others call them vices, but all the substances discussed in this book could be freely bought and sold at the beginning of the twentieth century. Nearly all of them are derived from plants that have been cultivated for thousands of years. 'Drugs'—in the modern sense of the word, which encompasses stimulants, narcotics, hallucinogens, alcohol and tobacco—have been a part of civilisation for millennia. When viewed through the long lens of human history, they have been under prohibition for barely a heartbeat. This book is about the people who made it so. It is a study of "that singular anomaly, the prohibitionist".[11]

Who are they, these prohibitionists? Are they misguided but ultimately well-intentioned social reformers, or do they suffer from what H. L. Mencken called "the haunting fear that someone, somewhere, may be happy"? Are they what Howard Becker called "moral entrepreneurs"—the architects of panic and the makers of deviants? For Becker, the moral entrepreneur is motivated by "some evil which profoundly disturbs him. He feels that nothing can be right until rules are made to correct it... The crusader is righteous, often self-righteous."[12]

Righteousness is a recurring theme in the pages that follow. At the heart of our story is America's fit of moral indignation at the start of the last century which led to an idealistic crusade against alcohol and opium. The USA's battle against the bottle, the subject of Chapter One, was the ultimate clash between the liberal values of the Founding Fathers and the Protestant morality of the first puritan settlers. The puritans won the battle but lost the war. Prohibition* lasted just under fourteen years and was brought down by the economic crash of 1929 which left the country unable to allow the lucrative drinks industry to remain in the hands of criminals. But before Prohibition collapsed, there was a brief, quixotic campaign to bring about a ban on the sale and manufacture of alcohol throughout the world. This little-known story is documented in the second chapter.

The USA never managed to persuade the rest of the world to ban alcohol, but it succeeded in leading an international campaign against opium which survives to this day. Partly born of the same zeal that spawned the Anti-Saloon League, and partly necessitated by foreign policy considerations, the global

---

* Throughout this book, I will capitalise Prohibition only when referring to the ban on alcohol in the USA between 1920 and 1933.

crusade against narcotics—the subject of Chapter Three—is now in its second century and, though it continues to flounder, is under no imminent threat of serious reform. When the world economy crashed again in 2008, no mainstream politician called for the narcotics industry to be legalised, despite an annual turnover that runs into the hundreds of billions of dollars.

The religious fervour and racist propaganda that started the prohibitionist frenzy of the 1910s have long since fallen out of favour, but the doctrine of prohibitionism remains keenly alive and is endlessly capable of producing unintended and unpredictable consequences, as in the case of Swedish snus—the only tobacco product currently prohibited in the European Union—and the stream of designer drugs that have emerged since the 1990s. These modern prohibitions are documented in Chapters Four and Five. In the closing chapter we will see how prohibitionism survives and thrives today and why, for so many people, utopia is only ever one more ban away.

1

Bone dry forever

Alcohol prohibition in the USA

"The non-drinkers had been organising for fifty years
and the drinkers had no organisation whatever.
They had been too busy drinking."
— George Ade, 1931

It was the night before Christmas Eve when the towering, bearded figure of Dr Diocletian Lewis arrived in the town of Hillsboro, Ohio. Preacher, lecturer, author, teetotaller, nutritionist, campaigner against the girdle and—according to one historian[1]—the inventor of the beanbag, Lewis was one of those enthusiastic all-rounders that the nineteenth century produced in abundance. His claim to be a doctor rested on an honorary degree in homeopathic studies but it was enough to attract patients when he practised medicine without a license in Buffalo, New York. In his forties, he began lecturing about the evils of alcohol and it was this obsession that brought him to Hillsboro's Baptist church on that wintry evening in 1873.

The lecture Dr Lewis delivered was one he had given many times before. Titled 'The Duty of Christian Women in the Cause of Temperance', it revolved around a story from his childhood in which his dear mother pleaded with a saloon-owner to stop selling booze to her alcoholic husband. When he refused, she returned with some friends to pray for his soul and the souls of his wretched customers. The story ended with the barman's heartstrings being pulled so hard that he not only ceased selling liquor, but took the temperance pledge of total abstinence himself.*

Directing his gaze at the women in the congregation, Lewis laid down the gauntlet and boomed: "Ladies, you might do the same thing if you had the same faith." For the God-fearing females of Ohio, this amounted to something between a wager and an incitement. Fifty of them immediately stood upright and resolved to face down Hillsboro's liquor men the very next morning.

The women were as good as their word and Christmas Eve saw a minor miracle in Hillsboro. Calmly and peacefully, the wives and mothers travelled from saloon to druggist and from druggist to grog-shop, holding prayer vigils and singing hymns. All but one of the town's alcohol vendors yielded to the call of temperance and pledged to turn their back on the demon rum.

So began the Women's Crusade which engulfed Ohio and went nationwide in the new year. Armed with no more than prayer and song, tens of thousands of women rallied to the anti-saloon cause in thirty-one states, a mass movement that shut down hundreds of saloons and poured countless gallons of liquor down the gutter. The fire of the Women's Crusade burned brightly through the winter and spring of 1874 but by the summer it had begun to fizzle out. Most of the saloons quietly reopened and if drinkers and bar-owners had ever sincerely repented, it did not take them long to slide back into their old ways. The legacy of the Hillsboro Pentecost lay not in boarded-

---

* Or so some historians have said. By Ernest Cherrington's 1920 account, Lewis told the less inspiring story of his mother failing on both occasions. (Cherrington, *The Evolution of Prohibition in the United States of America*; p. 170)

up dives and overflowing church halls but in the enduring memory of those who had witnessed it.

Amongst those who were inspired was Frances E. Willard, a thirty-five year old professor of aesthetics teaching at Chicago's Northwestern University. A committed Methodist who had twice taken the pledge of total abstinence in her youth, Willard was a fiercely intelligent and well-travelled Renaissance woman. She first read about events in Ohio in the pages of the *Chicago Evening Mail*, which was edited by her brother Oliver, but when the "whirlwind of the Lord" reached Illinois, Willard plunged headlong into the cause. The call of temperance could not have come at a better time for the young academic. On bad terms with the head of her college, she was forced to resign her post in June 1874. Passionate, but in need of a mentor, she travelled to Boston to meet the already legendary Dr Lewis, whom she later remembered as a "kind old gentleman",[2] before taking part in her first saloon vigil in Pittsburgh—her "Crusade baptism".[3]

In November, Willard joined several hundred battle-hardened teetotallers in Cleveland, Ohio for the inaugural national convention of what had become the Woman's Christian Temperance Union (WCTU). Immediately recognised as capable, educated and otherwise unemployed, she was swiftly appointed Corresponding Secretary and became the chief architect of the WCTU's Declaration of Principles, the cornerstones of which were "protection of the home" and "abolition of the liquor traffic."[4] Five years later, Willard became the movement's leader, a position she held until her death. As the WCTU's official history put it: "God's time had come for the deliverance of the pitiful victims of a pitiless liquor traffic."[5]

Ohio had become the cradle of Prohibition.

The liquor question

When the WCTU was formed in 1874, Americans spent over $1 billion a year on alcohol—four times as much as was spent on education. Even staunchly anti-prohibitionist historians have conceded that the rural saloon was "vile and sordid"[6] and that "such local disorder and crime as there was usually began in the saloons".[7] The human costs of American drinking habits in the late nineteenth century can never be fully quantified. Excessive consumption of spirits was well known to damage health, and addiction to alcohol by those who could least afford it undoubtedly led to secondary poverty, malnutrition, crime and violence. But it can be said with equal certainty that the sustained wave of temperance agitation that began in the 1870s and culminated fifty years later with Prohibition was not driven by an epidemic of drinking.

The peak of US alcohol consumption had long since passed. In the 1830s, Americans were drinking an average of 26 litres (seven gallons) of pure alcohol per capita, mostly in the form of spirits. By the time the women of Ohio began their offensive, this total had fallen to less than 8 litres (two gallons), with beer fast becoming the nation's drink of choice. Aside from the dip in the Prohibition-era, per capita alcohol intake has remained between two and three gallons ever since.[8]

These statistics do not tell the whole story. Because drinking was largely confined to white males whose religions allowed them to partake of alcohol, per capita consumption figures understate the quantities imbibed by drinking men, which was considerable by modern standards. Even so, the prevalence of alcohol and alcoholism in this period do not indicate a national crisis. A thorough academic investigation conducted in the 1890s estimated that half of the male population were occasional imbibers and a further quarter were regular, moderate drinkers. "Not more than 5%" were "positively intemperate", which is similar to the percentage considered alcoholics in many Western societies today.*

Nor were American drinking habits more excessive than those of other countries. The enemies of King Alcohol exaggerated many things in the long years leading up to Prohibition, but they never claimed that Americans were thirstier than their neighbours. An 1872 temperance pamphlet entitled *An Adequate Remedy for a National Evil* began as follows:

It is beyond a reasonable doubt that intemperance in the use of intoxicating liquors is pre-eminently the crime, the curse and the shame of the nation. *Not that we are more drunken than some other nations*, or that we as a people have no other vices. But this is the darkest stain upon our *Christian civilization*, and the chief hindrance to our social and financial prosperity. [emphasis added][9]

It was a distinctly Presbyterian interpretation of "Christian civilization", rather than any outbreak of binge-drinking, which thrust the liquor question to the forefront of the American consciousness in the late nineteenth century.

Prohibitionists tracked their lineage back to 1808, when the now forgotten Dr Billy J. Clark formed a total abstinence society in New York, but warnings about alcohol were almost as old as the Republic itself. As far back as 1785, the physician Benjamin Rush published his *Inquiry into the Effects of Ardent Spirits upon the Human Body and Mind, and its Influence upon*

---

* It is currently estimated, for example, that 6% of Englishmen drink at levels that are considered 'harmful'.[10] A further 20% are categorised as 'hazardous' drinkers, although the amount one needs to imbibe to fall into this category has been systematically reduced in recent decades, somewhat arbitrarily. Two glasses of wine a day would have been considered neither "positively intemperate" nor hazardous in the 1890s (except to prohibitionists). The 'harmful drinking' figures quoted above use a more sophisticated method which takes account of patterns of consumption, reasons for drinking, and addiction. As such, they are more likely to identify individuals who would be described as problem drinkers in any era.

the Happiness of Society, a pioneering study of the effects of drunkenness on physical and mental wellbeing. Alongside jaundice, coughing, belching, epilepsy, gout and liver disease, Rush observed "uncommon good humor, and an insipid simpering ... profane swearing ... a disclosure of their own, or other people's secrets ... a rude disposition to tell those persons in company whom they know, their faults ... immodest actions ... fighting; a black eye or a swelled nose ... extravagant acts which indicate a temporary fit of madness."[11]

Such observations remain stingingly true more than two centuries later, and yet Rush was no prohibitionist. Like many temperate men, he recommended the drinking of beer in preference to 'ardent spirits' and did not argue for suppression because even before he was born, prohibition had been shown to fail. The British had banned rum and brandy exports to the territory of Georgia in 1734 after hearing tales of endemic drunkenness reminiscent of the 'gin panic' that was then gripping England. In scenes that would be played out many times across the USA in the 1920s, the ban on spirits in Georgia led to a spate of moonshining, bootlegging and smuggling which only ended when the British repealed the prohibition eight years later.

The rapid decline in alcohol consumption after the 1830s can be partially attributed to the slew of temperance societies which surfaced in the years when the USA was 'the Alcoholic Republic'.[12] The American Temperance Society was formed in Boston, Massachusetts in 1826 and within five years boasted a membership of 170,000. The Society for the Suppression of Intemperance and its logical counterpart the Society for the Promotion of Temperance came into existence shortly afterwards. The Sons of Temperance, boasting a membership of 200,000, was joined by the Daughters of Temperance in the 1840s, and dozens of lesser groups emerged all over the country advocating teetotalism or, at the least, abstinence from spirits.

This first wave of anti-alcohol activity began as a campaign against hard liquor and for true *temperance*—which is to say, *moderation*. Although beer had traditionally been seen as a temperance drink—indeed, virtually a soft drink—it did not take long for temperance to evolve into teetotalism and, by the 1840s, the lure of prohibition had ensnared its more zealous recruits. In the decade that followed, thirteen states banned the sale and manufacture of intoxicating beverages. As in Georgia a century earlier, these laws served to make sneaks of honest men and turn brewers into criminals. Licensed saloons were closed down to make way for unregulated drinking dens and 'blind tigers'.* With prohibition exposed as a failure, twelve of the thirteen states repealed their dry laws and only Maine still had the legislation on its books when national Prohibition began in 1920.

After the failure of statewide prohibition came a lull. The evils of alcohol paled before the evils of slavery and it was slavery that preoccupied American minds in the years leading up to the Civil War (1861-65). When that conflict resulted in emancipation, the liquor question became the nation's most divisive political issue and remained so for the next seventy years.

Why then? Why America? The historian Edward Behr contends that the temperance argument flourished for lack of anything better to squabble about. After slavery was abolished there were, he writes, "no wars, no major social upheavals, no immediate, overwhelming cause around which public opinion might be mobilized in the interests of justice and freedom. The Prohibition issue became America's lasting obsession largely by default."[13]

---

* The term 'blind tiger' was coined to describe illicit drinking dens which exploited the loophole in nineteenth century prohibition laws which permitted complimentary drinks to be served at exhibitions of natural wonders. The 'wonders' being exhibited in such establishments were seldom impressive, as indicated by the later derivation 'blind pig'.

There is some truth in this. Hysteria over a liquid drug that had been ingrained in civilisation since antiquity could only thrive in a period of idle tranquility. But the absence of more pressing problems does not explain how the liquor issue became such a national obsession that the American Constitution had to be rewritten. Clearly, much more was at stake than the right to have a drink. The political waters may have appeared calm on the surface, but Americans on both sides of the Mason-Dixon line harboured a multitude of grievances and fears in the *postbellum* period. Those who saw themselves as custodians of American values felt threatened by mass immigration, racial integration, Catholicism and urbanisation, but so many of these "lasting obsessions" were best left unspoken that it was more prudent to express them through the rhetoric of temperance than to shout them out loud. It is no exaggeration to say that the battle between Wets and Drys between 1874 and 1933, although farcical in many respects, was nothing less than a fight for the soul of the United States. It allowed the simmering tensions between town and countryside, Protestant and Catholic, skilled and unskilled, Anglo-Saxon and immigrant to be expressed as a brawl between drinker and teetotaller. The battle for Prohibition was, as Joseph R. Gusfield argues in *Symbolic Crusade,* a struggle for status in a rapidly changing nation, instigated by those who felt their influence slipping away.

Armed with the response of indignation at their declining social position, the adherents of Temperance sought a symbolic victory through legislation which, even if it failed to regulate drinking, did indicate whose morality was publicly dominant.[14]

What better vessel to carry the fight for the Protestant, rural middle class than the anti-alcohol cause which had a ready-made template from earlier in the century and which targeted so many suspect groups? Who were the biggest drinkers if not the Irish and Italian Catholics? Who made the beer if not German immigrants? Where were the saloons most densely packed if not in the bustling, modern and increasingly Godless towns and cities?

Other countries saw temperance campaigns that emphasised moral suasion and self-reform. In Britain, teetotalism became a genuine working class effort for self-improvement. In other times and places, alcoholics have been treated with pity rather than contempt. There was none of that in the American prohibitionist crusade. To quote Gusfield again:

The coercive reformer reacts to nonconformity with anger and indignation. Sympathy and pity toward the victim have no place in his emotional orientation... In Prohibition and its enforcement, hostility, hatred, and anger toward the enemy were the major feelings which nurtured the movement.[15]

The inherent elitism of American prohibitionists was amply expressed by the WCTU's stated desire "to reform, so far as possible, by religious, ethical and scientific means the drinking classes".[16] The phrase brings to mind Oscar Wilde's quip about work being the curse of the drinking classes, but it also emphasises the top-down nature of the campaign and the distance between the reformers and those who were to be reformed.

Frances Willard described the Women's Crusade as "Home versus Saloon".[17] To the WCTU, the saloon was "the Devil's headquarters on Earth" while the home was "the citadel of patriotism, purity and happiness". For the wives of drinkers, it was the thirst for drink that took the husband out of the home for nights on end, it was the drinks industry that wrenched the hard-earned money from his hand and it was the drink that all too often led to domestic violence. What the ladies of the WCTU seldom acknowledged was that for the great majority of Americans, the saloon was the only alternative to church and home once the working day was over. It is no surprise that the protectors of religious and domestic life saw the saloon as a threat—it was their only rival. Nor is it a surprise that the second wave of temperance activity was ignited by the church-going homemakers of middle America. They gave no quarter to the millions of Americans who had no wives or children, nor could they relate to those for whom a saloon was a more luxurious and gregarious environment than the filthy tenements they called their homes. As one Illinois coal miner told a reporter:

"'Tis mighty easy to preach temperance, but it's the only decent place we fellows have to go. We have a newspaper to read, another fellow to argue with, and we can put our feet on the table and eat all the free lunch we want. We have a blooming fine fiddler who plays for us—say, what's a fellow livin' for—all work?"[18]

Temperance reformers in Britain responded to the squalour of the Victorian pub by creating alternative venues and activities which did not revolve around drinking. They understood that for millions of working men, the pub was the sole alternative to the drudgery of the factory and the boredom of the slum. Their American counterparts, being less familiar with the reality of inner-city life, placed excessive faith in the power of the law to make wretched men wholesome. Whether the battle was pitched as Home *versus* Saloon or Church *versus* Saloon, the prohibitionists could never accept that there were rational reasons for their countrymen to choose the saloon.

Distilling sentiment

Almost no one had a bad word to say about Frances Willard. Her first biographer concluded that "she was perfect; not in her deeds, perhaps, nor in her work, but in her soul."[19] When she died in 1898, 20,000 people visited her casket and the government commissioned a statue of her at a cost of $9,000 (the equivalent of $250,000 today) which still stands in Washington, DC. The *New York Times* recalled that "she possessed that unknown quality often called magnetism" along with a "ready wit, and a great fund of humor."[20] She worked phenomenally hard, averaging one speaking engagement a day in the 1880s, and was a woman of many interests. A progressive at a time when that most fatuous of political labels still had some meaning, Willard was a prohibitionist, a socialist, a scholar, a suffragette and—historians have generally assumed—a sapphist. Within weeks of joining the WCTU, she had added references to the living wage and the eight-hour day into its Declaration of Principles and when she became president in 1879, the organisation adopted the mantra of "'do everything". She called for the nationalisation of the telegraph, rail and telephone networks, votes for women and, later in life, became a great advocate of the bicycle as an "agent of temperance" (she wrote a whole book on the subject).

On the critical issue of prohibition, her slogan was "Agitate, Educate, Legislate". Since women were not able to vote, the WCTU aimed to empty the saloons by other means. Their role was to be a constant presence in community life and be always in the minds of those whom Willard called the nation's "opinion-manufacturers".[21] Wherever respectable people gathered, the ladies of the WCTU would be there with a fistful of literature, a jug of lemonade and an uplifting song. If there was a social event, they would be there. If there was a meeting in the town hall, they would be there. If a lawmaker came to town, they would certainly be there.

The women were playing a long game and they knew it. Willard was under no illusion that Prohibition would arrive overnight or even in her lifetime. As she wrote in her autobiography, the WCTU's mission was to mould minds in preparation for the battle to come.

While their enemy brewed beer, they have brewed public opinion; while he distilled whisky, they distilled sentiment; while he rectified spirits, they rectified the spirit that is in man.[22]

In the cause of distilling sentiment, no move was more inspired than Willard's decision to invite Mary Hanchett Hunt to speak at the WCTU's National Convention in 1879. Hunt was a former school mistress turned educational agitator who had successfully lobbied for what she called 'Scientific Temperance Instruction' to be taught to children in Massachusetts. Like Willard, her vision was to see a whole generation grow up believing that alcohol was a poison which must be banished from society. The voters of tomorrow, said Hunt, "must first be convinced that alcohol and kindred narcotics are by nature outlaws, before they will outlaw them."[23] To achieve this level of indoctrination, Hunt intended to place pressure on schools to teach anti-alcohol propaganda as if it was science.

Roused by Hunt's scheme, the WCTU formed the Department of Scientific Temperance Instruction in 1880 and began harassing teachers, school governors and politicians to the point of exhaustion. As Superintendent of this wing of the WCTU, the hard-nosed Hunt co-ordinated operations in what soon became a national campaign to place the prohibitionist's view of human biology—which placed an inordinate emphasis on the perils of alcohol—on the curriculum.

The WCTU was well suited to the task. Education was one of the few areas of nineteenth century life to be dominated by women. As teachers and mothers, WCTU members were in a position to apply constant pressure on school boards. As letter-writers and petition gatherers, they were able to inundate lawmakers with pleas and demands until, unable to see the problem with a little temperance instruction, the authorities capitulated.

The first scalp was taken in Vermont, which mandated statewide Scientific Temperance Instruction in schools in 1882. Thereafter, Hunt boasted that school boards across the country were under a "state of siege" and over the next two decades every state in America brought in legislation to impose the WCTU's view of drink as an unmitigated evil upon school children.

By the end of the century, Hunt wielded an influence over the nation's education system that was unmatched by any other private citizen. Without a personal endorsement from the former chemistry teacher, publishers found it almost impossible to sell physiology textbooks to schools. Having acquired this effective veto, Hunt began to turn the screw on what could be taught in American classrooms. She stipulated that "temperance should be the chief and not the subordinate topic and should occupy at least one fourth the space in textbooks."[24] Authors were compelled to either rewrite their work to suit the doctrine of total abstinence or be blacklisted by the Department of Scientific Temperance Instruction. Those who complied most cravenly would be lauded as the "greatest living authority" or "foremost scientist"[25] while those who were more deserving of such epithets were ignored or vilified.

The sole aim of Scientific Temperance Instruction (STI) was to frighten children into believing that alcohol was a toxic substance that could never be used in moderation. The medicinal benefits of alcohol were never mentioned, nor was the distinction between use and abuse. Amongst the 'facts' peddled in STI literature was the idea that most beer drinkers died from dropsy, that alcohol was addictive even if consumed in small quantities and that the children of drinkers were guaranteed to be degenerates.

One STI textbook told the story of a boy who "once drank whisky from a flask he had found and died in a few hours."[26] Another insisted that alcohol burns the flesh from the throat leaving it bare and raw. Above all, STI hammered home the message that fermentation turned food into a poison which could never be consumed safely. "This alcohol is poisonous," asserted one textbook. "It is in its nature, even in small quantities, to harm any one who drinks it."[27]

STI was veritable junk science. In 1893, a group of avowedly impartial academics founded the Committee of Fifty to consider the issue of alcohol use in America. It was, in the words of the sociologist Harry G. Levine, "the most comprehensive attempt to study the 'liquor problem' that had ever been tried in the United States" and remained so for decades.[28] After ten years of deliberation, the committee released a mammoth report in 1903 which reserved its harshest criticisms for Mary Hunt's propaganda machine. It described Scientific Temperance Instruction as "neither scientific, nor temperate, nor instructive."[29] The committee found that "much of the methods and substance of so-called scientific temperance instruction in the public schools is unscientific and undesirable."[30] They found that STI textbooks selectively quoted scientists in a way that misrepresented their work and in some instances fabricated quotations in their entirety; animal experiments were misleadingly cited as if they were directly applicable to humans; unsourced anecdotes were used in place of empirical evidence; the medical use of alcohol was deliberately overlooked and moderate consumption was demonised in a way that had no basis in sound science. Damningly, but accurately, the committee concluded that: "The textbooks are written with a deliberate purpose to frighten the children, the younger the better, so thoroughly that they will avoid all contact with alcohol."[31]

It was difficult for the WCTU to argue with this verdict. Hunt had explicitly declared that the objective of STI was to create "trained haters of alcohol to pour a whole Niagara of ballots upon the saloon."[32] But argue they did. The ageing prohibitionist retaliated with an apoplectic, unconvincing and hypocritical rebuttal which accused the Committee of Fifty of grossly misrepresenting the facts and being prejudiced against the doctrine of total abstinence. 100,000 copies of Hunt's response were sent to the nation's 'opinion-manufacturers' in 1904.

Hunt died two years later. Her financial records revealed that she had been receiving bribes from publishers and had been quietly siphoning royalties into a charity she had set up—a charity which also happened to have paid the mortgage on her palatial house in Boston. The WCTU covered their embarrassment by renaming Hunt's department the Scientific Temperance Federation and maintained its stranglehold on physiology textbooks until Prohibition collapsed in 1933. By that time, almost every American under the age of fifty had grown up being taught that alcohol transformed the heart into fat and turned blood into water.

Partisan politics

The seeds planted by Mary Hunt and Frances Willard took many years to bear fruit. Beneath the surface, minds were being moulded in the classrooms and town halls of America. Above the surface, however, the 1880s were a period of consolidation that was easily mistaken for stasis. Temperance crusaders had few tangible victories to celebrate during Willard's twenty year tenure as WCTU president and prohibitionists would later look back on this era as "the long, gray years of preparation."[33]

Those who were eligible to vote had, since 1869, been able to cast their ballot for the Prohibition Party. The party had been founded by a group of Methodists who had become disillusioned with Republicans who, like the Democrats, refused to commit themselves to prohibition. Thus began the Prohibition Party's unsteady lurch towards becoming a third force in American politics. The party fared better in every presidential election before peaking with over a quarter of a million votes in 1892, but its share of the national vote never exceeded 2.3%[34] and it was not pivotal to the success of the cause whose name it bore. The candidate in the 1900 election, John G. Woolley, later lamented that his party "had the principles, the passion, the courage, the endurance. But it could not get the votes."[35]

Like all single-issue parties, the Prohibition Party suffered from two problems. Firstly, only a fraction of those who supported its flagship policy were sufficiently obsessive to vote for its candidate in national elections. Secondly, having pictured themselves wielding supreme executive power, the party's leaders could not resist compiling a list of other policies to reform their country. The platform of the Prohibition Party thus became a curious amalgamation of the progressive left (women's suffrage, income tax, state education) with the religious right (Sabbatarianism, "free use of the Bible in schools").[36] Most of the former became law in the twentieth century while most of the latter fell out of favour. As a package, it was too daring and incoherent for middle America in the 1880s, but for a Christian Socialist like Frances Willard it was nectar and, in 1884, she officially aligned the WCTU with the Prohibition Party.

Willard's dalliance with partisan politics—she also flirted with the misleadingly named Populist Party—was a source of dismay for WCTU members who were already uncomfortable with their leader's socialist tendencies. Teetotal Republicans were not prepared to desert the party of Abraham Lincoln for a minority faction whose electoral prospects were negligible at best. In 1889, disaffected members walked out of the WCTU national convention and formed the Non-Partisan WCTU. An exasperated Willard asked how they expected America to go dry without a prohibitionist in the White House, but the rebels were more alive to reality. A vote for the Prohibition Party was almost always a wasted vote, and dry politicians, whether Republican or Democrat, were inevitably the losers.

The factionalism and infighting worsened in the 1890s. Both the Prohibition Party and the WCTU were divided over whether to fight for 'local option' laws, which allowed communities to go dry by referendum, or go all-out for the ultimate prize of national suppression. Eager prohibitionists who saw a national solution as both essential and feasible agreed with the founder of the Prohibition Party when he dismissed local option as "local nonsense".[37] On this issue, however, Willard was the pragmatist. She saw local option as the most viable approach to the liquor question in the short-term. A patchwork of dry regions across the country was surely preferable to a long wait in a wet land, but even as she displayed flexibility on this issue, Willard added pet projects such as anti-vivisection and prison reform to the WCTU's increasingly unwieldy agenda.

In an interview with the *New York Times* in 1896—two years before her death—Willard was optimistic about prohibition, but did not anticipate that she would live to see it.

"There is an entirely different atmosphere [these days]. We live in an impressionist age, and we judge by the atmosphere. It is more highly charged by prohibition ozone that it was years ago."

When asked what the final outcome would be, her language became still more flowery.

"Total prohibition salted down with salt sea waves. Not sad sea waves, for they will be joyful."

And when asked when these happy sea waves would arrive, she replied:

"Certainly in fifty years; perhaps in half that time, we move so rapidly."[38]

Willard's most optimistic scenario turned out to be correct—Prohibition was enacted 24 years later—but to say things were moving "rapidly" in 1896 was an excessively generous assessment of the WCTU in its third decade of glacial progress. 'Scientific Temperance' was doing a fine job of persuading the public that the crusade against drink was driven by health concerns rather than the religious beliefs of its overwhelmingly Baptist and Methodist adherents, but the prohibitionists were in the middle of a long fallow period which would outlive its sainted president. Not a single state went dry between 1890 and 1906, and many states voted to stay wet. No amount of "prohibition ozone" could disguise the fact that a national ban on alcohol remained a distant dream.

Eloquent and inspiring though she undoubtedly was, Frances Willard was part of the problem. Her "do everything" approach was the very opposite of what was required if the prohibitionists were to make any headway. Although the idea of Prohibition appealed to millions of Americans, not all of them supported votes for women, let alone the nationalisation of the theatres. Many of them, especially in the South, had yet to come to terms with the abolition of slavery. It was asking a lot for them to warm to someone like Willard, whose own supporters accused of "teaching Socialism and Anarchism".[39] For Prohibition to become a reality, it would take more than a few hundred thousand disenfranchised women in rural America trying to persuade their menfolk to vote for a party that had no chance of taking office. Rather than doing everything and achieving nothing, the temperance cause needed to please everybody except the drinkers. In short, it needed that staple of twentieth century politics: the single issue pressure group.

The Anti-Saloon League

On May 24 1893, a handful of professors, preachers and tradesmen gathered in the library of Oberlin College to discuss how best to turn Ohio dry. Foremost amongst them was the Reverend Howard Hyde Russell, a former lawyer who had undergone a religious conversion ten years earlier, at the age of twenty-eight, and attended seminary at Oberlin College. Now a Congregationalist pastor, Russell had spent several years lobbying for local option with veterans of the Women's Crusade and had witnessed the splintering of the WCTU with mounting dismay.

Russell needed no reminding that decades of temperance agitation had produced few solid gains. Of the eighteen states that had banned the sale of alcohol in the nineteenth century, twelve had repealed their prohibitions by 1893. Three of these would repeal in the next decade, leaving just Maine, Kansas and North Dakota, where enforcement was so half-hearted that they remained wet states in all but name.

The electoral fortunes of the Prohibition Party were only one notch above pitiful and it was inconceivable that they would ever send a man to the White House. The WCTU, meanwhile, was led by a controversial suffragette with eclectic political views who had divided her supporters by cosying up to the Prohibition Party. The remnants of the other anti-alcohol groups, such as the American Temperance Society, were more proficient as pamphleteers than lobbyists. Russell understood all this and, though a Republican himself, aimed to avoid the squabbles of the past by creating a temperance group that would remain strictly neutral in matters of politics and strictly pragmatic in matters of prohibition.

The result was the Anti-Saloon League whose charter explicitly set out its strategy:

The object of the League is the extermination of the beverage liquor traffic, for the accomplishing of which the alliance of all who are in harmony with this object are invited. The League pledges itself to avoid affiliation with any political party as such and to maintain an attitude of strict neutrality on all questions of public policy not directly and immediately concerned with the traffic in strong drink.[40]

Even the League's name seem designed to pacify moderate sentiment. As K. Austin Kerr noted, "it was the Anti-*Saloon* League, not the Anti-Liquor or Anti-Beer League".[41] Respectable people who took a glass of wine with their dinner could convince themselves—wrongly, as it transpired—that they had nothing to fear from a group that set its sights on the squalid saloon. The subtle deceit embedded in the Anti-Saloon League's name may or may not have crossed its founders' minds as they discussed their tactics in that college library. Perhaps it was subconscious, but the emphasis on the drinking venue, rather than the drink, reflected the true nature of the Home *versus* Saloon campaign. Russell and his colleagues were teetotallers to a man but, like the torch-bearers of the Women's Crusade, they saw the 'dives' and 'joints' as the real threat to the home, the Church and to progress itself. The aim was always Prohibition, to be sure, but the aim of Prohibition was to destroy what Russell called the "drunkard-making, heart-breaking, home-blasting, soul-damning, hell-crowding saloon."[42] They knew that legislation alone could never force every citizen into a life of total abstinence, but by destroying the "liquor traffic" and, therefore, the saloon, they believed Prohibition would lay waste to the least acceptable face of drinking in America.

Temperance folk believed that drinking was a remnant of a savage past that would wither and die in the coming age of science and education. As Andrew Sinclair says in *The Era of Excess,* the Drys' unshakeable belief in the righteousness of their cause led them to look upon drinkers as reactionaries whose "selfish imbibing was a last protest against progress".[43] Darwinian ideas appeared to support them. Willard explicitly applied the 'survival of the fittest' maxim to the war on drink in her later years, saying: "The fittest *has* survived. Food holds its place as a necessity; intoxicating drinks are losing theirs."[44]

Prohibitionists believed they were giving history a helping hand by attacking the liquor trade, but they also knew that prohibitory laws could never work without the support of the public. "The truth is," said Russell, "a strong public sentiment against the drink habit and traffic is the main thing. Without public demand no law can be passed, and it is worthless when it is passed."[45] Russell never questioned the role of education in bringing about "public demand". Imbued with the confidence that comes from absolute certainty in one's beliefs, he had no doubt that if the perils of alcohol were explained patiently, no rational man would drink again. The essence of the problem, therefore, was that the public were ignorant.

For this reason, Russell aimed to make the Anti-Saloon League a "public opinion building society."[46] By 1903, the League had over 100,000 donors, including the world's richest man, John D. Rockefeller, who pledged to add 10% to whatever was raised by other means. Most of this money was spent on paper and ink as the League pumped out a torrent of newspapers and books to make sure that those who had been indoctrinated with Scientific Temperance Instruction as children could be bombarded with the same pseudo-science in adulthood.

Its flagship newspaper, the *American Issue,* was launched in 1896 and was personally edited by Russell before he passed the torch on to his trusted lieutenant Ernest Cherrington. Twenty years younger than Russell, Cherrington was a devout Methodist who would go on to manage an empire of temperance literature on behalf of the League. An admirer of Mary Hunt, he would later remark that Prohibition would have been "practically impossible" without the enduring influence of her textbooks.

The sole institution with which the League wished to be aligned was the Protestant Church, and much energy was expended on ensuring that the feeling was mutual. "The church bodies," Cherrington later recalled, "held in their hands the destiny of the Anti-Saloon League."[47] In their efforts to make their cause synonymous with Protestant Christianity, League officials held monthly temperance meetings and annual 'Anti-Saloon Sundays' in churches up and down the country and, by the turn of the century, after "many years of difficult and persistent endeavour",[48] the alliance was secured. Pitching itself as 'The Church in Action Against the Saloon', the Anti-Saloon League drew on the support, donations and votes of millions of God-fearing Americans until it became a pressure group of such power that it was able to hold the President of the United States to ransom.

The Anti-Saloon League's affiliation with the Church was never likely to alienate its natural supporters, but its political strategy was more controversial. Having resolved to work only within the realm of the possible, the League at first seemed content fighting for reduced opening hours, fewer saloons and tighter licensing laws. Its policy was, as Cherrington said, "to go only so far and so fast in legislative efforts as the public sentiment of the state would justify."[49]

Hard-liners from the WCTU and Prohibition Party mistook this pragmatism for a lack of ambition. WCTU members were known to refer to Russell's organisation as the Into-Saloon League, and some of the more paranoid teetotallers even accused them of having been corrupted by the drinks industry. In their fervour, they viewed local option as a half measure and they believed that to regulate the saloon was to acknowledge its legitimacy.

The Anti-Saloon League, however, was happy to support any legislation that would dampen the appeal of drinking, whether it was Sunday closing, banning women from bars or prohibiting musical entertainment. Above all, they were firm believers in the right of local communities to decide whether liquor should be sold in their jurisdiction and they remained so until the very moment when they called for national Prohibition, at which point they firmly believed the exact opposite.

In its political dealings, the Anti-Saloon League displayed an almost sociopathic lack of sentimentality. For over thirty years, it bullied, browbeat and harassed politicians with a mercilessness that betrayed not a hint of affection for traditional party lines. The League promised to hold political candidates "to account" for their stance on the liquor question. In practice, this meant that any politician who displayed wet sympathies could expect a flashmob of monomaniacs to aggressively campaign for his opponent.

The League was indifferent to whether a politician abstained from drink in private so long as he could do a passable impersonation of a teetotaller in public or, failing that, would support prohibitionist legislation in government. Never fielding its own candidates, the League preferred to intervene in tightly fought elections which could be swung by a well-marshalled minority of dry voters. The first victim of this approach was Ohio's Senator Locke who was brought down by a co-ordinated dry attack in 1894. Over the next ten years, the Anti-Saloon League deposed more than 70 wet politicians in a flurry of rallies and a blizzard of pamphlets all over the country. Those who survived learnt to allow local option referendums and to campaign for the Drys when they did. The League's approach soon paid dividends. In 1902 alone, 93 municipalities in Ohio voted dry. Statewide prohibitions still eluded them, but towns and villages began to fall to the water-drinkers.[50]

The undisputed master of pressure politics was Wayne Bidwell Wheeler. A wily opportunist with a gift for persuasion, Wheeler nurtured a lifelong hatred of alcohol as a result of a pitchfork injury suffered at the hands of a careless drunk in his childhood. Wheeler was a twenty-three year old student at Oberlin College when the Anti-Saloon League was formed. Spotting an opportunity to pursue his twin ambitions of prohibition and power, he joined up and became one of the League's first full-time employees.

When Russell required a lawyer, Wheeler spent four years in law school to become the League's enforcer. Thereafter, this small, bespectacled and prematurely balding young man prosecuted over 2,000 violations of dry legislation, but it was as a lobbyist and rabble-rouser that Wheeler truly shone. H. L. Mencken memorably said of the man: "He was born with a roaring voice, and it had the trick of inflaming half-wits."[51] Wheeler is credited with inventing the term *pressure group*, and no one was more skillful or less scrupulous in applying pressure to wavering politicians. With Wheeler pulling the strings, the League's tactics of persuasion evolved into outright intimidation.

In 1905, Wheeler directed his considerable energy towards taking the scalp of the state's Governor, Myron T. Herrick. Herrick was a successful and popular Republican politician with a majority of 113,000 and ample campaign funds. His only mistake was to have trampled on a local option bill proposed by the Anti-Saloon League.

The League had taken on wet Governors in Nebraska and Arkansas before but, whilst they had seen their majorities greatly reduced, both politicians had survived. This time, the hyperactive Wheeler held hundreds of dry rallies in favour of his opponent—the Democrats had sensibly nominated a bone-dry candidate—and scurrilously accused Herrick of being in the pocket of the drinks industry. By now, Wheeler was one of more than thirty full-time League officials working in Ohio and the organisation could boast a membership in excess of 100,000. With consummate skill, Wheeler directed tens of thousands of floating voters from the church pews to the polling station and the unfortunate Governor was overwhelmed. Herrick lost the election and spent much of the rest of his political career in France where the fire of temperance barely flickered.

Herrick's defeat did not result in statewide prohibition for Ohio—that did not arrive until 1918—but it was a bleak warning to wet politicians that it was safest to drink in private and support prohibition in public. As a result of the Anti-Saloon League's tactics, attitudes towards alcohol in American public life would be characterised by rank hypocrisy for years to come. Politicians knew that they could placate their tormentors by supporting dry laws, but they also knew that they could placate drinkers by failing to enforce them. This unprincipled, if practical, fudging culminated in the disastrous farce of wet politicians lining up to vote for national Prohibition. If this was moral cowardice, it was Wayne Wheeler who made them cower. There was no shortage of mendacity and insincerity in American public life at the turn of the century, but Wheeler's mastery of the political dark arts guaranteed that they would define the politics of alcohol.

The brewers droop

If, as the Committee of Fifty believed, three quarters of American men were occasional or regular drinkers, and a further 5% were "positively intemperate", it was easy to surmise that only 20% of the male population were total abstainers. The proportion of non-drinking women was much higher but they could not vote and it should not have been beyond the wit of the drinks industry to rally at least some portion of the drinking majority to the ballot booth. From the outset, however, the liquor trade's response to the threat of Prohibition was so monumentally ineffective as to border on self-sabotage.

What the Anti-Saloon League routinely described as the 'liquor trust' never existed. Although the drinks industry was often portrayed as a highly organised and fiendishly clever puppet-master, this was a temperance fantasy. It could never have been a 'trust' (ie. monopoly) because it was made up of two rival industries—the brewers and the distillers—each of whom bitterly resented the other. Far from conspiring in smoke-filled rooms, the beer-makers and the spirits men eyed each other with an enmity befitting two competitors who had long fought over the same customers. Hamstrung as a lobbying force by mutual antipathy, the putative 'liquor trust' displayed a hopeless inability to unite against the common foe.

Of the two industries, the brewers were in the ascendancy. After the 1830s peak in alcohol consumption, beer drinking flourished at the expense of whisky. The invention of the refrigerator and the influx of immigrants from Germany and Eastern Europe both aided the rise of lager. The brewers themselves were predominantly German immigrants and they were the first to defend themselves at a political level. The United States Brewers Association was formed in 1862 as a response to a beer tax that was levied to pay for the Civil War. Tellingly, they had not bothered to form a trade organisation when the first wave of prohibition swept through New England in the previous decade. They were, however, ahead of the distillers, who took another 24 years to form the National Protective League (1886) and another seven before they created the National Liquor League.

In a rare show of unity, the two competitors worked together in 1882 to form the Personal Liberty League. Recognising that the issue was, at heart, one of constitutional freedom and individual rights, the organisation had some success in putting forward the alcohol industry's strongest arguments against prohibition—that it was un-American, that it had been shown not to work and that it eliminated an important source of tax revenue. But both industries were preoccupied with fighting federal tax rises and did not take either the WCTU or the Anti-Saloon League sufficiently seriously in the years when public opinion was being fomented. The Washington-based Personal Liberty League spent much time lobbying politicians on Capitol Hill, but was poorly placed to fight the countless local battles being waged by Drys up and down the country.

The beer-makers were secretly content to see a war being waged against strong liquor. Ardent spirits had been the traditional target of temperance campaigns in the past and the brewers did not anticipate their own products being banned in the future. Had they wished to rid themselves of this delusion, the brewers need only have read one of the millions of pages of prohibitionist literature flying off the presses in Ohio. Instead, they attempted to portray lager as a nutritious temperance drink while tacitly supporting the war against whisky and rum. The distillers naturally resented this cynical attempt to harness temperance sentiment for the brewer's own gain and the

Personal Liberty League fell apart in a blizzard of squabbling and recriminations.

Meanwhile, the Anti-Saloon League convinced itself—and many others—that it was fighting a war against a cartel of infinite cunning, without which Americans would not only abstain from drink, but would not even *want* to drink. It was a commonplace belief amongst temperance crusaders that they, and they alone, represented the true will of the people. Since the true will of the people was to be permanently sober, drinkers must be the unwitting victims of a drug-pushing industry whose nefarious activities would make Lucifer weep.

Seeking to explain the failure of temperance prior to the Anti-Saloon League's ascendancy, Ernest Cherrington wrote:

In short, the saloon controlled politics. It dictated political appointments. It selected the officers who were to regulate and control its operations. It had its hand on the throat of legitimate business. It defiantly vaunted itself in the face of the church. It ridiculed morality and temperance. It reigned supreme.[52]

This is sheer psychosis. There was plenty of corruption and bribery in every walk of life in nineteenth century America and the saloon business was no different (Cherrington failed to mention that the corruption invariably got worse when prohibition was enacted). The 'liquor trust' had no more political influence than any other American industry of its size. Considering the income the government received from alcohol taxes—which amounted to around a third of all federal revenue —the drinks trade was arguably *under*-represented. And far from 'reigning supreme', the drinks industry was a blundering, bickering mess which effectively gave the Anti-Saloon League a fifteen year head-start.

But however fictitious it was in practice, the spectre of a powerful drinks industry provided a suitable foil for prohibitionists, who proved to be far more effective in disseminating propaganda and subverting democracy than the drinks trade. Having demonised the industry, the Anti-Saloon

League was able to blame every setback on their enemies while attributing every victory to the good sense of the common man. Anyone who spoke out against the Anti-Saloon League must therefore be aligned with—and in the pay of—the brewers and distillers. This tactic of casting aspersions on the motives of their critics did not go unnoticed by contemporaries, as Fabian Franklin recalled in the 1920s:

> Throughout the entire agitation, it was the invariable habit of Prohibition advocates to stigmatize the anti-Prohibition forces as representing nothing but the "liquor interests." The fight was presented in the light of a struggle between those who wished to coin money out of the degradation of their fellow-creatures and those who sought to save mankind from perdition.
>
> That the millions of people who enjoyed drinking, to whom it was a cherished source of refreshment, recuperation, and sociability, had any stake in the matter, the agitators never for a moment acknowledged; if a man stood out against Prohibition he was not the champion of the millions who *enjoyed* drink, but the servant of the interests who *sold* drink.[53]

In truth, the major obstacle the Anti-Saloon League faced in its early years was not the drinks industry but the 'more-prohibitionist-than-thou' temperance groups that Howard Russell had formed the League to get away from. The spats with these *über*-zealots rumbled on, but as the League's strategy proved successful at the start of the new century, the various factions began to put aside their differences.

The WCTU had never been fond of the male dominated Anti-Saloon League, but relations became less frosty after Frances Willard's death from influenza in 1898. Having disentangled themselves from the Prohibition Party, the non-partisan WCTU returned to the fold, but the organisation's influence waned as its ageing members became fixated with the memory of their fallen leader. While the WCTU continued to campaign for a string of causes, including the newly formed Anti-Cigarette League that was formed a year after Willard's death, their greatest president cast a shadow that none of her successors were fully able to step out of.

The Anti-Saloon League, however, remained doggedly single-minded. Since haters of the bottle were at logger-heads on the other big political issues of the day, this was wise. Women's suffrage, socialism and racial integration, to name but three, had the potential to tear the movement apart. Whilst it might have seemed self-evident to progressives like Willard that prohibitionists should support the suffragettes—since it was assumed that if women got the vote, they would vote against the bottle—this view was by no means universal. The Anti-Saloon League had no more desire to poke this hornet's nest than they had to tackle the still more divisive issue of race.

There is no doubt that many prohibitionists felt that the Civil War had been won by the wrong side, nor can it be denied that when the Deep South states adopted prohibition, they did so, in part, to prevent black people drinking. With characteristic opportunism, the Anti-Saloon League was content to allow its speakers to exploit sentiment about blacks in whatever way was most expedient. To a progressive audience, the Drys argued that Prohibition would reduce the number of drunken lynchings. To a less enlightened audience, they warned of the dangers of "nigger gin" and told grim stories of drunken blacks raping white women.

None of this could be considered official policy since the League had no policy but Prohibition. It welcomed both trade unionists and industrialists, feminists and chauvinists, the Ku Klux Klan and abolitionists, liberals and conservatives—so long as they could keep their other passions to themselves when speaking on behalf of the League. Itching to impose their will on others, many prohibitionists privately yearned for a raft of laws to remake America in their own image, but these were best kept quiet if moderate voters were to be won over. Occasionally the mask would slip. For example, Herman Trent of the New Jersey Anti-Saloon League wrote a letter on the eve of Prohibition which he prefaced with the disclaimer that he was "speaking now in my personal capacity, and not as a member of the Anti-Saloon League". It read, in part:

I regard the anti-liquor crusade as merely the beginning of a much larger movement... If I had my way I would not only close up the saloons and the race-tracks. I would close all tobacco shops, confectionary stores, delicatessen shops, and other places where gastronomic deviltries are purveyed—all low theatres and bathing beaches.

Getting into his stride, he continued:

I would forbid the selling of gambling devices such as playing cards, dice, checkers and chess sets; I would forbid the holding of socialistic, anarchistic and atheistic meetings; I would abolish the sale of tea and coffee, and I would forbid the making or sale of pastry, pie, cake and such like trash.[54]

We cannot know how many League members Mr Trent spoke for when he wrote these words. Certainly, the drinks industry was correct when it warned that Prohibition was a slippery slope down which tobacco, coffee and free speech would slide if left unchecked. But, for the Anti-Saloon League, there would be plenty of time for the Anti-Cigarette League, the Anti-Profanity League and the Anti-Immigration League to blossom once drink was defeated. In the meantime, the Herman Trents were mostly kept on message while the League rolled on.

Christ's bulldog

One crusader who was never afraid to speak her mind was the hatchet-wielding vigilante whose destructive exploits in the saloons of America provided a dramatic interlude in the story of Prohibition and whose behaviour seemed to confirm every negative stereotype of the temperance obsessive.

Born in Kentucky in 1846, Carry Amelia Moore spent her teenage years moving from place to place as her family attempted to avoid the ravages of the Civil War. At the age of twenty, she settled in Holden, Missouri where she met and married Dr David Gloyd, a notorious alcoholic who was dead within two years. In 1877, she married the more wholesome David Nation, a timid lawyer and Methodist minister who was almost twenty years her senior. This marriage of convenience gave David a homemaker and provided Carry with financial security. Above all, it gave Carry A. Nation a striking name that she viewed as a sign of providence.

Nation's second marriage was no happier than her first. She would later attribute her "combative nature" to her squabbles with him. Together, they embarked on an ill-fated attempt to run a cotton plantation in Texas before moving to the town of Medicine Lodge, Kansas in 1889. There, Nation divided her time between her work as an osteopath, jail evangelist and president of the local WCTU.

Kansas had been officially dry since 1880, but even the most God-fearing communities rarely enforced prohibition with any vigour and there were enough reports of illicit drinking in the state for the *New York Times* to send a reporter to investigate in 1891. Although the journalist concluded that prohibition was "reasonably enforced", his report provides an insight into what reasonable enforcement meant in practice. Four cities had saloons operating with the thinnest of veneers as legitimate businesses, with the front room acting as a shop and the back-room as a drinking den. In Wichita, sixty saloons operated with the full knowledge of the authorities who imposed regular fines upon them as a *de facto* business tax. Numerous other 'joints' and 'houses of bad character' existed for those who knew where to look.[55]

Carry Nation knew exactly where to look. If the smell of drink did not give the 'dives' away, the stream of men heading in and out could not fail to. At first, she prayed and sang in the illicit liquor joints of Medicine Lodge, just as Diocletian Lewis would have wanted, but when this failed to yield results she took a more forthright approach.

On the morning of June 6 1900, Nation awoke hearing the voice of Jesus telling her: "Go to Kiowa and I'll stand by you."[56] "I understood," she later recalled, "that it was God's will for me to go to Kiowa to break, or smash the saloons."[57] After wrapping several bricks in newspaper, she climbed into her buggy and made the twenty mile trip south to the town of Kiowa. She spent the night at a friend's house before rising early the next morning and destroying the mirrors and bottles in three "dens of vice". She then stood up in her buggy and shouted, rather incongruously, "Peace on Earth, good will to all men!"

At the age of 54, Carry A. Nation had finally found her calling in life and it lay in fanatical violence against liquor and all those who drank it. Little more was heard from her for the next six months and the attack on Kiowa was widely viewed as a one-off protest from an eccentric grandmother, but two days after Christmas, she set off for the ostensibly dry, but in reality saturated, city of Wichita. Recognising that a brick could only be used once, she bound a rod of iron to the end of a cane and set about the luxurious Carey Hotel, throwing rocks at a picture of a naked woman that hung behind the bar and using her new weapon to smash more mirrors and bottles. After doing likewise in a bar across the street, she was clapped in irons and taken to jail where she spent the first of twenty-two periods of incarceration in her new career as a saloon smasher.*

The new year saw more destruction and greater notoriety. Returning to Wichita on 21 January, Nation announced herself by raising her fist in the air and yelling: "Men of Wichita, this is the right arm of God and I am destined to wreck every saloon in your city!"[58] Accompanied by three women from the WCTU, she set to work on two "murder shops" with rocks, iron rods and

---

* Her obituary in the *New York Times* said she was jailed twenty-two times. Her most sympathetic biographer Fran Grace put the figure at "over thirty".

hatchets, only stopping when the owner of the second saloon put a revolver to her head. She then ran into the Carey Hotel (again) and attacked a waiting policeman with a poker before being overpowered and returned to jail.

Showing considerable leniency, the chief of police released the teetotal delinquent on bail on the condition that she smash no more saloons until noon the following day. Nation's first act as a free woman was to stand on the steps of the police station and inform the waiting crowd that she would recommence her reign of terror as soon as the clock struck twelve. In the event, she could not control herself for even that long. A few hours later, she caused a sensation by "slapping Sheriff Simmons in the face, taking hold of his ears, and giving him a rough handling generally."[59]

After another night in the cells, Nation made off for the nearby town of Enterprise at the invitation of the local WCTU and destroyed another dive for which she received a black eye at the hands of the saloon-owner's wife. The following morning, she was severely beaten and pelted with rotten eggs by four prostitutes hired by the same proprietor. She wisely departed the town before further retribution could be wrought and headed south to Hope to begin what the *New York Times* was already describing as "the usual operations". Noting that there were two saloons in the town, the newspaper reported that "the liquor people there are terror-stricken at the knowledge of her coming."[60] Nation then moved on to Topeka, where she was assaulted by the wife of a saloon-owner, and remained there for much of February, often behind bars, doing herself no favours by addressing the town's judge as "your dishonour" whilst standing in the dock.

By this time, Nation had become synonymous with the hatchet and her every move was being reported by the national press. In faraway New York, a woman describing herself as "a second Carry Nation" had destroyed a saloon and other copycat smashings took place in Kansas, Illinois and Indiana.[61] It was a measure of Nation's infamy that the *New York Times* dedicated an editorial to her in 1901, albeit an unflattering one. Nation's main claim to fame, the newspaper opined, "is that she is a crank and a monomaniac, and that she has perpetrated a great deal of damage to glass and glassware with the cheerful irresponsibility of a moral paretic."[62]

This was not the worst that was said of her. Nation wrote in her memoirs that after her antics in Kiowa she "never explained to the people that God told me to do this for some months, for I tried to shield myself from the almost universal opinion that I was partially insane."[63] This comment reveals a certain degree of self-awareness in the woman but "partially insane" remains a fair assessment. Her mother died in an insane asylum and her daughter Charlien would later be institutionalised. Carry was never officially certified, but it is likely that she would be diagnosed as mentally ill were she alive today, as people who hear the voice of God often are.

Neither jail, nor injury, nor death itself held any fear for 'Christ's bulldog' (a title she bestowed on herself). Violence against women was far from rare in those days, but even the most vicious degenerate drew the line at striking a little old lady. Not so in Nation's case. In one week in Kentucky, she was knocked to the ground after slapping a cigarette out of a man's mouth and was attacked with a chair by an opportunist saloon-owner who spotted her walking down the street. She came close to being lynched in Wichita and was fortunate to escape with her life on several other occasions.

Saloon-owners had ample reason to hate and fear a woman who was capable of causing thousands of dollars' worth of damage in a few minutes. Since they operated illegally and without insurance, an attack from the lady with the hatchet could mean bankruptcy or jail, and Nation received death threats on a regular basis. She published the worst of her hate-mail in her short-lived newspaper, the *Smasher's Mail*, under the heading 'Letters from Hell and Elsewhere among the Wicked'.[64]

In August 1901, as Carry Nation languished in jail once more, her husband petitioned for divorce after twenty-seven gruelling years. David Nation charged his wife with neglecting her family, abandoning her home and holding him up to public ridicule. In an interview with the press, he confirmed the view of many an armchair psychologist when he claimed that his wife "smashes saloons because her first husband died of drink". With simmering resentment, the teetotal church minister added that "she keeps telling me that I may do the same."[65]

Divorce liberated Carry Nation from the last shackles of conventional life and, now under the management of a publicity agent who kept his own drinking a secret, she rolled into New York City where she was thrown out of the police headquarters by a Commissioner who told her she was crazy. "That's what all the vicious rum-soaked creatures in Kansas thought also," she replied, "but they're wrong. I've shown them things, and I'll show you things before I finish!"[66]

And so she did. Over the next eight years, the great hatcheteer saw the inside of prison cells from San Francisco to Pittsburgh. Jobless, husbandless and with an unending stream of court fines to pay, she created a cottage industry selling miniature souvenir hatchets and, in 1904, published her autobiography, *The Use and Need of the Life of Carry A. Nation,* which sold 60,000 copies.

As her fame grew, she desired to be taken seriously as a lecturer and lay preacher. The militant wing of the WCTU continued to cherish her fearless views, but invitations to speak in churches dwindled and, in 1903, Nation appeared in vaudeville theatre playing the role of an obsessive saloon smasher in the stage adaptation of the temperance best-seller *Ten Nights in a Bar-Room.* Two years later, she moved her operations to Oklahoma with the specific aim of having prohibition written into the new state's constitution. When this was achieved in 1907 it marked the resurgence of statewide prohibition in America for which Nation could take some credit.

A trip to the British Isles in 1908-09 demonstrated her international renown and was to be her swan-song. Now in her sixties, she spoke to a packed house in Cambridge, appeared in the music halls of London and was still in robust enough physical shape to lay waste to a pub in Newcastle-upon-Tyne, for which she received the customary arrest. She found the British to be more hostile to temperance than the people of Missouri. In Glasgow, she was greeted by a mob of 3,000 who forced her to postpone her assault on the Scottish pub. Instead she was escorted by police to a nearby temperance inn. In Dundee, she enquired of the receptionist at a hotel, "Young man, do you sell drink here?" "No," replied the man, looking into the face of the world's most famous anti-alcohol crusader, "but you can get what you want next door."

Shortly after returning to America, Nation sold her hatchets and used the proceeds to buy a farm in Arkansas that she renamed Hatchet Hall. She died of heart failure two years later. The last words she uttered in public were reputed to be: "I have done what I can."[67]

Nation was a figure of fun to drinkers and a source of embarrassment to many abstainers. The cause of temperance had little to gain from being represented by a woman who was at least half-mad. A stranger to diplomacy, she called the Anti-Saloon League "traitors", she despised both Republicans and Democrats, and only had time for the moribund Prohibition Party. She applauded the assassination of the wet President McKinley, saying "no one's life was safe with such a murderer around" and was jeered off stage for describing the current President Roosevelt as a "cigarette fiend".

In the twilight of her career, the *New York Times* ran an editorial advising both "foes and friends alike" to remember that "her peculiarities are due to a long-recognized form of mild insanity and that she should receive more of pity than of either encouragement or derision."[68] The newspaper reflected the metropolitan view of an eccentric woman from the midwest who dressed like a Salvation Army widow and whose God was of the fire and brimstone variety, but in America's heartland, Nation was taken more seriously and she was capable of surprising warmth, wit and charisma when talking about her war on "saloonacy".

If raising the profile of the liquor question was her aim, Carry Nation's whirlwind career can be considered a qualified success. Her fame eclipsed that of even Frances Willard, whose temperament could not have been more different, and, by offering a more violent, latter-day version of the Women's Crusade, her antics reinvigorated the temperance movement during otherwise lean years. The WCTU and the Anti-Saloon League were cautious about endorsing her publicly—only the Prohibition Party would have her speak at its convention—but many prohibitionists were cheering her on in private. By drawing attention to the lax enforcement of local prohibition laws, authorities were shamed into taking action and hundreds of saloons were closed down. In that sense, she did what she could.

And yet, in the final analysis, Prohibition depended less on violent fanaticism from teetotallers than on the apathy of drinkers. While questioning the sanity of Carry Nation, the *New York Times* exhibited the same nonchalance about the drink question that allowed the prohibitionists to prevail.

Nobody here really cares much what happens to those particular traffickers ["the liquor-selling class"], for, though a good many of us patronize them more or less frequently, most of us are ready to admit, when it comes to a matter of argument, that they might easily be in a better business.[69]

The author of this editorial evidently had no problem with someone buying alcohol but, like many Americans of the time, he failed to comprehend that if one man was to have the right to buy, someone else must have the right to sell. The *New York Times* was no more in favour of prohibition than were the legion of imbibers in the city which bore its name. Nonetheless, it was keener to condemn the way Carry Nation conducted herself than to condemn what she stood for.

What did its readers have to fear from prohibitory laws anyway? If Nation's crusade showed anything, it was that such laws did not stop people drinking. For those who liked to wet their whistle "more or less frequently", it would take the reality of Prohibition to hit home before selling drink became an activity worth defending. Writing in 1923, Charles Hanson Towne remarked that Prohibition "came upon us like a phantom, swiftly; like a thief in the night, taking us by surprise."[70] This is plainly nonsense. The drink question had been the most talked about issue in American politics for decades. It was not as if the temperance crusaders had made any secret of their intention of bringing about national Prohibition; a more vocal set of campaigners would be hard to imagine. And yet, to New Yorkers like Towne, the threat had never seemed real, even as one state after another capitulated to the prohibitionists. Since it was not illegal for drinkers in dry regions to order alcohol by mail order from wet regions, local prohibition was primarily a problem for the poor who depended on the saloon. For the middle class, as Towne recalled, "it was mighty easy to give a dinner party with plenty of liquid refreshment. All one had to do, it seemed, was to lift the telephone receiver in Bangor, and ask that Boston send over a supply of whatever one desired."[71]

Mugged by the reality of Prohibition, Towne rued what he called the "national insincerity" that had existed prior to 1920 when middle class opinion-makers had vaguely approved of the anti-saloon movement while feeling certain that their own drinking habits would go untouched. It took Prohibition to rid them of their hubris. Until then, few were prepared to speak up for the drinks industry, and the "traffickers" were pitifully inept at doing so themselves. Since the efforts of the 'liquor trust' to fend off Prohibition were a shambles, and short-sighted drinkers chose to live in denial, the shrewd and vastly better organised Anti-Saloon League took the initiative.

The battle of Ohio

By the time Carry Nation hung up her hatchets, the Anti-Saloon League was in full swing. The first decade of the twentieth century saw the patchwork of dry towns, villages and counties grow denser. By 1906, 35 million people—over a third of the population—lived in officially dry territory.

The Anti-Saloon League was active in forty states and employed hundreds of full-time staff dedicated to ousting wet politicians. Casualties of the League's negative campaigning littered the political landscape, as Ernest Cherrington later recalled:

The thousands of political graves which were to be found in almost every state of the Union, due to the active work of the League, had come to be a constant and wholesome reminder to the political leaders everywhere that this new movement, backed by the Christian citizenship in the counties, cities and villages of the several states, had come to hold the balance of power wherever temperance issues were involved in political campaigns.[72]

The League did not have things all their own way. They could coerce politicians into putting dry legislation before the people with their "wholesome reminders" but they could not force the people to vote for prohibition. Towns and counties continued to reject anti-liquor laws. Others tried them once and repealed them. After a failed experiment lasting eight years, South Dakota repealed statewide prohibition in 1897. Vermont and New Hampshire did likewise in the following decade, leaving Maine as the last state from the great prohibitionist wave of the 1850s still standing.

There was a message there for those who chose to listen. Almost six decades after Maine had gone dry, every indicator had shown that prohibition did not work. It had failed to achieve its stated intention of prohibiting drinking, it had failed in its more modest ambition of *reducing* drinking and it had succeeded only in bringing forth a succession of unwanted and unintended consequences that had brought the whole system of law into disrespect. The saloons had been replaced by 'blind tigers', soon to be known as 'speakeasies'. Legitimate drinks had been replaced by contraband and home-brew. The drinking remained, the drunks remained and the death, vice, violence and squalour remained.

This was hardly a secret. As far back as 1888, G. H. Thompson had applauded the "zeal and indefatigable energy of the noble men" who had campaigned for prohibition, but was forced to conclude that "prohibitory laws have disappointed the sanguine hopes of their honest advocates and done little to reduce drunkards."[73]

In the same decade, the *New York Nation* said of a dry law then under consideration:

Such a law, if enforced, would be disobeyed and evaded to an extraordinary degree, even by people of reputable character. It is a matter of history that the drinking habits of society are as old as the race itself, and to attempt their eradication by special legislation, is an absolutely hopeless undertaking.[74]

In the face of these uncomfortable facts, true believers merely shrugged. This time, they said, things would be different. The fog of self-delusion grew thicker and by 1907, the League felt ready to push for prohibition in the most temperance-minded states of America. Oklahoma and Alabama were the first to fall. Mississippi, Tennessee, Georgia and both Carolinas soon followed suit, motivated by a desire—as one contemporary put it—"to keep liquor away from the negroes."[75]

Jolted awake by this spate of statewide prohibitions, the liquor industry sprang into something approaching action. In response to a temperance movement that had seemed toothless just a few years earlier, the distillers formed the National Model

License League as a direct alternative to the Anti-Saloon League. While their enemies pushed prohibition, the National Model License League preached true temperance, with an emphasis on tougher licensing and regulation. Eager to remind the public that prohibition was "un-American" and "a costly absurdity", the National Model License League called for saloons to be limited to one for every 500 people, for drunks to be arrested, and for licences to be revoked whenever saloons breached the law.[76] Its president, Thomas Gilmore, released a statement to let Americans know that a long overdue house-cleaning had begun:

Society is moving forward and the saloon must move forward or be outlawed. The edict has gone forth that men must be sober if they would be free, and few men would now contend that a man possesses an inherent right to overthrow his reason.

The edict has gone forth that saloons must obey all laws, that they must not sell to intoxicated men nor to habitual drunks nor to minors, that they must not exhibit improper pictures nor connect themselves with gambling resorts—in a word, that the saloons must not be a nuisance.[77]

Still wary of the distillers, America's brewers declined to join the National Model License League and only awoke to the threat of statewide prohibition in 1908 when the fight came to Ohio.

Ohio was the spiritual home of both the brewers and the Baptists. It was there that Diocletian Lewis had sparked the Women's Crusade thirty-five years earlier and it was there that both the WCTU and the Anti-Saloon League had been born. But it was also the home of America's biggest beer companies and the Ohio Brewers' Association would not be moved. Between 1908 and 1913, the beer-makers' chief tactician, Percy Andreae, was given $1 million to fight the Anti-Saloon League on home soil. An intelligent and practical libertarian, Andreae was astute enough to recognise, as the National Model License League had, that the key to beating the Anti-Saloon League lay in reforming the saloons themselves.

Despite the efforts of the Drys, the number of saloons had been increasing for many years, both in Ohio and across the nation. In the cities, there was one 'dive' for every 300 people and as numbers rose, standards declined. Faced with more competition and fewer customers, saloon-owners actively solicited trade on their doorstep, sold to children and lured in customers who could ill-afford to spend more money on drink. Sidelines such as gambling and brothel-keeping helped to pay the bills. Consequently, as Andrew Sinclair noted, "at the moment when the progressive wave of reform was pressing for better conditions of life, the old city saloon was becoming worse."[78]

What seemed like bad luck for the brewers was, as usual, largely self-inflicted. They owned two-thirds of America's saloons and had been given every opportunity to put their public houses in order. It took them years to realise that the saloon was the most visible face of their industry and that the unscrupulous behaviour of bar-owners and the often squalid conditions within were the best advertisement for prohibition. British publicans had fought off the temperance movement by self-regulating and Andreae now urged American brewers to clean up their act, personally taking charge of the 'vigilance bureau' at the Ohio Brewers' Association and employing private detectives to check that saloons were following his new code of conduct.

This eleventh-hour conversion to self-reform, combined with a concerted lobbying effort, denied the Anti-Saloon League the statewide ban it most craved. Since the defeat of Myron T. Herrick, every Governor of Ohio had been a committed Dry. The brewers had been unable to unseat any of them but they took encouragement from several dry counties voting to go wet and, in 1912, the unthinkable happened when Ohio became the only state in the nation to amend its constitution to allow the licensing of intoxicating liquors. This effectively trampled all over the local prohibitions that had been enacted by three-quarters of the counties in the state. A livid Anti-Saloon League complained that less than half of the electorate had cast a ballot in the referendum but this hardly invalidated the result and, in any case, a low turnout was more likely to hinder the brewers than help them.

Set on revenge, the Anti-Saloon League put statewide prohibition before Ohio voters no fewer than four times between 1914 and 1918. Betraying the myth that the 'liquor trust' had deeper pockets than the prohibitionists, Wayne Wheeler admitted that the objective was to exhaust the finances of the brewers. "What we plan to do," he said, "is make the saloon, the distillery, and the brewery elements bankrupt themselves trying to keep Ohio wet. And we will succeed. We will wear them down, and wear them out."[79]

They did not succeed in bankrupting the brewers and the League's tiresome demands on the electorate only served to demonstrate how divided the nation remained on the liquor question. Having lost twice with a much increased turnout in 1914 and 1915, the Anti-Saloon League lost again two years later by just 1,137 votes out of over a million cast. When they finally won in 1918, the vote was still very tightly split with 51.4% in favour and 48.6% against. Such a narrow margin of victory, on the League's home turf and at the fifth time of asking, was a less than compelling mandate for one side to impose its will upon the other. As any student of American politics knows, Ohio is reputed to be a barometer of public opinion. It did not bode well for the Drys that they had to fight tooth and nail to win a slim majority in America's bellwether state.

'The Next and Final Step'

While the Anti-Saloon League went head-to-head with the brewers in Ohio, the campaign for statewide prohibition elsewhere was stalling once more. Alabama repealed its law just two years after enactment and prohibition referendums in Missouri, Oregon, Texas and Florida all went the way of the Wets. By 1913, nine states had prohibition laws on their books, only three more than had been the case when the Anti-Saloon League began operations twenty years earlier.

Faced with these facts, Wayne Wheeler expected the campaign for national Prohibition to take another twenty years before it bore fruit, but statewide prohibitions were not the only marker of success. When local option laws were taken into account, 46 million people—more than half the population— were living in dry areas and, from 1913, the Drys enjoyed a run of good fortune which allowed their mission to be achieved within just seven years.[80]

In February 1913, the Sixteenth Amendment was ratified, bringing about a system of federal income tax for the first time. This new source of revenue eased the government's reliance on alcohol taxes which hitherto had provided as much as half of all federal income. When speaking publicly, Drys had always insisted that Prohibition would save the taxpayer a fortune by emptying prisons, hospitals and asylums. In private, they were conscious that Prohibition would create a gaping hole in the government's budget. People would still have money to spend after Prohibition, of course, and those who did not spend it on illicit moonshine would spend it on something taxable, but politicians knew that soda water and candy could never be taxed as exorbitantly as booze. A federal income tax offered a way of compensating for the expected shortfall and had long been supported by prohibitionists.

The following month saw the passage of the Webb-Kenyon Act which banned the transportation of intoxicating beverages into dry states. At a stroke, the mail order liquor business that had been such a solace to Wets living in prohibitionist communities was destroyed. It was an unexpected and electrifying victory for the Drys, who took particular satisfaction from the Senate overriding President Taft's veto to get the legislation through. A jubilant Cherrington declared the ban to be the "crowning achievement" of the Anti-Saloon League and immediately used his editorial pulpit in the *American Issue* to call for a Constitutional Amendment to ban the sale and manufacture of alcoholic drinks throughout the USA.

Twenty years after that inauspicious meeting in an Ohio library, the Anti-Saloon League was on the brink of the promised land. The prohibitionists' long-standing commitment to allowing communities to set their own alcohol policy was dropped like a stone. They now argued that Americans living in dry territory—who were, they did not fail to mention, the majority—were having their rights infringed by the production of alcohol in neighbouring towns. Smuggling was a fact of life, they admitted, and the only way to truly prevent drink being bootlegged into dry regions was to turn the whole nation dry. They demanded what would today be called a 'level playing field'.

With the end in sight, Ernest Cherrington became the League's chief strategist for the final push and set about his work with gusto. He was acutely aware that time was against the Anti-Saloon League. America's rate of immigration and urbanisation was showing no sign of slowing down. In 1860, one in five Americans lived in the cities. By 1913, the figure was two in five and soon the urban masses would be an intemperate majority whose votes would forever block national Prohibition.[81] The electoral system was rigged in favour of the countryside, and therefore the Drys, but Cherrington knew the League had to act quickly and he made plans for a five year campaign. The Anti-Saloon League's general superintendent, Purley A. Baker, called for a blitzkrieg of posters, pamphlets, books and newspapers, and told his followers:

"This is not spectacular work. It is siege work, but it brings lasting victory... The masses are utterly without knowledge. They will not seek knowledge. It must literally be forced upon them when they are not looking... We must put modern advertising business sense into our propaganda. Well-prepared circulars for the different classes mailed into the homes, attractive posters hung everywhere..."[82]

The Anti-Saloon League had every tool of propaganda at its disposal. Four years earlier, they had built a large printing press in Westerville, Ohio which a staff of seventy kept running all day and all night. Not a single page printed was unrelated to the battle against drink. As the first of Mary Hunt's "trained haters of alcohol" entered middle age, the American Issue Publishing Company aimed to increase production of temperance literature from an already impressive one and a half tons a day to ten tons a day. The mighty *American Issue* had a monthly circulation of half a million and Cherrington now added a further four publications to the fold: the *American Patriot* ('A Magazine for the Home'), the *Worker* (aimed at the labour movement), the *National Daily* and the *New Republic*.

In June 1913, Purley Baker negotiated a partnership with the WCTU's Scientific Temperance Federation which gave the Anti-Saloon League access to the vast archive of anti-drink pseudo-science that had been built up since the 1880s. After adding their own patented brand of melodrama and morality plays to the mix, the League produced more fliers based on Scientific Temperance material than anything else it printed at the Westerville plant.[83]

Alcohol, these 'fact sheets' confidently asserted, was responsible for 90% of crime, 80% of poverty and 70% of insanity. It had been "scientifically demonstrated" that 77% of children born to intemperate parents were degenerate.[84] All nonsense, but who needed science when you had prose like this?

This is the indictment; the liquor traffic is the criminal; the people are the victims; God is the judge; science, reason, religion, motherhood, and posterity are the jury; and the verdict is, GUILTY in every unprejudiced, unpurchasable, and just court. And the sentence of the national conscience is that this mother of all abominations, and father of all lies, and son of all villainies, this covenant with death and agreement with hell, shall be carried bound to the place of execution at the holy of holies of the temple of the nation at sunrise on the next general election, and there stoned with Christian ballots that it die.[85]

For the benefit of children and the barely literate, temperance cartoons showed men rowing towards Niagara in a canoe marked 'Moderation' and cigar-smoking saloon-owners oozing malevolence in their shop doorways. No character appeared more often in temperance cartoons that the saloon-owner. With his clean apron and sinister smile, he was the physical manifestation of the seductive immorality of the liquor trust. Fat from the earnings of his hapless customers, he stood in stark contrast to the wretched housewife stranded at home with a baby in her arms and hungry children around her ankles.

In November 1913, the Anti-Saloon League celebrated its twentieth anniversary in Cleveland, Ohio, where the WCTU had been founded 39 years earlier. Baker used the occasion to officially announce that the League was ready to take what he called the "next and final step." He urged supporters to put politicians under the deepest scrutiny and to broadcast aloud any hint that they might waver on the liquor question. He told his almost exclusively Protestant audience to portray the battle for Prohibition not as the religious crusade it so clearly was, but as an evidence-based policy rooted in sound science.

"The narrow, acrimonious and emotional appeal is giving way to a rational, determined conviction that the traffic being the source of so much evil and economic waste and the enemy of so much good, has no rightful place in our modern civilization."

A few weeks later, on 10 December 1913, Ernest Cherrington led more than a thousand prohibitionists to the steps of the

Capitol in Washington, DC and presented a draft of the Constitutional Amendment to Congressman Hobson who greeted them as brothers.

Captain Richmond Pearson Hobson was the League's ace in the pack. Variously described by historians as "a person of virtually unlimited moral indignation"[86] and a "peculiarly objectionable crank",[87] Hobson made a name for himself as a naval hero in the Spanish-American War before retiring at the age of thirty-two to spend the rest of his life searching for new enemies to vanquish. Hobson was a man born to raise panic. The first of his obsessions was that Japan was intent on overwhelming the United States by military force and he spent several years preaching against the 'yellow peril' which, it seemed, could only be countered by drastically increasing the size of the navy. He continued to rail against Japanese supremacy after becoming Congressman for Alabama in 1905, but when this thinly veiled attempt to solicit naval expansion failed to capture the public's imagination he turned instead to the cause of temperance.

Hobson worked on a speech entitled 'Alcohol: The Great Destroyer' which brought together every myth and half-truth about the demon drink that had been uttered in the previous hundred years. Alcohol, he proclaimed, was a poison in all its forms; it had no benefits; it could never be consumed safely in moderation; nearly half of all deaths in the United States were directly attributable to drink; the saloon was an "assassin"; each saloon killed three men a year, and one in five children born to drinkers was "hopelessly insane". To this compendium of Scientific Temperance, Hobson added his own tidbits of information. By some calculation or other, he deduced that "alcohol is ten thousand times more destructive than war" and that beer was "vastly" more dangerous than distilled spirits.

Like others before him, Hobson was keen to interpret the liquor question through the eyes of a muddled Social Darwinist, asserting that: "Science has proved that this nation must become sober or die." Alcohol, he said, made men of all races commit "unnatural crimes" although the white man—"being further evolved"—was less susceptible than blacks.[88] Still obsessed with the Japanese, Hobson warned of what would befall America if it allowed itself to be brought down by alcohol:

The Chinese and Japanese want to come to this country. They are not degenerates. Don't despise the yellow man. The Romans despised the barbarian. Nature will not have a family of degenerates. If we are not careful, before our grandchildren have left the scene, they will hear the hoof of the yellow man's horse.[89]

As a *bona fide* non-smoking, teetotal war hero with a gift for oratory, Hobson was the darling of the Anti-Saloon League and soon became its highest paid speaker, delivering his hour-long lecture hundreds of times across America. On December 22 1914, he delivered it once more, this time to Congress, for a year had passed since the Constitutional Amendment was first introduced. He began the speech by attacking the liquor trust and concluded with an appeal to progress:

There can be but one verdict, and that is this great destroyer must be destroyed. The time is ripe for fulfillment. The present generation, the generation to which we belong, must cut this millstone of degeneracy from the neck of humanity.[90]

The debate was lively. The most eloquent of the Wets, Julius Kahn of California, explained the futility of trying to "regulate all human conduct by laws, laws, laws"[91] and noted that even statewide prohibition had done little to quell the appetite for, and the availability of, ardent spirits. "Prohibition is not temperance", he said:

Temperance harms no one, on the contrary it does good. Prohibition, on the other hand, has generally resulted in making men liars, sneaks and hypocrites.

In keeping with the national mood, the Congressional vote was tight. The Drys won a narrow majority of 197 to 189 but this fell short of the two-thirds majority required for the Bill to progress. Prohibitionists shrugged and treated it as a dress rehearsal.

A few months later, the seeds of America's War on Drugs were sown when the Harrison Narcotic Tax Act attempted to rid the country of opium. This law represented a further shift towards state regulation of private behaviour. Never slow to miss an opportunity to advance his cause, Wayne Wheeler equated drink with opium and exploited the supposed hypocrisy of clamping down on one "habit-forming drug" but not the other. "A national evil requires a national remedy," he said. "The liquor traffic is a national evil... The Federal Government realised that such evils must be dealt with by the nation. This is why the Harrison Anti-Narcotic Act [*sic*] was passed."[92]

A leading proponent of both the Harrison Act and the Sixteenth Amendment was William Jennings Bryan, a native of Nebraska who was, in the words of Edward Behr, "an unspeakably boring, flatulent windbag".[93] A career in politics naturally beckoned and Bryan was the presidential candidate for the Democratic party on no fewer than three occasions. He lost every time, and by an increasingly wide margin, and by 1908 his political career seemed over.

Like most politicians—and *all* presidential hopefuls—Bryan had always skirted around the liquor question for fear of alienating voters. Despite being a devout Presbyterian and a teetotaller—he had signed the pledge at the age of twelve—Bryan would not officially endorse even statewide prohibition until 1914. The following year, aged 55, Bryan resigned from the Wilson administration in protest at President Wilson's supposedly anti-German attitude, and dedicated the rest of his life to Prohibition, women's suffrage and the campaign to ban the teaching of evolution in schools.

Capable of delivering up to ten heartfelt speeches a day, Bryan shared Hobson's obsession with race degeneracy, and yearned for the "purer blood" and "stronger race" that would surely accompany Prohibition.[94] He also provided a fine entry for any anthology of bad predictions when he forecast that: "Our nation will be saloonless for evermore and will lead the world in the great crusade which will drive intoxicating liquor from the globe."[95]

Bryan's coming out as a torchbearer of alcohol suppression came at an opportune moment for the Anti-Saloon League. Richmond Hobson was defeated in the 1914 election, thus bringing to an end a Congressional career which saw the great orator propose prohibition amendments on more than twenty occasions.[96] The man who defeated him, Oscar W. Underwood, was a defiant Wet who described Prohibition as a "tyrannous scheme to establish virtue and morality by law"[97] and the Anti-Saloon League chose to hold fire on presenting a new resolution to Congress until after the elections of 1916. Just as the prohibitionists had hoped, those elections resulted in Drys outnumbering Wets in Congress by more than two to one. The political class had been largely purged of outspoken drinkers and the Anti-Saloon League was ready to resubmit the Constitutional Amendment.

With 300,000 donors and an annual income of $2.5 million,[98] the League had offices in all 435 congressional districts.[99] They had trebled the circulation of the *American Issue* in just three years. The Supreme Court had declared the Webb-Kenyon Act to be constitutional. Prohibition was supported by a wide range of industrialists and businessmen including—with shameless self-interest—the *Coca-Cola* company. More than half of all saloons were concentrated in just fourteen cities and the Anti-Saloon League could do without all of them and still get their Constitutional Amendment.[100] Above all, twenty-three states had now passed statewide prohibition. If not now, then when?

The brewers' last stand

The Wets were wholly unprepared for the Anti-Saloon League's final assault. While the drinkers were, as George Ade later recalled, "too busy drinking", the brewers had been lulled into a false sense of security by their success in Ohio. It took the *American Issue* to declare that "The Time Has Come" for the *American Brewers' Review* to warn its readers that "Prohibition is no longer a local issue. The last stage has been reached. Prohibition is a national danger."[101]

Suddenly finding themselves drinking in the last chance saloon, the panicked liquor industry lived up to every stereotype of pork barrel politics, bribing politicians, throwing money at lobbyists, employing journalists and buying up the *Washington Post* to install the wine-quaffing Arthur Brisbane as its editor. The brewers and the distillers finally buried the hatchet in 1913 and worked together to form the National Association of Commerce and Labour with Percy Andreae appointed president on an astronomical salary of $40,000 a year (close to a million dollars in today's money). It did not take long for the media to identify the true source of this industry front group—nor that of the Civic Liberty League, the Manufacturing and Business Association and all the other auspiciously named trade organisations that suddenly sprang up on the eve of Prohibition —but the unravelling of this subterfuge scarcely mattered. The recriminations and sibling rivalry soon returned and the brewers withdrew their money.

The drinks industry attempted to counter a hundred years of temperance literature with a burst of its own propaganda, not realising that the time for words had long since passed. The Wets could never match the Anti-Saloon League for mawkish yarns and, as the sun began to set, they fought their corner with a fury that was characteristically counterproductive. Had they discussed their public relations strategy more calmly, they might have conceded that they were unlikely to win over many Drys by complaining about the "cowardice of weaklings who want the government to protect them from their own lack of self-control",[102] nor would they win the hearts of progressives by warning that Prohibition would put the country on a slippery slope that would lead to mixed race marriages and women getting the vote.[103]

They were on firmer ground when appealing to personal liberty and protesting against the "widespread campaign of misleading and invented statistics". Their contempt for "the belief that evils resulting from the excessive use of liquor can be cured by prohibitory laws" was quite justified,[104] but the key argument remained the industry's contribution to the economy. Aside from the $300 million brought to the US government in alcohol taxes every year, the industry claimed to be responsible for one and half million workers who were amongst the best paid in the country. All this may have been true but the introduction of income tax had neutered the economic argument and temperance folk had answers to the rest, although not always very rational ones. ("Go and talk to the wife or the gray-haired mother of the drunkard about personal liberty," was one popular rebuttal.)[105]

There was no end to the industry's gaffes. Fearing that women's suffrage would seal their fate, the liquor men became noisy opponents of the universal franchise, thereby angering at least half the population. The Anti-Saloon League responded by officially endorsing women's suffrage in 1916, the only time it took a political position on anything other than alcohol. The League had every reason to make this rare excursion into partisan politics; Ernest Cherrington wrongly, but understandably, predicted that repealing Prohibition would be "next to impossible" once women had the vote.[106]

In a final act of self-destruction, albeit one which could not have been foreseen, the brewers attempted to rally beer-drinkers of German extraction by throwing money at the German-American Alliance. The Alliance was a powerful lobby group with two million members and the brewers felt they had achieved a publicity coup when, in 1913, German-Americans complained that Prohibition was an attack on "German manners and customs, and the joviality of the German people."[107] It no longer looked such a masterstroke a year later when the First World War broke out and tales of German atrocities began appearing in every newspaper.

Wayne Wheeler was about as interested in the "joviality of the German people" as he was in the profits of the beer-makers. He rushed to capitalise on the brewers' misfortune by asking the American public to question whether the loyalties of the predominantly German brewers lay with Uncle Sam or with the land of their ancestors. Wheeler repeatedly made the unfounded accusation that the German-American Alliance was "crippling the army and navy" by funding America's enemies[108] and told the *New York Times* that "the liquor traffic aids those forces in our country whose loyalty is called into question at this hour."[108] No less tenuously, he insisted that the army was "hamstrung" by the liquor traffic's ownership of 100,000 delivery vehicles which could, he suggested, be put to better use in the muddy fields of Flanders.[110]

The First World War was the "murderous stroke of luck"[111] which settled the drink question in favour of the prohibitionists. Without it, Prohibition may still have come to America, but the wave of hot-headed jingoism that erupted in 1917, combined with the desire to make postwar America a sober land fit for heroes, made Prohibition inevitable. Not only did the war arouse public suspicion of the brewers as the enemy within, but it forced the US government to consider acts of authoritarianism which would have been unthinkable in peacetime. As the state embarked on a mission to seize industry, fix prices and ration fuel, it became difficult to defend the use of wheat and barley to make products which half of Americans viewed as luxuries and the other half viewed as a plague on mankind.

In June 1917, two months after the United States declared war on Germany, President Wilson drew up the Food and Fuel Control Bill to conserve essential supplies, including wheat. The Anti-Saloon League decided that the time was right for a show of strength. Exerting its unparalleled influence over legislators in Washington, the League blocked the Bill until it was satisfied that the President would severely limit the amount of food that could be used to ferment alcohol. Wilson, who was personally inclined towards temperance rather than prohibitionism, was forced to write a begging letter to the League, appealing to their patriotism and reminding them that "time is of the essence". Bishop James Cannon, the League's notoriously cold-hearted legislative superintendent, told him that so long as he banned the production of ardent spirits he was free to carry on at his own discretion. It was a sign of the White House's pathetic subservience to this private interest group that Wilson felt compelled to write back, thanking the League for their co-operation and commending their willingness to compromise as "admirable proof of their patriotic motives."[112]

But Wilson chose to do no more than the League had explicitly commanded. Spirits were banned, but beer and wine were left untouched. A furious Wayne Wheeler responded with a new resolution to ban all intoxicating beverages as part of the 1918 Agriculture Appropriation Bill. Again masquerading as a wartime necessity, this law effectively prohibited the production of *all* alcoholic drinks, effective from July 1919. Senators, three-quarters of whom were ostensibly dry, voted resoundingly for its implementation but, inconveniently—and contrary to all military expectations—Germany surrendered nine months before the start date. Any lingering belief that the Anti-Saloon League had supported the ban for patriotic reasons was dispelled by its violent insistence on maintaining it despite the Armistice.

As a result of his earlier 'treachery' on the beer issue, Wilson was now reviled by prohibitionists and was unable to get his other legislation through Congress without capitulating to the

Anti-Saloon League on the appropriation bill. Consequently, the President signed this emergency wartime measure into law ten days after peace was declared, but by then it was a sideshow. Fifteen months earlier, the Senate had drafted the Eighteenth Amendment to prohibit "the manufacture, sale, or trans-portation of intoxicating liquors" in the United States of America. By the end of 1917, the amendment had breezed through both Houses and awaited ratification by the states. Had Congressmen been allowed to vote by secret ballot, it is likely that the amendment would have been thrown out. As it was, under scrutiny from 50,000 League activists and 300,000 WCTU members, the politicians took the path of least resistance. Wets eased their consciences by telling themselves that they had not voted for Prohibition *per se*, but had only allowed the states to make their choice. For some, voting dry was an act of political expediency. Others found it possible to genuinely believe in Prohibition despite being drinkers themselves. For those who were capable of making or acquiring their own beer and cider, it was difficult to imagine life changing radically under the new law and whatever sacrifices were to be made would be a price worth paying to reform the blacks, the immigrants and the working class.

With their fully stocked cellars of wine and whisky, politicians imposed Prohibition on America in the sure knowledge that it would barely affect them personally. This hypocrisy was no secret at the time. Fabian Franklin wrote in 1922 that "nothing is more notorious than the fact that a large proportion of the members of Congress and State Legislatures who voted for the Prohibition Amendment were not themselves in favour of it... Not the least of the causes of public disrespect for the Prohibition law is the notorious insincerity of the makers of the law, and their flagrant disrespect for their own creation."[113]

Politicians were not alone in succumbing to cant and mendacity. The Anti-Saloon League had created a climate of institutionalised hypocrisy in which millions of Americans convinced themselves that Prohibition was morally laudable while expecting to remain immune from its consequences. Decades earlier, the Governor of Rhode Island, which had indulged in a fleeting experiment in prohibition between 1855 and 1863, made the crucial distinction between public will and public opinion; the latter reflecting what one ought to think, the former reflecting what one actually did.

"The attempt to enforce prohibition is a thankless undertaking, for, though it may represent public opinion, the carrying out of a law is almost wholly dependent upon the public will, as contra-distinguished from the public opinion. Without a will, the way cannot be found."[114]

Never was the gap between public expression and private behaviour wider than when Congress and the Senate rubber-stamped the Eighteenth Amendment in 1917. Whether intimidated by the League, infused with their own sanctimony or bewitched by the notion of forging a pure nation from the ashes of war, lawmakers unleashed a Noble Experiment which would expose the nation's insincerity in the starkest terms.

By November 1918, with the war at an end, fourteen states had ratified the Eighteenth Amendment. Another twenty-two would have to do the same to achieve the three-quarters majority necessary to amend the Constitution. Displaying their perennial talent for shutting the stable door after the horse had bolted, the National Association of Distillers picked this moment to publish its *Anti-Prohibition Manual*, which provided "a quick and easy means of answering arguments offered by 'dry' speakers". It was, boasted its editor, "the only book of its kind in existence."[115]

The drinks industry was counting on a long, drawn out campaign. If the amendment was not ratified within six years it would be withdrawn and, in a final show of hubris, the liquor men expected to be able to hold out that long. In the event, a flurry of activity over the next two months culminated on

January 17 1919 when Nebraska became the thirty-sixth state to ratify.

Rejoicing at the news that the Drys had crossed the finishing line, Senator Kenyon, one of the architects of the Webb-Kenyon Act, told the Senate:

"This marks the successful ending of the greatest moral battle waged in this country since the abolition of slavery. The power of the saloon is ended in the United States. As it passes to its grave it can go with the knowledge that it has been responsible for more misery and crime, more destruction of homes and debasement of character, more poverty, sorrow and tears than any other agency the world has ever known. No one will weep over its demise. The United States will be a better, more prosperous nation, its citizens will be more happy and contented than ever."[116]

The Senator was correct in his first observation. The battle over Prohibition had divided America like no other issue since the Civil War. And he was at least part-right in blaming the saloon for many social ills. But it would take fourteen years of organised crime, corruption, deceit, theft, poisonings, cripplings, blindings and shootings to prove him disastrously wrong about the happiness of his nation under Prohibition.

As Nebraska's most famous son, William Jennings Bryan took particular delight in seeing his home state put the final nail in the coffin of the liquor traffic. It was he who predicted that America would "lead the world in the great crusade which will drive intoxicating liquor from the globe." For a short time the triumphant Drys believed they could do just that.

2

Prohibition averted

The campaign for a dry world

"Prohibition has made nothing but trouble."
— Alphonse Capone

On January 4 1920, thirteen days before Prohibition came into force, a headline in the *New York Times* announced the new goal for the forces of temperance:

Now for another World War, waged against demon rum

The newspaper reported that the World League Against Alcoholism was gathering a $50 million fund to bring about global prohibition within ten years. Agents of the Anti-Saloon League were being dispatched around the world to offer advice to like-minded Drys in Britain, Scandinavia, Australia and India who were eager to follow in America's foot-steps.[1]

For the water-drinkers, worldwide prohibition was the inevitable next step. Prohibition in the USA was believed to be irreversible. So long as thirteen states stood firm, it would be impossible to find the three-quarters majority necessary to repeal the Constitutional Amendment. Since 45 states had ratified the Eighteenth Amendment, repeal seemed phenomenally unlikely. The Drys' faith that Prohibition would last forever was further boosted by the knowledge that the Nineteenth Amendment, which gave the vote to women, had been passed by both Houses and was months away from ratification.

With the domestic situation apparently secure, the Drys cast their gaze abroad. Their rationale for embarking on this orgy of cultural imperialism borrowed heavily from earlier rhetoric. Just as statewide prohibition had been threatened by wet states, so too was nationwide prohibition threatened by wet nations. "A strongly organized liquor traffic anywhere is a menace to prohibition everywhere," said Ernest Cherrington.[2] For America to be truly free of liquor, argued the Drys, every other nation must be the same.

The plan for global prohibition had taken shape a year earlier when Cherrington created the World League Against Alcoholism and appointed himself General Secretary. Cherrington rallied his troops by telling them that twenty-five years earlier only one in sixteen Americans had lived under prohibition but now, thanks to the leading role of the United States, one in sixteen of the *world's* population was free from the liquor trade. What else could this mean but that global prohibition was imminent?[3]

Only a movement delirious with victory could regard being hopelessly outnumbered as a sign of providence. Even if one disregarded the fact that a large proportion of the dry one-sixteenth resided in just one country, it soon became clear that many of those who lived under Prohibition bitterly resented it. Ignoring these facts entirely, Cherrington insisted that if the Anti-Saloon League could achieve so much as stumbling pioneers, then surely the rest of the world could achieve total abstinence now that the Americans had mapped out the road to success.

World prohibition now sounds so outrageously fanciful that it is hard to believe the idea was ever seriously entertained, but the prohibitionists had some reason to be optimistic. Severe restrictions on the drinks trade had been introduced in many countries during the First World War. The Australian WCTU had succeeded in closing the pubs at six o'clock in the evening, a piece of temperance legislation that remained in place until 1965. Norway had banned strong drink during the war and, in 1919, had voted to keep the restrictions in place. Canada had brought in national prohibition in the last months of 1918, much to the disgust of the soaking wet citizens of Quebec.

A majority of New Zealanders had voted for prohibition in 1911, albeit without reaching the 60% majority required for legislation. Finland and Iceland were already dry (the latter did not legalise beer until 1989). Russia brought in prohibition in 1914, ostensibly as a war measure, and the Bolsheviks were happy to keep the proletariat sober after the revolution of 1917. A foreign observer noted that the Russian working class had become smarter, cleaner and better nourished, and some teetotal socialists questioned whether the revolution could have taken place at all had the workers remained addled by vodka.

The worldwide crusade was not, therefore, starting entirely from scratch. Although the Anti-Saloon League was invisible outside of the United States, the WCTU was active in dozens of countries. Part of Frances Willard's 'do everything' strategy had been to form the World Woman's Christian Temperance Union, which had hundreds of thousands of members by the time its new president, Anna Gordon—who had been Willard's secretary—announced the goal of world prohibition in 1918.

In addition to the various arms of the WCTU, a handful of European temperance groups gave the World League Against Alcoholism an aura of genuine internationalism. While Lucy Page Gaston led the Anti-Cigarette League in America, her younger brother Edward co-ordinated the International Prohibition Federation in London. This alliance of thirteen teetotal societies had been fighting for a dry world for a decade before it joined forces with Cherrington's outfit. In 1919, it changed its name to the Worldwide Prohibition Federation and vowed to create a "dry Europe by 1930".[4] Accompanied by the United Kingdom Alliance for the Suppression of the Traffic in all Intoxicating Liquors and Switzerland's International Bureau Against Alcoholism, the World League Against Alcoholism set about its gargantuan task.

Cherrington identified the Scandinavian countries as the prime targets for prohibition. Australia and New Zealand were considered "promising fields" while Japan was seen as the most likely candidate in the Far East. He conceded that mainland Europe offered fewer immediate prospects, especially in the wine-drinking, Catholic countries, but the banning of absinthe in France, Switzerland, Holland and Belgium was seen as a foothold for more comprehensive restrictions in the years ahead. But it was Great Britain, with its breweries, distilleries, merchant navy and—above all—empire, that was identified as the key to unlocking the rest of the world. The Anti-Saloon League concluded that: "Without prohibition in the British Isles world prohibition becomes a mere dream. With prohibition in the British Isles world prohibition is inevitable."[5]

Great Britain

The British temperance movement had followed the trajectory of its American cousin for much of the nineteenth century. A campaign for moderate drinking emerged at the end of the 1820s and was soon accompanied by a movement for teetotalism—the doctrine of total abstinence having a simplicity and rigour that made it more appealing to social reformers.

During the industrial revolution, gin had triumphed at the expense of ale, leading to a serious moral panic over the 'gin craze' in the first half of the eighteenth century. One need only look at Hogarth's famous paintings of 'Gin Lane' and 'Beer Street' (1751) to see how contemporaries contrasted the miserable depravity of gin to the peaceful joviality of beer. A series of laws restricting the sale of gin brought the panic to an end in the 1750s and contemporary accounts suggest that public drunkenness declined in the last decades of the eighteenth century.

The 1820s brought new fears. Criminal convictions rose fourfold between 1811 and 1827 while sales of gin appeared to rocket after 1825.[6] All this coincided with the opening of the first 'gin palaces'. Spacious and lavishly decorated, these emporia offered a taste of vulgar modernity to the London hordes and were viewed by some as a mortal threat to the traditional public house. The gin palaces were, as Peter Haydon writes in *The English Pub,* "incongruous surroundings for poor people to get drunk in. What offended middle class sensibilities was not that the poor were getting drunk (they had always been getting drunk), but that they were getting drunk in opulent surroundings that were lavish out of all proportion to the status of the customers."[7]

It seems likely that the surge in criminal convictions had more to do with improved policing than a drink-fuelled crime wave.[8] It is also likely that the rise in gin sales documented in official records reflected a shift from drinking smuggled liquor to buying legitimate products after the tax on spirits was slashed in 1825.[9] But whatever the truth behind the statistics, the triple whammy of crime, gin and opulence was enough to renew concerns about working class inebriation.

In 1831, the British and Foreign Temperance Society became the country's first major temperance association. Based in the south of England, and led by the Bishop of London, it sought to persuade the public to shun spirits for beer. As it happened, this was also the policy of the government, whose solution to the gin panic was classically liberal in its rationale and execution. In an attempt to turn drinkers from the juniper to the hop, Parliament passed the 1830 Beerhouse Act which permitted anyone to open a beerhouse and slashed taxes on ale and cider. Since beer was considered to be a true temperance drink, the Act was presented as a public health initiative. By dangling the carrot rather than wielding the stick, it was hoped that entrepreneurs would rush to open up respectable beerhouses and give working men and women a more wholesome alternative to the gin palaces.

The government's ruse worked only too well. Within weeks of the law coming into effect, the Reverend Sydney Smith made an observation about England's 'sovereign people' that has become much quoted:

The new Beer Bill has begun its operations. Everybody is drunk. Those who are not singing are sprawling. The sovereign people are in a beastly state.[10]

By the end of the 1830s, 46,000 beerhouses had been added to the nation's 45,000 pubs.*[11] So successfully had the Beerhouse Act reinvigorated the British taste for ale that it was subsequently amended to make the drinks industry less of a free-for-all, but not before a significant teetotal movement had been born.

One of several theories for how the word 'teetotal' came into existence gives the credit to a Lancashire plasterer named Richard Turner who suffered from a stammer and told the Preston Temperance Society in 1833 that he would be "reet down out-and-out t-t-total for ever and ever."[12] This anecdote may be apocryphal, but the time and place fit. Preston was the cradle of teetotalism and 1833 was the year in which Joseph Livesey gave his first 'Malt Lecture'.

Livesey was a Preston-born cheesemonger with a talent for oratory whose semi-scientific lectures about the brewing process

---

* Alcohol was always more readily available in Britain than in the USA. The number of saloons in America peaked at around 1 per 300 people. In 1831, there was one licensed premises for every 168 people in England and Wales.[13]

were crucial in challenging long-held beliefs about beer as a temperance drink. For centuries, it had been assumed that ale offered essential sustenance, vitality and strength. Livesey called this "the great delusion". The amount of nutrition in a pint of beer was, he said, "trifling"; it would be much better to simply eat the barley from which it was made.[14] He gave his audiences a detailed explanation of the brewing process, showing them how the nutritional content of hops and barley was steadily eroded until there was practically nothing left. For his dramatic finale, Livesey evaporated a quart of ale and set fire to what remained, thereby demonstrating that at the heart of beer lay nothing but neat spirits.

Livesey was no scientist and his analysis of the beer-making process was "riddled with errors and unjustified assumptions".[15] His 'Malt Lecture' greatly underestimated the calorific value of beer, which did indeed provide working men with much needed energy. But he was correct in two important respects—a penny spent on food provided more calories than a penny spent on ale, and the psychoactive ingredient in beer was no different to the psychoactive ingredient in spirits; it was the same alcohol in both drinks. This had not been generally recognised until Livesey gave his lectures; conventional wisdom held that beer and spirits were fundamentally different drinks. By demonstrating that this was not so, Livesey had a profound effect on the temperance movement. Abstaining from hard liquor was no longer enough because beer-drinkers were, in effect, spirits drinkers.

In the 1830s, teetotalism became the dominant brand of temperance for working class men in the north of England. There had been teetotallers in Britain before, of course, but a life of total abstinence could be a lonely business in the nineteenth century and it was only now that they began to form associations. At a time when life revolved around the factory and the pub, temperance meetings provided alternative social venues to "enable teetotallers to survive in a drink-ridden society."[16]

Teetotal societies, coffee shops and temperance hotels helped to deliver pledge-takers from temptation while offering companionship and support to reformed drunkards. As a support group for the voluntary abstainer, they were indispensable, but when the lonely extremist suddenly finds himself surrounded by like-minded people, the result is often greater fanaticism.

In 1839, the teetotal movement was split when its most abstemious members embraced the 'long pledge' of not allowing alcohol in the home and not offering drinks to others. If the conventional short pledge of total abstinence demanded a certain amount of isolation from the wet majority, the long pledge required followers to be almost hermetically sealed. This was not a practical option for the middle class, most of whom already considered the short pledge to be excessively austere. Regarded as utterly eccentric by mainstream society, the long pledge nevertheless gained a foothold in some insular working class communities where militancy was worn as a badge of honour.

Popular teetotalism in northern England was very different to the anti-saloon movement in the USA. Although British temperance groups were typically founded by wealthy men from the church and industry—whose motives ranged from heartfelt compassion to a desire to squeeze more productivity from the workforce—teetotalism became a genuine working class movement for self-improvement. Its roots in the industrial cities of the north of England ensured a compassion for the common man that was seldom displayed by America's predominantly rural Drys. Moral suasion was their weapon and although they had some political objectives, such as shorter pub opening hours, it was not until they heard the news of America's first statewide prohibition in Maine that their legislative programme became more aggressive.

In 1853, two years after the Maine Law, a group of Quakers formed the Manchester-based United Kingdom

Alliance for the Suppression of the Traffic in all Intoxicating Liquors and within three years had 30,000 members. They were under no illusion that a national ban on alcohol was a realistic short-term goal and instead campaigned for local option, known in Britain as local veto.* This, however, still required political action at the national level. A law would have to be passed in Westminster to give local authorities the power to ban drink within their jurisdictions. To this end, the Alliance submitted the Permissive Bill to Parliament in 1864. If passed, this would have allowed a community to outlaw the sale of alcohol if a two-thirds majority could be achieved in a local referendum. It was an idea entirely at odds with the free trade politics of the day and MPs described it as "sheer tyranny and intolerance of the worst sort" which was designed to "permit you to prevent me doing what you don't like and I do."[17] They voted against the bill by an overwhelming margin.

The Alliance pressed on regardless, submitting the same bill to Parliament for a decade, always with the same result. What else could this single-issue pressure group do? In some ways, the Alliance was a precursor to the Anti-Saloon League. It refused to align itself with any political party, it worked for local option as a forerunner to national prohibition, it blamed drinking on the drinks industry, it sought to influence politicians at a personal level and it was a professional political lobby group which made no pretense of being a social club. But unlike the Anti-Saloon League, it failed to bring about legislation. When British prohibitionists asked politicians whether they would support the Permissive Bill, they received a politician's answer. Those who gave them assurances of solidarity in private usually failed to

---

* Mancunian prohibitionists were a force to be reckoned with. In the 1870s, they successfully lobbied for Dog Kennel Lane to be renamed Maine Road in tribute to the first US state to go dry. Manchester City football club's stadium, built in 1923, was given the same name until it was demolished 80 years later.

vote dry in Parliament and, crucially, the Alliance lacked the political clout to unseat those who betrayed them.

The Alliance could not claim, as the Anti-Saloon League later would, that they had the support of the silent majority. Its prohibitionist aims were opposed even within the broader temperance movement. Amongst its bitterest critics was Joseph Livesey, who regarded prohibitionists as misguided souls who had missed the whole point of temperance. From his perspective as a moral suasionist, abstinence from alcohol was a hollow act if it was the result of state coercion. He had no doubt that choosing a life of teetotalism was empowering, but to force it upon a man was to rob him of his maturity and self-reliance. Livesey also mocked the Alliance's pretensions of being at war with the drinks industry when there was palpably so much public demand for drink. Until that demand was curtailed, he said, suppression was futile.

The battle between the moral suasionists and the prohibitionists created a third rupture in the temperance movement, following on from the schism between the anti-spirits crusaders and the teetotallers, and the subsequent rift between the short-pledgers and the long-pledgers. The Alliance struggled to garner support in the south-east of England, where teetotalism was not widely popular, and even fellow teetotallers in the North, such as the Band of Hope (founded in Leeds in 1847), were by no means always inclined towards coercion.

In the broader society, the aristocracy was too fond of its drink to demand abstinence from the working class. Lord Randolph Churchill once made the astute observation that: "The aristocracy and the working class are united in the indissoluble bonds of a common immorality."[18]* This unofficial

---

* His son, Winston, described Prohibition as "an affront to the whole history of mankind" in 1932.[19] A thirstier MP than most, the younger Churchill had lost his parliamentary seat in Dundee to the prohibitionist Edwin Scrymgeour ten years earlier. Scrymgeour was the only candidate of the Scottish Prohibition Party ever to become an MP.

alliance between the gentry and the workers—which was wholly absent in the United States—meant that Victorian reformers found themselves opposed from above and below whenever they attacked traditional pastimes such as blood-sports and prize-fighting. The drink issue was no different.

The other great institution of the establishment, the Church of England, also refused to endorse teetotalism, let alone prohibition. In 1873, a survey found that only 660 of the nation's 23,000 Anglican ministers abstained from drink,[20] and although the Anglicans contributed to the temperance movement by forming the Church of England Temperance Society in 1862, the organisation was accused of being, as one aggrieved teetotaller put it, "very much Church and very little temperance."[21] Some Anglicans regarded the 'born again' experience of taking the pledge, with its obvious similarities to baptism, as an explicit rival to the Christian faith and so it was left to the Methodists and Quakers to persuade the British public to live without alcohol.

Deprived of support from the aristocracy, the Church and most of the medical establishment, prohibitionists were always on a hiding to nothing in the United Kingdom. But if prohibition was not on the menu, lesser restrictions remained palatable. Rather than fighting drinking *per se*, nineteenth century temperance legislation focused on reforming the public house. The bourgeois view of the pub as a "great underworld of sex, indecency, depravity, crime, cock-fighting, gambling, plotting and subversion"[22] was much the same as American progressives' view of the saloon. It was not an entirely inaccurate picture. Even the passionate anti-prohibitionist Charles Hanson Towne, writing in the 1920s, *after* the drinks industry had cleaned up its act, described the London pub as "a notoriously shocking place":

In the meanest sections of the city, I have witnessed scenes which made one realize that Dickens did not exaggerate when he drew a character like Bill Sykes. I have seen thinly clad, anemic children waiting on the steps of a public house for not only their fathers, but their mothers, to emerge. And when they finally did so, they were so drunk that they could scarcely toddle to their wretched homes.[23]

For most city dwellers, the working week extended at least half-way into Saturday, leaving Sunday as the only day on which to have a drinking binge. The resulting hangovers meant that 'Saint Monday' had long been an unofficial day of rest. This was one tradition that mill-owners were keen to see die out and they joined forced with the Sabbatarians to fight for a sober Sunday. In 1848, pubs were ordered to close at midnight on Saturday and not reopen until 1pm on Sunday. Seven years later, the Sale of Beer Act prohibited pubs from opening for more than six hours a day but this hugely unpopular law was relaxed after a protest against it turned into a riot in London's Hyde Park.

Efforts to tame British drinking reached their zenith in 1872 when Gladstone's Liberal government passed the Licensing Act. Pubs were forced to close at midnight in the city and 11pm in the countryside—a severe curtailment of traditional drinking practices which was much resented by drinkers, publicans and brewers alike. The Liberals lost the next general election, brought down, so it was said, "in a torrent of gin and beer".[24]

Alcohol consumption continued to rise. The booming economy of the 1870s saw urban wages grow as never before and with new prosperity came a spike in drinking not seen since the 1830s. Paternalists saw the concomitance of higher incomes and greater drunkenness as further evidence that if a working man was given a horse, he would ride to hell on it. "The rise of wages coming upon a class of men ill-prepared for it, was a positive evil of the highest degree", said one reformer.[25]

Not for the last time, the working man proved to be wiser than his betters gave him credit for. 1876 saw the peak of both alcohol consumption and pub numbers. Wages kept rising in the 1880s but drinking declined and continued to do so for decades. The temperance movement could take little credit for this. By the close of the century, the local pub, which had once been practically the only social venue for the urban masses, found itself competing with football, rugby, music hall, libraries, parks and railway travel. Beer and gin had to compete with tea, coffee, lemonade and—crucially—clean water, as drinks that could be consumed without fear of contamination. Teetotallers were often inclined to ignore the social deprivation and misery that led to heavy drinking, but as living standards improved and alternative leisure activities became available, fewer people felt compelled to use alcohol as an escape hatch.

By 1900, the prohibitionist element represented by the United Kingdom Alliance was a busted flush. The attention of the working class shifted towards the labour movement in the last decades of the nineteenth century and the temperance cause withered. By reining in the worst excesses of the trade, the 1872 Licensing Act appeased the moderate majority and dampened the flame of suppression. Political lines began to be drawn. So unpopular had the Licensing Act been with publicans and brewers that they became staunch Tory supporters in the 1870s. Seeing nothing to lose from dropping its nonpartisan approach, the Alliance then cosied up to the Liberals, whose growing thirst for reform made them natural bedfellows in the fight for alcohol regulation, if not prohibition.

The landslide election of 1906 resulted in a huge influx of teetotal Liberal MPs and a Licensing Bill which would have closed a third of Britain's 96,000 pubs. This radical reform became the subject of intense public debate culminating in another rally in Hyde Park which attracted hundreds of thousands of protesters. Although the Bill was passed in the House of Commons, it was rejected in the House of Lords, where the Tories were dominant, and the most controversial alcohol legislation of the century was killed off. Having lost nine by-elections while the licensing debate raged, the Liberals never again attempted to take on the pub industry in peacetime. When Britain's most draconian and enduring drinking restrictions arrived, it came in the fog of war rather than under the cloak of temperance.

In August 1914, in an effort to save resources and keep munitions workers sober, the government used the Defence of the Realm Act to reduce pub opening times to six hours a day, double the tax on spirits and triple the tax on beer. Pubs were forbidden from selling hard liquor on Saturdays and were made to close all day on Sundays. Three English counties went further and made it illegal to purchase a drink for another person, thus criminalising the practice of buying a round.

It was ironic that the most severe anti-alcohol laws in British history were introduced under the premiership of Herbert Asquith, whose legendary devotion to drink led him to be nicknamed Squiffy. David Lloyd George, who succeeded him in 1916, was a more convincing frontman for temperance. Having campaigned against the bottle for many years, the Welshman proclaimed in 1915: "We are fighting Germany, Austria, and drink, and, as far as I can see, the greatest of these deadly foes is drink."[26] As Prime Minister, Lloyd George reduced the country's beer production by two-thirds, reduced the alcohol content of ale by one third and continued the wartime policy of hefty tax hikes on beer and spirits. By 1919, the duty on a barrel of beer was almost ten times higher than it had been before the war.

The combination of higher prices, rationing and shorter opening hours forced alcohol consumption into a nose-dive from which it has never fully recovered. This brought undoubted public health benefits. Deaths from liver cirrhosis fell by half and, by 1918, convictions for drunkenness were a sixth of the pre-war total. (Neither can be wholly laid at the door of the austerity measures since millions of young men were on active duty abroad.) But having endured five years of weak beer and extortionate prices, the British were in no mood to hear talk of total prohibition. That, however, is what William "Pussyfoot" Johnson set out to give them.

"Pussyfoot" Johnson

"Pussyfoot" Johnson was a journalist-turned-enforcer who earned his nickname sneaking around Indian reserves in Oklahoma carrying out raids on grog-shops and saloons. An anti-liquor activist since the 1880s, Johnson wrote to Wets posing as the proprietor of 'Johnson's Pale Ale' to ask them how to defeat the water-drinkers. When they offered their advice, he gleefully handed their letters to the Prohibition Party and had them published in the newspapers. In his later years, Johnson cheerfully admitted that he "had to lie, bribe and drink to put over Prohibition."[27]

Spotting a man after his own cynical heart, Wayne Wheeler welcomed him into the Anti-Saloon League and appointed him editor of the Anti-Saloon League's short-lived *New Republic* magazine. In 1919, with Prohibition ratified but not yet enforced, Pussyfoot became the leading ambassador of the World League Against Alcoholism.

His first port of call was London. If he expected a Kansas welcome, he was destined for disappointment. While speaking in the Strand, he was pelted with stones and manhandled by a mob of medical students who grabbed him, hoisted him onto a stretcher, covered him in flour and carried him around central London chanting "What won the war? Rum!" and "We've got Pussyfoot, meow! Send him back to America!" The police did nothing to stop them.[28]

Johnson took all this with remarkable serenity, even lighting a cigarette as he was paraded through the streets. Events only turned sour when a stone caught him in the eye and he had to undergo surgery to have the wounded peeper removed. This unfortunate injury turned into a publicity coup for Johnson. From his hospital bed, he smilingly told reporters that he bore his assailants no ill will and the students later apologised. Suddenly the subject of popular sympathy, Johnson became the acceptable face of Prohibition and the *New York Times* called him "a jovial dry" and "the kind of prohibitionist that the most devoted opponents of prohibition have a fondness for". British temperance activists immediately adopted the slogan "Pussyfoot's eye will make England dry".

If opponents of prohibition had a fondness of Johnson—and that was debatable, the English had burnt him in effigy a few days earlier—they remained less keen on his cause. Prohibition was not without its supporters in the UK—two million people signed a petition to outlaw the sale of alcohol in 1916—but, by the end of the war, Britain was a more sober nation than it had ever been before. The sovereign people were no longer in a "beastly state" and prohibitionists were unable to induce the moral panic required for more draconian action.

A year after Johnson's mauling in London, WCTU president Anna Gordon and Anti-Saloon League founder Howard Hyde Russell set sail for Britain to distill sentiment against the liquor trade. Their visits had little impact. Aside from a few Calvinist patches of Scotland which went dry in the early 1920s, the British never came close to prohibition. What they got instead were temporary restrictions which became permanent. Pub opening hours were relaxed a little in 1921 but remained limited for the rest of the century. It was still impossible to buy a drink in a pub on a weekday afternoon as late as 1987, and 11pm closing remained mandatory until 2005. Nor did alcohol taxes ever fall back to pre-war levels. On the contrary, there were large annual rises for four years after the First World War and raising duty on alcohol (and tobacco) has been the first instinct of every cash-strapped government ever since.

"Pussyfoot" Johnson predicted that England would be dry within his lifetime (he died in 1945), but then he was something of an optimist. He also declared that Denmark was "drying up"[29] despite being heckled on a visit there, and said the same of Canada, where he was jeered off stage. By April 1921, he was of the belief that India was "on the verge of ruling out liquor" with

New Zealand and Norway to be dry within a year. Mexico would be "bone-dry" within five years, he insisted, and, perhaps most implausibly, France was "giving serious consideration to the question of prohibition."[30] In reality, the most likely candidates for prohibition were the Scandinavian countries where a Protestant majority and an established temperance movement had already set the stage.

Referendums

Like the Anglo-Saxons, the Nordics had been bitten by the temperance bug in the 1830s. In Scandinavia, as elsewhere, the anti-drink crusade was dominated by evangelical Protestants and started life as a non-coercive campaign against hard liquor, the only twist coming in Finland, where alcohol was seen as a problem of the rural peasantry rather than the urban masses. The shift to prohibitionism in mid-century mirrored that of the United States and, by 1919, the temperance lobby had successfully agitated for restrictions on alcohol despite all the Nordic countries remaining neutral during the war.

These restrictions ranged from fairly mild in Denmark* to total prohibition in Finland and Iceland. Norway had dodged the prohibitionist bullet by limiting alcohol sales but Sweden had been on the brink of prohibition for several years. By 1909, it was clear that a slim majority of Swedes favoured a ban on alcohol sales, but they were thwarted by a young doctor named Ivan Bratt who wrote a book entitled *Can the Temperance Issue be Resolved without a Total Ban?*. Bratt was no stooge of the liquor trade—he sat on Stockholm's Temperance Committee—but for

---

* Protestant countries with a preference for spirits were usually guaranteed a successful temperance crusade and yet Denmark resisted anti-alcohol extremism. The historian Sidsel Eriksen attributes this to the Danes' rejection of Methodism in favour of the less temperance-minded Lutheranism.[31]

him the answer was yes. As an alternative to prohibition, he proposed an overtly paternalistic and egalitarian rationing system which permitted a set amount of hard liquor to be sold, ranging from four litres a month for a married man to nothing at all for married women.

After personally buying up a large share of Stockholm's off-license industry, Bratt managed to have his system made law in 1917 and the drinks industry became a state monopoly. At the same time, the drinking age was raised to 25, beer was weakened and ration books were withheld from criminals and drunks.

Many Swedes found the new alcohol rations too meagre for their thirst and deeply resented the measure, but if drinkers disliked Bratt's innovation, prohibitionists hated it with a passion usually reserved for the liquor trade itself. The World League Against Alcoholism feared any legislation that addressed excessive drinking unless it banned alcohol outright. It preferred to fight a rampant drinks industry than one that was heavily regulated. Consequently, Ernest Cherrington described the Bratt system as one of "the most formidable rivals of prohibition in Scandinavia, Finland and the British Isles."[32]

If Bratt's intention was to hold off the prohibitionists—as it surely was—his success was not immediately resounding. The rationing system pacified those Swedes who were only moderately anti-alcohol, but when a national prohibition referendum was called in 1922 the result was still too close to call. This was the moment the World League had been waiting for. Seeing Sweden as "the key to the dry situation in the whole of the Scandinavian peninsula",[33] Cherrington despatched Anti-Saloon League members to give Nordic prohibitionists a little American know-how. The much travelled Pussyfoot Johnson was shipped off, as was the Reverend David Ostlund who set about organising the Swedish Anti-Saloon League. (The involvement of an American pastor in Swedish affairs brought events full circle, as it had been the roaming American teetotaller Reverend

Robert Baird who had formed the Swedish Temperance Society back in 1837.)

When the referendum was held on 27 August 1922, newly enfranchised Swedish women obligingly voted in favour of prohibition, but men voted against it in slightly higher numbers and the Wets secured a victory by the extraordinarily tight margin of 51% to 49%.

Bitterly disappointed, the Drys regrouped in Toronto for the World League's first international convention. There, delegates were told that the whole of northern Europe was "ripe for prohibition". Reverend Ostlund took the platform to insist, unconvincingly, that "we did not win but we did not lose, either" and said that "Bratt, in his castle in Sweden with his brandy and his liquor, is trembling",[34] an absurd mental image that managed to convey paranoia and bravado at the same time. This was pure self-delusion. It was widely understood by neutral observers that the referendum had killed off any hope of prohibition in Sweden for a generation.

Efforts to suppress the liquor traffic in other countries were undermined by the mounting evidence of Prohibition's failure in America. In April 1920, as Pussyfoot Johnson recovered from his eye operation in a London hospital, the *New York Times* complemented him on his valour but issued an early warning that all was not well with the Noble Experiment back home.

One likes him and his joyous temperament so well that it is almost rude to remind him that, in his regretted absence, a strong reaction against his favorite doctrine has manifested itself in the United States.[35]

There had been no honeymoon for Prohibition. Within hours of the clock striking midnight on 17 January 1920, government officials had closed down two illegal stills in Detroit[36] and police in Chicago were investigating the theft of $100,000 of medicinal whisky by six masked men.[37]

Soon the trickle became a flood. Illegal stills and home brewing equipment were assembled in their hundreds of thousands. The Californian vineyards became prolific producers of grape juice, the price of which increased from $10 to $100 a ton as Americans took to wine-making on a grand scale. For those who had the money, foreign wines and whiskies were available in the speakeasies that could be found in every city, or from the boats anchored just off the American coast.

By 1922, Charles Towne was lamenting that America had become "a nation of self-appointed law-breakers" and "the laughing stock of Europe".[38] Enforcement of Prohibition was farcical or nonexistent in several of the country's most densely populated states. Authorities in New York City respected neither the spirit nor the letter of the law while Chicago was fast becoming a swamp of corruption, bootlegging and crime. When prosecutions were brought against offenders, juries refused to convict and judges refused to jail. In dripping wet New York, the first 4,000 prosecutions came and went without anyone going to prison.

This kind of news could not easily be hidden from the rest of the world and, by 1922, New Zealand offered the only serious possibility of a dry gain for the World League Against Alcoholism. With a plebiscite due in December, Pussyfoot Johnson once again set off to tell floating voters that, contrary to what they might have read in the newspapers, Prohibition in the United States had been a roaring success.

New Zealand temperance activists felt cheated that alcohol was still on sale at all. A majority had voted dry in a referendum in 1911 without reaching the three-fifths majority required to change the law. A second referendum was organised in 1914 but this time the vote went against them. A third referendum took place in April 1919, by which time the Drys had managed to change the system in favour of a straight majority. As the results were counted, a dry win seemed certain. With close to half a million ballots cast, the prohibitionists led by 15,000 and the Drys were ready to uncork the milk in celebration as they waited for the votes of servicemen stationed in Europe to be counted.

But when the ballots arrived, it transpired that of the 39,000 soldiers who voted, 31,981 cast their ballots for the Wets. Prohibition was forestalled once more.

American soldiers waiting to return to their now dry homeland might have grumbled that their Kiwi comrades had at least been consulted on the matter, and they were consulted again eight months later when the Drys put yet another referendum before the people. This time the Wets won by the wafer-thin margin of 1,327.

Still, the prohibitionists would not give up. As Pussyfoot Johnson prepared to rally supporters in advance of yet another referendum in 1922, one New Zealand journalist wondered what exactly this tranquil country was trying to protect itself from.

We have no saloons such as America had. In some of the hotels there are lax barmen and lax proprietors, but generally the hotels are very decently managed. There are only 1,100 liquor licenses in the country and really no drink evil for the prohibitionists to attack. There is drink and that is enough for them.

It is not because New Zealand is suffering from drink that the prohibitionists desire to turn the country dry, but because they believe that drink is itself an evil. They committed themselves in a solemn way to the theory that even the most abstemious man is suffering from drink. The 'soak' who drinks twenty whiskies a day is only ten times drunker, they declare, than the man who takes two drinks a day, one at lunch and one at dinner.

Mr Johnson can hardly bring much in the way of fanaticism to the aid of prohibitionists who think and speak like that.[39]

Alas for the fanatics, the monocular Mr Johnson could not convince voters that the newsreels showing American lawlessness and gangsterism were figments of their imagination. When New Zealanders went to the polls for the fifth time in December 1922, the wet majority was a still slender 16,138, but it was sufficient to finally put the matter to bed.

The collapse of prohibition

The World League never came close to generating the $10 million a year that Cherrington believed was necessary for a successful global campaign. Its revenue peaked at $75,000 in 1922 and dwindled to practically nothing when the Anti-Saloon League was forced to spend its time maintaining Prohibition at home rather than engaging in its increasingly quixotic foreign adventures.

Despite their bombastic optimism, most of Europe was a no-go zone for prohibitionists. Those not already inclined towards teetotal Protestantism were off limits and the wine drinkers of mainland Europe viewed the fermented grape as food, no matter what temperance folk might tell them. Even the more supportive Methodists of northern Europe often found Pussyfoot Johnson and his Anti-Saloon League colleagues too brash and zealous.

Unbeknownst to the World League, the fifth New Zealand plebiscite was the last time a national referendum would offer the chance of a dry gain. In 1922, Iceland legalised wine after the Spanish threatened to boycott their fish and, in the same year, Lenin responded to the huge hole that prohibition had blasted in the state's finances by legalising beer. In a surprisingly bourgeois move by the fledgling Bolsheviks, wine had been legalised the previous year. Thereafter, the Russians began to gradually allow stronger liquor to be sold, culminating in the long-awaited legalisation of vodka in August 1925.*

Norway voted to legalise spirits in 1926, thereby overturning its partial prohibition. Tellingly, the reasons given for Norwegian liberalisation were very similar to the reasons given for banning strong drink in the first place.

---

* Records show that the number of illegal distilleries unearthed by Russian police during prohibition rose from 1,825 in 1914 to 73,000 in 1924.[40]

(1) to drive bootleggers out of business;
(2) to decrease drunkenness;
(3) to increase revenues;
(4) to eliminate completely the rapidly mounting costs of prohibition enforcement;
(5) to decrease the death rate.[41]

A report in the *Canadian Medical Association Journal* gave an insight into Norway's experiment in prohibition:

Difficult of execution, severe measures were added in 1920, 1921 and 1922. With the addition of each restraint, however, the situation became worse. The actual consumption of alcohol during this period decreased, but the problems of alcoholism increased. There were more arrests for drunkenness than before prohibition, there were more cases of acute alcoholism in the hospitals, and there were more crimes due chiefly to excessive drinking.

In 1922, the Norwegian Government, realizing that prohibition was, in its essence, a mistake, began to repeal restraining measures. The result was that the consumption of alcohol *increased*, but the arrests and disorders *decreased*. [emphasis in the original][42]

The journal's Canadian readers were all too familiar with these symptoms of prohibition's failure. A temperance campaign running parallel to that of the USA had been pursued by the Dominion Alliance for the Total Suppression of the Liquor Traffic in Canada since the 1870s. Working in conjunction with the Canadian WCTU, this overwhelmingly Protestant, anti-French pressure group succeeded not only in putting national prohibition to a referendum in 1898 but won the popular vote. Typically, however, the vote was astonishingly close (another 51%/49% split) and the government nobly refused to act on such a slim majority, particularly since four out of five Quebecers had voted against.

Local option created a patchwork of dry regions in Canada but total prohibition eluded Drys until the First World War provided the usual patriotic spring-board into the promised land. Shortly after the war, Quebec wasted no time in shaking off the shackles of prohibition and, one by one, the rest of Canada followed. By 1930, only Prince Edward Island—the only province to have been dry before the war—still had the law in operation and valiantly continued to do so until 1948.

The collapse of Canadian prohibition was more than a moral defeat for the World League Against Alcoholism. American prohibitionists had been happy to publicise cross-border smuggling in the early days of Prohibition because it seemed to strengthen their case for global action. In his 1922 book *America and the World Liquor Problem*, Ernest Cherrington told readers that Quebec was importing ten times as much whisky as it had in the previous ten years combined, with the clear implication that most of it was being illicitly transported into the USA. 1,000 cases of contraband were being smuggled over the Canadian border every day, he said, and nine million gallons of intoxicating beverages were being smuggled into the USA every month.[41] Cherrington hoped that such figures would shame the Canadian government into clamping down on the illicit trade, but once Canada abandoned prohibition and tacitly encouraged the lucrative cross-border trafficking, the millions of gallons of whisky being imported into America from the north only served to prove that the law was unenforceable.

But enforcement was all the Anti-Saloon League had left once public support had ebbed away. Wayne Wheeler never involved himself in the World League, believing that global prohibition was "too grand a scheme" and "impractically idealistic."[44] He had enough on his plate as the Anti-Saloon League's chief enforcer and it was a role he seized with vindictive glee. In 1926, Wheeler encouraged the US government to begin poisoning the nation's supply of industrial alcohol which, as everyone knew, was being used to make moonshine. The contaminant chosen for the purpose was 'Formula No. 5', a concoction of methanol, pyridine bases and benzene, which could cause blindness and death. For Wheeler, the resulting fatalities were a cause for mirth. "If a man wishes to violate the

Constitution of the United States," he chuckled, "he should be free to commit suicide in his own way."[45]

The Anti-Saloon League had always said that alcohol was a poison and now they made it so. Over the Christmas of 1926, 46 people died after drinking poisoned alcohol in New York City alone, with hundreds of others blinded, brain-damaged and hospitalised. Wheeler cheerfully announced that the government would soon be doubling the toxic dose.[46] Before Prohibition was over, 10,000 lives were lost to alcohol deliberately contaminated by the government.[47]

To this ghoulish tally must be added the tens of thousands of poisonings from badly distilled bootleg liquor and dubious patent medicines, such as the infamous Jamaica Ginger, or 'Jake', a brew so toxic that a single batch left five hundred drinkers in Wichita paralysed for life. It is estimated that 40,000 Americans were left permanently crippled by Jake during Prohibition. We must also include the many murdered victims of the mobsters who became the new 'liquor trust' in the age of Prohibition. Murders and assaults rose by a third between 1920 and 1933 and only began to fall after the Eighteenth Amendment was repealed.

Within a year of the Christmas poisonings, Wheeler himself was dead. At the age of 57, the dry kingpin's punishing work schedule finally took its toll and after he succumbed to a heart attack in September 1927, *Time* magazine observed that "the brains of the Anti-Saloon League died with him".[48]

With or without the practical Mr Wheeler, the chances of Prohibition being overturned remained remote. Wets pinned their hopes on a victory for the Democratic nominee Al Smith in the 1928 election. The first presidential hopeful to publicly oppose Prohibition, Smith was disadvantaged by being a Catholic running against the popular Herbert Hoover at a time of economic prosperity. The Republicans won by a landslide and exuberant Drys predicted that no candidate would ever dare run on a ticket of repeal again.

Taking Hoover's victory as a renewed mandate for Prohibition, the Anti-Saloon League launched a crackdown on drinkers. In 1928, the League's legislative superintendent Bishop Cannon drafted the Jones Law, which increased the penalty for a first offence from six months to five years imprisonment. Fines rose from a thousand to ten thousand dollars. Failing to report an offence—as countless people did every minute in the speakeasies of America—was punishable by three years in prison. The supine members of the House and Senate both passed the law by three to one.

The Anti-Saloon League's overt lurch towards brutal suppression cost them dearly in the eyes of millions of Americans who were already weary of this flagging experiment in social control. Exasperated by the WCTU's claim to represent American womanhood, Pauline Sabin formed the Women's Organization for National Prohibition Reform in May 1929 and joined the Association Against the Prohibition Amendment (formed in 1918) in campaigning for repeal. Five months later, a crash in share prices on Wall Street heralded the start of the Great Depression and the beginning of the end for Prohibition.

The Depression was to the Wets what the First World War had been to the Drys—a convenient crisis which crippled their opponents. Donations to the dry cause dropped off as the economy went into free fall and the Anti-Saloon League was in no fit state to defend itself from the resurgent Wets, who could now count the formerly dry press baron William Randolph Hearst amongst their number. Like John D. Rockefeller, Hearst turned against Prohibition once it became clear that it was doing little for sobriety and much for lawlessness. For the newspaper magnate, the draconian Jones Law was the final straw.

As America moved into the gloomy 1930s, the old gang of prohibitionists was falling apart. Wayne Wheeler and Purley Baker were both dead. William Jennings Bryan was long gone, collapsing and dying four days after famously defending creationism against Clarence Darrow at the Scopes 'monkey trial'. Pussyfoot Johnson retired from the movement in 1930 and lived out his remaining fifteen years on a farm in New York. Richmond Hobson gave up on the cause in 1930 after admitting that Prohibition was "useless" until people were "ripe for reform." Lest he be accused of learning a lesson, he dedicated the rest of his life to drug prohibition.

Finally, Bishop Cannon, the man who had once held the President to ransom over Prohibition, endured a spectacular fall from grace when he was exposed as a crook and an adulterer. The bent bishop, whose own colleagues described as "cold as a snake", was acquitted of charges of stealing election funds but a proven affair with a secretary, combined with evidence that he had been a war profiteer, put an end to his career in public life.

In 1932, another Democratic politician, Franklin D. Roosevelt, stood for election with the promise to repeal Prohibition. This time, the wet candidate was a Protestant who was up against an unpopular opponent at a time of economic despair and he won with 57% of the vote. The Twenty-first Amendment was drafted before Roosevelt had even taken his oath of office. It contained just three sentences and promised only to repeal the Eighteenth. Congress and the Senate both passed it by a three to one majority and it was submitted to the states on February 20 1933. America was wet again within ten months, with Utah taking the honour of being the thirty-sixth state to ratify the new Amendment, thus making it law, on December 5 1933. The state of Maine—the home of prohibition since 1851—ratified it the very next day.

The Anti-Saloon League remained standing and—as we shall see in a later chapter—lives on today under another name, but the World League Against Alcoholism was already a distant memory and hopes of exporting prohibition overseas had died. After holding out for fourteen years, Finland finally repealed prohibition in 1931. An indication of the failure of the Finnish law came when wet Sweden officially complained about the volume of illicit drink coming in from their supposedly dry-as-dust neighbour.[49]

The Twenty-first Amendment left little Iceland to fly the flag for national prohibition, but having already legalised wine to appease the Spaniards, Iceland did the same to spirits in 1935, and only the sale of beer remained illegal. When asked why the law apparently encouraged the drinking of ardent spirits but forbade the drinking of ale—thus turning the original vision of the temperance movement on its head—Icelandic public health advocates explained that beer was more harmful because it was cheaper. If drunk by the pint, this was indisputable, and this twisted logic was enough to keep the ban on beer in place for decades. When it was finally repealed in 1989, Iceland had the highest per capita membership of Alcoholics Anonymous of any country in the world.[50]

3

Opium

The dawn of the War on Drugs

"Every form of addiction is bad, no matter whether
the narcotic be alcohol or morphine or idealism."
— Carl Jung, 1962

The valiant act which made Richmond Hobson "the most kissed man in America" took place off the coast of Cuba on 3 June 1898. The United States had declared war on Spain six weeks earlier and its navy was hunting enemy ships hiding in an inlet off the Caribbean Sea. The Spanish boats were well concealed and too heavily armed for the Americans to risk a direct attack. Instead, a plan was devised to scuttle the *Merrimac*, a notoriously unreliable coal-carrying vessel, in the shallowest part of the harbour to block the Spaniards' escape route. It was a dangerous strategy. The *Merrimac* would have to sail alone up a narrow stretch of water under heavy bombardment and the crew, assuming they made it to shallow water alive, would have to detonate ten explosives and abandon ship before returning to their comrades on a small catamaran. Twenty-eight year old Lieutenant Hobson was the first to volunteer and, accompanied by six other brave men, set sail for what seemed likely to be his final mission.

What happened next can be filed under 'heroic failures'. Under a hail of unfriendly fire, the crew navigated the old steamboat to its destination without suffering any casualties but were only able to detonate two of the explosives. Instead of blocking the shallow part of the harbour, the ship sailed helplessly on for another hour before sinking slowly and pointlessly into the deep. Hobson and his men made it onto the catamaran unscathed, but the tide took them further upstream into the hands of the Spanish sailors who became their captors.

For Hobson, the *Merrimac* mission was only the first brave but futile endeavour to which he would devote his energies. For the rest of the world, the Spanish-American War—which the USA won two months later—was to have an unexpected but enduring consequence. In defeat, the Spanish relinquished control of Cuba, Guam, Puerto Rico and the Philippines to the Americans, thereby burdening the USA with the nucleus of an empire. This raised important questions about how the new imperial power should behave. Would it rule its dominions with the hypocrisy and greed with which it associated European empire-builders, or would it work to spread American decency and Christian morality?

In the Philippines, one issue emerged as a testing ground for American ethics. There, the Spanish had long held a government monopoly on the sale of opium for the benefit of the islands' minority Chinese population. Filipinos were not allowed to smoke the drug, but the Chinese appetite for the poppy was world famous and their habitual consumption had gone unquestioned for decades. Would the United States continue to sanction the opium-smoking habit in the Philippines? The answer to that question would have profound implications for millions of drug users in the twentieth century and gave the most kissed man in America his third chance to be a hero.

The plant of joy

Opium has been used in medicine and recreation for over five thousand years. Known in Mesopotamia as the 'plant of joy', it was subsequently cultivated by the Egyptians, Greeks, Romans and Persians. There is an allusion to opium being mixed with wine in Homer's *Odyssey* and opium-eating was endorsed by Hippocrates, the father of modern medicine, in the fifth century BC. In its natural habitat of the Middle East, where Islamic law proscribed alcohol, opium was used for centuries as a social lubricant. Arab merchants may have introduced the drug to China as early as 400 AD and certainly no later than 800 AD. Portuguese, Dutch and English sailors ensured that, by 1650, opium was widely used throughout Europe and Asia.

Its medicinal uses are many and varied. Opium and its derivatives are effective treatments for cholera, dysentery, diarrhoea, coughs and sleeplessness, as well as being powerful killers of every kind of pain. In the 1660s, Thomas Sydenham—England's 'Shakespeare of medicine'—declared that "among the remedies which it has pleased Almighty God to give to man to relieve his sufferings, none is so universal and so efficacious as opium".[1] It was Sydenham who developed an alcoholic tincture made with opium, sherry, cinnamon and saffron which he called laudanum. The many varieties of this concoction were immensely popular for generations to come, with angst-ridden writers such as Edgar Allen Poe, John Keats, Thomas De Quincey and Samuel Taylor Coleridge amongst its most famous habitués.

For most of opium's history, the line between medical, recreational and religious use were blurred. Given that the poppy offered "the keys to Paradise"[2]—as De Quincey put it—no civilisation that became familiar with the drug was likely to be entirely free of hedonistic abuse. By the time De Quincey published his overwrought autobiography *Confessions of an English Opium-Eater* in 1821, the agonies and ecstasies of excessive opium use—including the risks of overdose and addiction—had long been recognised.

And yet, by the middle of the nineteenth century, opium's image as one of nature's greatest and most versatile remedies was much the same as it had been in Homer's day. By the middle of the twentieth century, however, its non-medical use had been banned worldwide, its medical use was strictly regulated and those who bought and sold opiates in any form were liable to prosecution, imprisonment and, in some countries, execution.

The demonisation of the poppy at the end of the nineteenth century coincided with science's newfound ability to unleash its most potent derivatives—morphine and heroin. In a misguided attempt to wean a relative handful of users off opium, doctors and pharmacists unwittingly brought vastly more addictive and dangerous drugs onto the market. When narcotics prohibition was introduced to atone for this mistake, it was sadly ironic that the lethal derivatives were best placed to prosper in the age of smuggling.

The battle against drugs in the twentieth century was, in large part, a fight to undo the damage done by scientific advancement. As well as unlocking the psychoactive substances nestling in the poppy, Victorian scientists also created the hypodermic syringe. It was this technological development, combined with advances in pharmacology, that unleashed opium's destructive potential.

But it was a much earlier breakthrough in drug delivery that sowed the seeds of narcotics prohibition. It may seem strange to describe smoking as a scientific breakthrough, but this dosing method was unknown in Europe until Christopher Columbus encountered American Indians in 1493. It took another century for the habit of tobacco smoking to take hold in the Old World and a further fifty years before the craze of opium-smoking began in China.

The Chinese opium-smoking habit was itself an unintended consequence of prohibition. Emperor Chongzhen banned tobacco by imperial decree in 1644, just a few years after European sailors first brought the dreaded weed to Chinese shores. Initiated in the art of smoking but deprived of tobacco, the Chinese stuffed their pipes with the drug they had known for centuries and found the results to be pleasing. It was a habit that the Chinese government, and later the world, would spend years trying to eradicate.

Opium Wars

As Britain's mighty East India Company ruled the waves in the eighteenth century, countless tons of tea and silk were shipped into the United Kingdom from China. England soon developed a tea-drinking habit that would become a national obsession, but it did so at a cost to the economy. The coffers of the Chinese treasury weighed heavy with silver while British reserves were gradually depleted. By the 1790s, the one-way traffic of the East India Company's Oriental shipping routes had created a significant balance of payments deficit which the British government was keen to reverse. The Chinese exported much and imported little because, as the Emperor Qianlong damningly explained, they simply had no use for foreign goods:

"Our Celestial Empire possesses all things in prolific abundance and lacks no product within its own borders. There was therefore no need to import the manufactures of outside barbarians in exchange for our produce."[3]

Those who were familiar with the markets of the Far East knew that the Emperor was wrong. There was one import the Chinese *did* want and it was being produced "in prolific abundance" in Britain's Indian colonies. What little opium that was grown in China was of poor quality, whereas Bengali opium was ideal for smoking. Fortuitously, the East India Company happened to have a monopoly on Bengal's opium industry.

The only inconvenience was that opium had been illegal in China since 1729 and those caught selling the drug could be sentenced to death by strangulation. The severity of the punishment was of little concern to foreign entrepreneurs since the law did not prohibit imports—in fact, it allowed imports to be taxed—but in 1799 the Emperor Kia King responded to a perceived epidemic of opium-smoking and enacted a total ban.[4]

Thereafter, opium traffickers had to be more careful, but not much. Chinese officialdom was notoriously corrupt and Britain's opium traders had to do little more than offer a bribe, anchor their ship off the coast and wait for the Chinese to ferry their loot ashore. It was impossible to deny that this constituted smuggling, albeit with the tacit approval of the British government, and so the East India Company forbade opium to be delivered in its own ships and instead encouraged British privateers to export thousands of chests of the drug to China while maintaining the monopoly on production in Bengal. With this arrangement in place, business was unfettered by the Emperor's ban. By the late 1830s, British opium exports to China were eight times what they had been in 1790 and thirty times what they had been in 1767.[5] It is reasonable to assume that rates of addiction increased by a similar magnitude.

The balance of trade deficit was soon reversed and, with Britain's opium stocks demonstrably worth more than all the tea in China, it was the Emperor's turn to lament the loss of his silver.[6] Faced with insouciant smuggling and a rising tide of opium-smoking, liberalisers in the Chinese government urged the Emperor to legalise the drug and enjoy the tax revenues. But those who favoured suppression warned that legalisation would turn the opium-smoking craze into a veritable frenzy. The prohibitionists won the argument and whilst the Emperor admitted that stamping out opium was a practical impossibility, he reaffirmed his moral stance, declaring that "nothing will induce me to derive a revenue from the vice and misery of my people."[7]

Instead of liberalisation, a brutal crackdown on opium traffickers was launched in December 1838. The first casualties were the crew of a Chinese cargo boat who were strangled to death after being caught ferrying opium back to harbour from a British ship. A few months later, three hundred smugglers, mostly British, were rounded up and forced to hand over their entire stock of opium. The seized cargo happened to be virtually the whole year's supply—20,283 chests—and was worth £2 million (the equivalent of £90 million today). The loss of so great a shipment was of no small concern to the British exchequer, not to mention the Chinese opium habitués who suffered rocketing street prices in the weeks that followed.

It was not, however, enough to incite military aggression from London. That came in June 1839 when a Chinese peasant died during a fight with drunken British sailors in a village inn. The authorities demanded that the murderer be tried in a Chinese court but naval officers claimed to be unable to identify the guilty man. In retribution, the Chinese cut off all trade with the Western 'devils' and gathered a military force to attack Macau, where the wives and children of British merchants were living.

The war that followed was, as Martin Booth described it, "little more than a series of skirmishes, British occupations of various towns and insignificant naval clashes".[8] Battles were few in number and the Chinese lost them all, with the British navy comprehensively outclassing China's little wooden boats. By August 1842, Shanghai had fallen and the British marched to Nanking where a peace treaty was signed. Not the least of its provisions was the seizure of Hong Kong and a payment of £4 million to reimburse the British for their confiscated opium.

The First Opium War had a more pugnacious sequel in 1856-60 after trigger-happy Chinese sailors attacked a suspected pirate ship sailing under a British flag. The crew were released unharmed and the matter would have been forgotten as a minor diplomatic incident had it not been for deeper resentments on both sides. The Chinese were still smarting from their earlier military humiliation while the British were aggrieved by the failure of the Chinese to allow greater access to their markets. When negotiations failed to release the alleged pirate ship, the British declared war. Within a year they were joined by the French, who sought retribution for the execution of one of their missionaries, and together they conquered Peking and destroyed the Emperor's Summer Palace.

China's surrender led to an agreement that effectively legalised the opium trade by placing an excise tax on every pound of the Indian drug that was imported. All talk of ending the trafficking of opium was silenced for a generation. British revenue from the sale of the drug to China—which had doubled between the Opium Wars—doubled again between 1860 and 1880.[9]

Britain's show of strength had paid off handsomely, but for the Chinese, defeat in the Opium Wars was a lasting source of shame which confirmed their view that they were being oppressed by "foreign devils" wielding "unequal treaties". A seething hatred towards the West was fostered for decades to come and opium came to symbolise the nation's emasculated decline. For the rest of the century, Chinese nationalists would portray opium-smoking as a debilitating and deadly plague forced on the Celestial Empire to enslave a proud people for Western profit. This, indeed, is how some British anti-opiumists viewed events at the time, but it is not the whole truth. It is a version of history that ignores China's historic appetite for the drug and the eagerness with which Chinese merchants peddled the Indian shipments once they arrived.[10] The British had certainly profited from the opium trade, as had the Portuguese, the Dutch and the Americans, but opium use in China long preceded the East India Company. When not growing it themselves, the Chinese had been importing the drug from India and the Middle East for over a thousand years.

Nor was the use of opium necessarily, or even usually, debilitating. In China, it was typically taken in moderation and in a civilised setting with the same ritual and decorum with which the English were then consuming Chinese tea. Deaths were extremely rare when the drug was smoked or eaten, and although many users could be classed as addicts, their habituation rarely led to ill health or criminal behaviour so long as prices remained low.

If Britain can be fairly accused of forcing a drug into China against the will of its Emperor, it is far from clear that it did so against the will of its people. Nevertheless, the sheer volume of opium being shipped into China by British privateers in the nineteenth century was, at the very least, disrespectful to national sovereignty. It lowered prices, increased availability and rendered any attempt to enforce prohibition futile.

Opium in Britain

The British government presented the Opium Wars as an unfortunate consequence of China's reluctance to embrace free trade. The drug trafficking aspect was downplayed in Parliament and the word 'opium' did not feature in either of the treaties that ended the wars. For those who could not see the irony in forcing people to accept free trade, globalisation was a more laudable aim than supplying narcotics, but some in Britain were as ashamed of their country's victory as the Chinese were of defeat. Several public figures spoke out against the "immoral" trade in opium, including Sir Stamford Raffles and William Gladstone. Gladstone said that he had never heard of "a war more unjust in its origins" than the First Opium War and confessed to standing "in dread of the judgements of God upon England for our national iniquity towards China."[11]

There had always been a moral ambivalence about the British opium traffic. Warren Hastings, the Governor of Bengal in the late eighteenth century, was happy to encourage the sale of opium to the Chinese while maintaining that it was "a pernicious article of luxury, which ought not to be permitted but for the purpose of foreign commerce only."[12] There was hypocrisy in Gladstone too, who was known to take a few drops of laudanum to steady his nerves before a speech. This was far from unusual, but it underlined the moral inconsistency of condemning the drug abroad when it was flourishing at home.

And how it flourished. By the 1860s, opium was being taken for almost everything by almost everyone. With few genuine cures for disease, physicians relied heavily on the poppy to alleviate pain and suffering, but since few working people could spare the money to visit a doctor, opium was generally bought from local shops and used in accordance with family wisdom and traditional knowledge.

Laudanum could be openly purchased by any man, woman or child in grocery shops, pubs and pharmacists. It was used for everything from hangovers to cholera. It was taken to induce sleep, to relieve aches and pains, and to tackle depression and *ennui*, as well as treating coughs, rheumatism, diarrhoea and toothache. Patent medicines such as Godfrey's Cordial, Mrs Winslow's Soothing Syrup and Street's Infant Quietness made it possible for everyone, young and old, to take opium without even knowing it. Whether used to treat illness or alter mood, the British self-medicated on a grand and growing scale. Between 1830 and 1860, imports of opium rose from ten to forty tons a year.[13] It seems unlikely that such quantities were being used for purely medicinal purposes.

With opium use practically universal amongst the British population, the risk of widespread addiction was very real. No statistics exist to tell us how many Victorians were hooked on the drug, but the list of famous habitués—Keats, George IV, Coleridge, Clive of India and Walter Scott to name but a few—suggests that opium addiction was either confined to wealthy men of leisure or was a much wider phenomenon that went unnoticed because working class habitués were able to feed their habit cheaply and inconspicuously. Either way, addiction was far from unknown. Thomas De Quincey's *Confessions of an English Opium-Eater* was the first detailed account of what we would now consider to be the modern drug addict. Published in 1821 and reprinted throughout the century, this sensational best-seller trod a fine line between cautionary tale and opium advertisement. Like the 1995 film *Trainspotting*, *Confessions* was accused by some of glamourising drug addiction while others saw it as a graphic warning of the dangers. Split into two sections—'The Pleasures of Opium' and 'The Pains of Opium'—*Confessions* was, in truth, a little of both, even if De Quincey could not resist making references to opium's seductive charms when discussing the many 'pains'.

As human beings, both De Quincey and the poet Samuel Taylor Coleridge were self-absorbed egotists whose petulance became insufferable on drugs. Their life stories demonstrate that junkies were prone to lies, immaturity and self-pity long before drugs were outlawed. From the historian's perspective, it is unfortunate that they became the public face of opium use in Britain, since their melodrama and debauchery were not representative of the drug's endemic use in the rest of society. De Quincey was, however, right when he said that the ready availability of opium meant that "happiness might now be bought for a penny, and carried in the waistcoat pocket".[14] Cheap enough for all but the poorest to acquire, an opium habit posed little risk to health or livelihood so long as the drug remained affordable, and it did—opium duty was abolished in 1860. Several contemporary observers were surprised to find that opium addicts led long and ordinary lives. Robert Harvey noted in 1894, for example, that he was "much struck by the fact that the use of the drug was much more common than I had any idea of, and that habitual consumers of ten and fifteen grains a day seemed none the worse for it; and would never have been suspected of using it."[15]

Inevitably there were casualties. Opium was responsible for a third of fatal poisonings[16] and, as in ancient Rome, opium overdose was a popular method of suicide.[17] Such is the art of murder that we can only guess how many deliberate poisonings were wrongly included amongst the hundred or so 'accidental narcotic poisonings' recorded in official statistics each year. Of the truly accidental overdoses, some were the result of shopkeepers absent-mindedly substituting opium for another product, or individuals mistaking laudanum for something milder. The rest involved users overestimating their tolerance or misjudging the strength of their powders, tinctures and syrups.

The saddest cases involved infants. More than half of all opium overdoses involved children under the age of five. A number of these were surely infanticides. The rest were the result of laudanum and 'soothing syrups' being spooned out by over-worked mothers before they disappeared into the mills and factories of industrial Britain. Opium was one of the few effective treatments for sickly children, and for women who endured long working hours without any form of childcare, the temptation to send a restless baby to sleep with patent medicines was not easy to resist. In the mid-1860s, between forty and fifty children under the age of five died each year from opiate overdose.[18] In the context of the appallingly high infant mortality rate of the time, which saw 150 babies die for every 1,000 live births,[19] narcotic poisonings made a negligible contribution to overall mortality, but it could not be denied that these deaths were both shocking and preventable. It was this perceived scandal of infant doping, combined with public unease about the Opium Wars, that gave rise to a ripple of anti-opium sentiment in the mid-nineteenth century.

Concern about opium use focused almost exclusively on the working class, leading some historians to portray the anti-opium campaign as part of a Victorian struggle to control the masses.[20] This is not entirely convincing. The nature of the drug is to make people docile rather than disorderly. An unscrupulous ruling class bent on social control should have tipped laudanum down the workers' throats. In fact, there was little effort expended in either encouraging or discouraging adult use of the drug. The public's right to consume opium in limitless quantities was not seriously challenged until the twentieth century and those who objected to the drug on moral grounds made no distinction between middle and working class use. Those who campaigned for public health and better living standards focused on the working class for the simple reason that it was they who were most likely to dope their children and to suffer secondary poverty through addiction.

Broadly speaking, there were three types of anti-opiumist. Some, mainly Liberals, were repelled by Britain's role in the international opium traffic and the wars fought to maintain it. Others, principally doctors, believed that domestic opium consumption needed to be curtailed to reduce deaths from overdose and accidental poisoning. A noisy third contingent, mostly made up of Quakers, regarded any form of addiction to sensuous pleasures as a moral evil in need of banning.

Although there was some agitation against drug use in Victorian Britain, it would be very easy to exaggerate the scale of anti-opium feeling. Even the anti-opiumists' natural bedfellows in the temperance movement were largely unmoved. Only three of the country's prominent teetotallers were active in the battle against opium, compared with forty-one who campaigned against slavery, thirty-nine who were involved in the peace movement and twelve who campaigned against animal cruelty. Twice as many teetotallers were involved in the obscure and inconsequential anti-tobacco campaign than were involved in the anti-opium movement.[21]

When the domestic opium trade was finally regulated in the late 1860s, it was not to pacify a small band of anti-opiumists but to satisfy doctors and pharmacists who insisted that they, and they alone, should be permitted to sell the drug. The physicians and druggists hardly lacked a financial incentive for wanting to become the sole retailers of a product worth millions of pounds a year. Although there were sincere concerns about opium overdoses and the 'massacre of the innocents', ulterior motives were laid bare when the pharmacists resisted calls from the General Medical Council for tough regulations that would allow opium to be sold only to a person known to the seller. This was too stringent for the street chemists, who shared the doctors' desire to limit sales to registered vendors but not at the expense of limiting the number of potential customers. If the two professions were united in wanting a duopoly on the poppy, only the doctors were sincere in wanting an end to self-medication.

After warning of an epidemic of illicit dealing if regulations were made too rigorous, the pharmacists prevailed. The 1868 Pharmacy Act banned the sale of opium in the traditional outlets of the community shop and local pub, and restricted it to chemists and doctors. Now labelled with a skull and cross-bones, opium could no longer be sold to children and all sales had to be registered. This had an immediate effect on opiate deaths amongst children, which fell by half and declined further as the century wore on. Adult deaths from accidental overdose fell by a third and remained at a level of three per million thereafter.[22]

But aside from these modest regulations, it was business as usual. The law was self-regulating, patent medicines were exempt and any adult could continue to buy any quantity of opium for any purpose. As an article of prohibition, the Pharmacy Act was mild indeed and it was the only law passed to restrict the sale of opium prior to it being banned outright fifty years later. Nevertheless, it represented the first faltering step towards the full medicalisation of drug use in Britain.

In the 1870s, the anti-opium movement coalesced around the Society for the Suppression of the Opium Trade, which was founded by the Darlington born Liberal MP, Joseph Pease. The Society was made up of a selection of clergymen, missionaries, politicians, doctors and temperance folk, most of whom, including Pease, were Quakers. Their concern about the abuse of opium was real enough, but it was Britain's supposed abuse of the Chinese that compelled them to act. The Society named its newsletter the *Friend of China* and petitioned the government to "withdraw all encouragement from the growth of the poppy in India, except for strictly medicinal purposes, and to support the Chinese government in its efforts to suppress the traffic."[23]

Joseph Pease brought anti-opium resolutions before Parliament four times in the 1880s and was repaid with comprehensive defeat on every occasion, but the Society scored a small victory in 1893 when the third Gladstone administration set up a Royal Commission of nine experts to investigate the health and social effects of opium use. The Commission's remit was limited to the drug's use in India, which few considered to be a major problem,* and after two years' research and a three month trip to the colony, the committee published a 2,500 page document which delivered, as the *Lancet* put it, "a crushing blow to the anti-opium faddists."[24] Not only was it a ringing endorsement of the *status quo* in India, but it gently suggested that the public had been misled by the anti-opium campaigners.

As the result of a searching inquiry, and upon a deliberate review of the copious evidence submitted to us, we feel bound to express our conviction that the movement in England in favour of active interference on the part of the Imperial Parliament for the suppression of the opium habit in India, has proceeded from an exaggerated impression as to the nature and extent of the evil to be controlled.[25]

---

* It is worth asking why the Indians were largely immune from the ravages of opium addiction despite its cheap abundance in their country. Part of the answer perhaps lies in the Indian preference for eating the drug, although the Commission heard from various witnesses who claimed that eating opium was *more* hazardous than smoking it. It is more likely that the Indian habit of using opium moderately for religious, quasi-religious and medicinal reasons gave a structure to opium use that discouraged excess.

Dismissing the "gloomy descriptions presented to British audiences", the Commission concluded that opium was little more than the Asian equivalent of alcohol. Noting the "universal tendency amongst mankind to take some form of stimulant with which to comfort or distract themselves",[26] they reported that many of the 723 witnesses who gave evidence regarded alcohol as the greater evil. Opium did not shorten life, they said, and was rarely addictive because only 1% of the morphine content was delivered when smoked. There was much truth in this, but a little less truth in their assertion that prohibiting opium in India would be an act of cultural imperialism (a strange concern from an imperial power) and very little truth in the claim that Indian prohibition would not reduce opium-smoking elsewhere.

Those anti-opiumists who dismissed the Commission's report as a whitewash—which is to say, almost all of them—had some cause for complaint. Opponents of the opium trade had been outnumbered seven to two on the panel and, by focusing on the drug's use in India, the Commission could fairly be accused of ignoring the real issue of Chinese contraband. Furthermore, many of the witnesses interviewed by the Commission had been carefully selected by officials in India who profited from poppy cultivation.

Biased it may have been, but the Commission was sincere in its belief that the evils of opium had been much exaggerated by those who sought to ban it. So compelling was the case *against* prohibition that one of the two anti-opiumists on the panel, the Liberal MP Arthur Pease—brother of Joseph— changed his mind about the whole issue and was asked to resign from the Society for the Suppression of the Opium Trade. It was the start of a fruitless decade for the Society, whose demands were ignored until another Liberal government took power in 1906.

In retrospect, the most remarkable feature of the Victorian anti-opium lobby was how small it was. Compared to almost any other nineteenth century reform movement, agitation against day-to-day opium use was negligible. In the light of the drug's extensive consumption, the absence of a major anti-opium crusade seems odd, as Terry Parssinen noted:

Given that opium was a cheap narcotic, and that the condition of life might well have disposed the working classes to use it as an intoxicant, one cannot help but be struck by the lack of public concern about its use. Either opium was used infrequently as an intoxicant, or middle class investigators overlooked it. In any case, it was insignificant as a social issue.[27]

It is unlikely that Victorian reformers, who campaigned against a whole range of moral vices, would have turned a blind eye to inebriety brought on by opiates, so we must assume that such intoxication was rare. At a time when a bottle of laudanum cost less than a bottle of gin and was almost as easy to obtain, it is surprising that opium was little used as a drug of abuse.* Before 1868, there were no restrictions on the sale of opium whatsoever, and even after the Pharmacy Act the only people forbidden from buying it were children. Despite a largely unregulated market, millions of poor, semi-educated Britons self-medicated with opium in a way that rarely disrupted, and often facilitated, a life of hard work. Not only did opium use reach an equilibrium during this period—albeit after a

---

* Several Victorian authors, including Wilde, Dickens and Conan-Doyle, used the setting of the London opium den in their work. In *The Man with the Twisted Lip*, Sherlock Holmes spends an evening in an opium den where he finds a man with "yellow, pasty face, drooping lids and pin-point pupils, all huddled in a chair, the wreck and ruin of a noble man." The wasted opium fiend stands in stark contrast with the great detective who is razor sharp from his cocaine injections. All this made for good fiction, but there were fewer than one hundred Chinese living in the city at that time and there cannot have been more than a tiny handful of opium dens scattered around the East End.[28] Although attractive to novelists, the idea that opium dens were a common feature of London's night-life is a myth.

substantial rise in mid-century—but its consumption began to fall in the 1880s, thirty years before it became a forbidden fruit.

While alcohol reigned supreme as Britain's preferred recreational drug, opium assumed a more functional role as a medicine, sedative and anti-depressant. The closest modern day equivalents would not be heroin and cocaine but *Valium* and *Prozac*, if one can imagine these drugs being as readily available as aspirin. Opium never competed with alcohol as a social lubricant, nor was it smoked for hedonistic purposes. This was the crucial difference between opium use in Britain and opium use in China. Had opium been used primarily for recreation, it would surely have been subjected to greater moral opprobrium. That is exactly what happened in China and, as we shall now see, in the United States.

Caves of oblivion

One morning in January 1848, James W. Marshall, the owner of a sawmill in Coloma, California, found several gold nuggets in a river. This seemingly fortunate discovery was to be his ruin. In the Gold Rush that followed, his employees deserted the sawmill to prospect for gold, he was forced off his land by avaricious miners and he died penniless 37 years later.

Amongst those who descended on California in the heady days of the Gold Rush were thousands of Chinese immigrants. Some worked down the mines and on the railroad. Others settled in and around San Francisco working in laundries, restaurants and grocery stores. A small minority set up brothels, gambling pits and opium dens to cater for their compatriots in their short hours of leisure.

While the economy boomed, relations between the Chinese and Americans were frosty, but not openly hostile. In the 1870s, the boom turned to bust. The Gold Rush had passed, the railways were completed and it was the Chinese who were blamed for low wages and job scarcity. With his distinctive language, dress and customs, the Chinese immigrant had never blended into the American West, but when the economy bombed, he was victimised without mercy. Resented for sending home money that could have been spent in America, and loathed for crossing picket lines at work, the Chinese became the victims of appalling acts of violence, such as when seventeen Chinese men and boys were hanged by a lynch mob in Los Angeles.

The smoking of opium—an activity almost entirely confined to the Chinese—became both a symbol of their otherness and the proof of their immorality. It was true that the Chinese had brought opium-smoking to California, just as they brought it to the other states they settled in, notably Nevada, Texas and New York. It was also true that of the 10% of Chinese immigrants who were women, a very large number were prostitutes. But both dope and whore were confined to the ghettos of Chinatown for the pleasure of poorly paid, unmarried Chinese labourers—the 'coolies'. If white labourers substituted alcohol for opium, they would have found that the Chinaman's life of hard work, gambling and occasional brothel-creeping was not so very different from their own, but ignorance of the Oriental lifestyle was a symptom of the Chinese's failure to integrate and it cost them dearly.

By 1879, the Chinese were being described as "an unmitigated evil" in the Nevada State Senate.[29] Their laundries and bakeries were portrayed as cauldrons of disease. Journalists who were sent to investigate the opium dens were repulsed by the smell of the drug and disorientated by the darkness of the dives.* Newspapers were overwhelmingly negative towards both the Chinese and opium-smoking in the last decades of the

---

*A word much used by Carry Nation in relation to saloons, the word 'dive' is actually a corruption of 'divan', the low beds upon which opium-smokers reclined.[31]

nineteenth century as they railed against "vile, pernicious dens of debauchery" and "caves of oblivion".[30] Anti-opium news stories and editorials appeared regularly for the rest of the century, often accompanied by calls to outlaw the drug and put an end to Chinese immigration.

Opium was blamed for fires, prostitution, theft, violence, mental illness, organised crime and death, but what really irked the anti-opiumists was the drug's rising popularity with young, white Americans. Beginning in the 1870s, a small number of gamblers, pimps, students, bohemians and—strangely— sportsmen began to dabble with the Oriental thrills of opium. It was said that the Chinese deliberately lured in America's youth, making addicts of the boys and seducing the girls. "What other crimes were committed in those dark fetid places when these little innocent victims of the Chinamen's wiles were under the influence of the drug, are almost too horrible to imagine," said the anti-opiumist Samuel Gompers. "There are hundreds, aye, thousands, of our American girls and boys who have acquired this deathly habit and are doomed, hopelessly doomed, beyond the shadow of redemption."[32] That Gompers was the president of the American Federation of Labor writing in a book entitled *Some Reasons for Chinese Exclusion* is probably no coincidence.

The idea that the ghettoised Chinese actively solicited trade from whites was at odds with their reputation for insularity, just as the image of the lusty Chinaman was incongruous with opium's recognised tendency to dampen sexual desire, but it was enough to spark a moral panic and legislation inevitably followed. Opium dens were banned in several towns in the north-west of America from 1875, with San Francisco the first to do so. The bans were largely ineffective. Opium dens had always operated semi-covertly and setting one up was a simple affair compared to fitting out a speakeasy or a saloon. If contemporary accounts are to be believed, the dives were far from ostentatious at the best of times and, although the police carried out raids periodically, little more than a room, a pipe and a stash of opium was required for operations to resume.

Thirteen states banned the smoking of opium between 1877 and 1890. Notable for being the first laws to ban the *consumption* of a drug in American history, they were poorly enforced and failed to achieve the unspoken aim of keeping whites away from opium. Nevertheless, the very fact that the smoking of opium was singled out when morphine, laudanum and any number of opium-laced patent medicines were widely available betrays the racial bias.

Anti-opium laws came on the back of a wave of legislation that restricted, taxed and disenfranchised Chinese labourers. As early as 1862, California passed the self-explanatory 'Protect Free White Labor Against Competition with Chinese Coolie Labor and to Discourage the Immigration of the Chinese into the State of California Act'. That law was later ruled unconstitutional, but in 1882 the federal government passed the Chinese Exclusion Act which suspended all immigration from China for ten years. By this time, the 'coolies' were almost universally regarded by press, public and politicians alike as an unwanted presence. That Chinese immigration was a great evil that had brought vice, immorality and disease to America was a conventional wisdom endorsed by presidents, trade unions and newspapers as diverse as the *New York Times* and the *Salt Lake Tribune*.

A monument to shameless racial bigotry, the Chinese Exclusion Act was a blot on the United States' reputation as the home of huddled masses. Insofar as it was an anti-drugs policy, the idea was simple: if the government could not get rid of opium-smoking, it would get rid of opium-smokers. In one sense, it worked. The country's Chinese population dwindled from 100,000 to 60,000 between 1890 and 1920.[33] As a means of controlling opium use, however, it was a failure. The police were as incapable of closing down the opium dens as they had ever been and the last decades of the nineteenth century saw a substantial rise in opium use amongst whites which negated any effect from a declining Chinese workforce.

Penalties stiffened and legislation proliferated in the early years of drug prohibition as legislators sought to remedy the failure of one law with another. Fines for visiting opium dens increased from $10 to $1,000. Prison sentences were handed out to whites and Chinese alike. The Chinese Exclusion Act was renewed for another ten years in 1892 and extended indefinitely in 1902. (The law was not repealed until 1943 when the US and China found themselves in an alliance against Japan.) As more states banned the smoking of opium, some talked of the need for a nationwide ban on the drug. Others proposed forcefully deporting the Chinese.

Meanwhile, medical opinion was hardening against opiate use generally and opium-smoking in particular. In 1892, the *Journal of the American Medical Association* condemned the smoking of opium as "an aid to the perpetration of illegal and vicious acts"[34] and called for a ban on imports of smoking opium (which differed from crude opium). At the turn of the century, the Committee on the Acquirement of the Drug Habit came to much the same conclusion, adding that: "If the Chinaman cannot get along without his 'dope', we can get along without him."[35]

Morphine

Opium-smoking attracted the headlines in late nineteenth century America, but it was a sideshow in the grander scheme of the nation's drug addiction. No reliable figures exist for the number of opium-smokers, but in addition to perhaps 15% of a dwindling Chinese population,[36] the habit was confined to "thieves, sharpers and sporting-men, and a few bad actors".[37] Since the number of opiate addicts has been estimated to have been in the region of 200,000,[38] the great majority of habitués either ate or drank their opium or were hooked on its high voltage derivative, morphine.

The typical drug addict in the 1890s could not have been more different to the popular image of the opium fiend. The average user was female, white, middle-aged and affluent. In most cases, she was introduced to opiates by her doctor after suffering from chronic pain or gynecological problems. Her drug of choice was morphine. Her preferred delivery system was the hypodermic syringe.

Morphine was first isolated in the early nineteenth century, at a time when scientists isolated a number of important alkaloids, including caffeine and nicotine, from their parent plants. Named after Morpheus, the god of sleep in Greek mythology, this pure white crystal was not widely used in medicine until the invention and mass production of the hypodermic syringe in the 1850s.*

From the perspective of the medical profession, morphine had several advantages over opium. Its purity allowed for carefully measured doses and its potency—ten times stronger than opium—made it more effective in killing pain and inducing slumber. The syringe allowed efficient administration without the gastric upsets that were associated with opium-eating. In the early years of its medical use, morphine was not thought to be addictive, especially when administered hypodermically. These beliefs could not have been more wrong, but they led to morphine injections being recommended as a cure for opium addiction in the 1870s and the drug was recklessly over-prescribed. Seeing it as a panacea, doctors administered it for every ache and pain with the same relish with which they had previously dished out opium, but a fortnight's use was enough for addiction to take hold and morphine's power

---

* In the nineteenth century, syringes were used to inject under the skin rather than into veins. According to Davenport-Hines, intravenous injection was not practised until the 1910s when heroin addicts pioneered the technique.[39]

as an analgesic was matched by the severity of the withdrawal symptoms. Many physicians made the fundamental mistake of leaving patients with a syringe to self-medicate. Others became hooked themselves; by 1910, one in fifty doctors were addicted —ten times the rate in the general population.

Morphine was more expensive than opium and only those who could afford to see a doctor and buy the drug could develop a habit. This excluded the ethnic minorities and social pariahs who came to be associated with cocaine, marijuana and smoked opium. By the end of the nineteenth century, morphine use was more widespread than any of these drugs, but the respectability of its habitués shielded them from moral censure. With the syringe giving their addiction a veneer of medical treatment, morphine addicts tended to be regarded as patients rather than junkies,* as indeed many were. Purely recreational use was frowned upon, but morphine addiction was seldom explicitly hedonistic and the line between pleasure and pain-relief remained blurred. In some cases, morphine use was a legitimate response to constant pain. For others, it was a lifelong addiction that had begun with an injury or illness that had long been forgotten.

The same could be said of the other major group of addicts in nineteenth century America. It is not known how many soldiers who fought in the Civil War became hooked on opiates, but with 375,000 wounded and ten million opium pills dished out in army hospitals, the number is likely to run into many thousands.[40] Not for nothing was opium addiction known as the Soldier's Disease, nor was it a coincidence that opium consumption in America began to decline after the 1890s, just as the Civil War veterans were dying out.

By the 1880s, the medical profession's honeymoon with morphine had turned sour and doctors awoke to the widespread

---

* An anachronistic term in this context, the word 'junkie', or 'junky', was not coined until young men began taking heroin in the 1910s. Its origin comes from the belief that addicts sold scrap metal to feed their habit.

addiction their earlier profligacy had caused. The next generation of medical students were taught to use the drug only in the last resort and although physicians continued to supply opiates to their older patients, it was expected that when they died, the morphine epidemic would die with them.

By the end of the century, doctors had less need for opium and morphine than they had at its start. The invention of aspirin provided a safer form of relief from minor pains, and chloral, bromides and codeine were increasingly prescribed for a range of other ailments. The latter was also derived from opium but it was weaker and therefore less addictive. Then, in 1898, a new drug came on the market which promised to help morphine users shake off their addiction. Promoted with the claim that "addiction can scarce be possible", this miracle cure—diacetylmorphine—was sold under the brand name of Heroin.[41]

Prohibition by diplomacy

Two events in 1905 laid the foundations for what would become the War on Drugs. For the Chinese, the nineteenth century had been an era of oppression and humiliation at home and abroad. Britain had twice used her military might to force opium on them and their emigrants were vilified in the United States. After defeat in the Second Opium War, China was forced to accept European merchants, American industrialists and Christian missionaries, all of whom were unwelcome to traditionalists. In the face of Western military supremacy, the Peking government was helpless to resist, but an embittered faction of students, conservatives and nationalists gathered to reclaim the sovereignty of the Celestial Empire, culminating in the viciously bloody Boxer Uprising of 1898-1901 which defeated by an army drawn from eight nations. This third military humiliation, combined with Allied atrocities during the war, only entrenched hatred of the 'barbarians' and in May

1905, Chinese merchants led a popular boycott of American goods which largely shut down China's ports to US shipping. The embargo was explicitly carried out in protest at the "national disgrace" of the Chinese Exclusion Act being extended indefinitely, thereby leading to a permanent ban on Chinese immigration into America. As one of the boycott's figureheads declared: "China, the sleeping lion, has awakened."[42]

The dramatic deterioration in Sino-American relations alarmed politicians in Washington who had for too long taken Chinese subservience for granted. Consternation rose when the boycott began to eat away at exports in 1906. If Americans were bearing the brunt of China's antipathy towards the West, the persecution of Chinese immigrants in the US gave it the air of comeuppance. In a private moment, President Theodore Roosevelt admitted that "we have behaved scandalously toward Chinamen in this country."[43] But just as Roosevelt was coming to terms with the consequences of cultural imperialism in China, the question of what to do with the fruits of its military imperialism in the Philippines demanded an answer.

The issue of opium-smoking in the Philippines had rumbled on since the Americans had 'liberated' the islands from the Spanish in 1898.* Debate was interrupted in 1902 by an outbreak of cholera—fortuitously, one of the diseases that can be treated with the poppy—but the state-owned opium monopoly America had inherited from the Spanish remained a test of the new empire's moral credentials. To some, the opium monopoly was a financial boon worth $600,000 a year. To others, it was a national embarrassment that fostered a wicked vice. The Right Reverend Charles H. Brent was firmly in the latter camp and it was he, a Canadian born missionary, who fought most vigorously for an end to the opium traffic. Brent first travelled to

---

* They then had to be liberated from the Filipinos themselves in the Philippine-American War (1899-1902). That conflict produced another American 'anti' group when Mark Twain founded the Anti-Imperialist League.

the Philippines in 1902 as the colony's first Episcopal bishop. Sincere in his convictions and compassionate in his intentions, Brent's attitude towards intoxicating drugs did not encompass shades of grey. One of his supporters described his attitude to opium thus:

"His point of view is, and doubtless will continue to be, missionary, and vocal with idealistic zeal at every stage. He is the uncompromising enemy of compromise. To him this question is a moral question; he is scornful toward every suggestion of expediency."[44]

Believing drugs to have no virtues and many dangers, Brent was of the opinion that—as David Musto put it—"recreational use of narcotics should be prohibited, their traffic curtailed on a world scale, and a scourge eliminated from the earth."[45] He intended to start with the Philippines.

The US came tantalisingly close to maintaining the opium monopoly. In 1903, a bill to retain the *status quo* was put forward by the government and received the approval of the Philippines' Governor-general (and later US President) William Howard Taft. The bill was on the brink of becoming law when it came to the attention of Wilbur Crafts, the founder and superintendent of the International Reform Bureau. A Methodist preacher of puritan stock, Crafts was gaining a reputation as a "reform fanatic" who crusaded against alcohol, cigarettes, Sunday baseball, carnival rides and close dancing.[46] It was no surprise that he also opposed recreational drug use and was repelled by the government's plan to facilitate opium-smoking in the Philippines. Crafts organised a letter-writing campaign which gave the White House sufficient evidence of popular outrage for Roosevelt to veto the bill.[47] Instead, Bishop Brent was sent to the Far East as part of a three man fact-finding mission to investigate the opium problem and find a solution.

There was little doubt what solution Brent, at least, would arrive at. "The question is first and foremost a moral one," he wrote in 1903. "The consumption of opium is not merely a personal weakness; it is a social vice, i.e. a crime... if the matter is a moral one there should be no more license allowed than in murder or stealing."[48] Travelling to the Philippines, Brent and his two colleagues found a Chinese population of 70,000 (5% of the total) and 190 opium dives. The Spanish system of allowing the Chinese to smoke opium while prohibiting its sale to native Filipinos had apparently been effective—the committee found that opium use amongst Filipinos was "insignificant"—and so the case for prohibition was instead made on the basis of precaution. "The danger", concluded the committee, "lies in the tendency of the vice to grow and spread, until the number of victims, now inconsiderable, may at some future time reach a point where it shall constitute an alarming evil."[49]* Such a contagion had never occurred in three centuries of Chinese settlement in the islands, but, perhaps mindful of the spread of opium-smoking in the United States, the committee called for total prohibition. When Brent's Philippine Commission published its report in 1904, it recommended that the opium monopoly remain in place for three years to allow Chinese habitués to disaccustom themselves from the habit. Thereafter, all opium traffic and trading would be abolished. This policy was adopted by the US government and was passed by Congress in March 1905.

By the summer of 1906, two seemingly unrelated problems were converging upon a single solution. While President Roosevelt worked to repair relations with China, Bishop Brent concerned himself with making a success of opium prohibition in the Philippines. Having now spent several years in the Far East, Brent was familiar with the scale of the international opium traffic and knew that the Philippines' vast, unwatched coastline was a smuggler's delight. He concluded that the only

---

* In a letter written in 1903, Brent made this scenario appear inevitable, writing: "If license is allowed any section of the community to consume opium it will be only a matter of time before vast areas of untainted life are polluted."[50]

way to eradicate drug use in the Philippines was to wage a global war against opium. The way to break the back of the opium trade, Brent believed, was to curtail demand in China and starve the British of their key market.

In July 1906, the bishop sent Roosevelt a letter explaining that "the sole hope for the Chinese is in concerted action [against the opium trade]"[51] and asked the President to consider building partnerships with other countries. Roosevelt took the hint. Seeing a way to curry favour with the Chinese by assisting them in their efforts to eradicate opium-smoking, he and Brent made plans for an international summit to discuss the narcotics problem.

Events abroad began to favour the anti-opiumists. The British were not blind to the implications of rising Chinese nationalism. "If we succeed in getting justice from Americans now," said one Shanghai lawyer at the height of the embargo, "we may then boycott the nation that forces opium down our throats."[52] In 1906, ten years of Conservative government came to an end and the Liberal party swept to power. While the Conservatives had maintained a course of studied inaction on the opium issue, many Liberals shared the view of Joseph Pease that the opium trade was "morally indefensible".[53] Having been committed to abolishing it during their long years in opposition, the Liberals took only a few months to hammer out an agreement with the Chinese to phase out opium trafficking within ten years.

Encouraged by events in London, the Chinese launched a new crackdown on opium-smoking in September 1906. Few expected this campaign to yield more success than previous efforts, but this time the government was able to harness the revived spirit of nationalism and, though its methods were brutal, the crusade against this most symbolic of evils won widespread support.

Meanwhile, Brent and Roosevelt busied themselves with plans for an international opium summit due to be held in

Shanghai in 1909. Twelve other countries had agreed to attend, but at the insistence of the two opium trading giants, Britain and the Netherlands, the meeting was designated a commission rather than a conference, which is to say that it would not have the power to make a binding treaty. Closely involved in proceedings was Hamilton Wright, an Ohio-born public health specialist endowed with a magnificent moustache and a penchant for social change. Having spent several years studying tropical diseases in India and the Far East, Wright returned to America believing opium to be "the greatest curse which humanity has ever known".[54] He and Brent were, as one historian described them, "moral entrepreneurs of the purest kind"[55] and it was they who planted the seeds of worldwide drug prohibition in the twentieth century.

As the USA prepared to lead the world in a crusade against the opium menace, Hamilton Wright noticed that America had an embarrassing lack of anti-drugs legislation of its own. This oversight was not a reflection of any lack of will. Most US states had banned or regulated the sale of opiates and a national ban would have been acceptable to politicians in Washington were it not for the constraints of federal government. Restricted by the Constitution and deprived of a national police force, lawmakers were limited in how far they could regulate private behaviour and voluntary transactions. The difficulty of banning a product nationwide was one reason why the Anti-Saloon League required a Constitutional Amendment in 1919. A similar amendment banning recreational drugs would almost certainly have been ratified if there had been a satisfactory definition of 'recreational' and if there had been time to put it before the states. Time was short, however, and the absence of a grass-roots equivalent of the Anti-Saloon League was an indication of how little interest Americans had in the issue.

With the Shanghai summit fast approaching, anti-opiumists demanded a gesture of prohibition in order to, as the Secretary of State candidly phrased it, "save our face in the conference at Shanghai."[56] Opium-smoking was the obvious target. It was the issue closest to China's heart and the habit had long been demonised in the United States. Its users were perceived as social deviants and had no political influence. Nor would there be any outcry from industry since no American companies were officially involved in the opium trade.

Unable to forbid either the act of smoking or the sale of opium, Brent and Wright drew up the Smoking Opium Exclusion bill to ban the importation of smoking opium. After a brief delay, the bill was passed by Congress while the Shanghai commission was in session on February 9 1909. A jubilant Bishop Brent, who was chairing the meeting, proudly announced the passage of the legislation to delegates and, although there is no record of any of them being impressed, the ban on opium-smoking set the standard for American leadership in the War on Drugs. It began what Musto calls "an American tradition in narcotic control—enactment of strict domestic legislation in the United States as an example to other nations."[57]

The Shanghai meeting was a qualified success. The thirteen nations represented—Austro-Hungary, Britain, China, France, Germany, Italy, Japan, the Netherlands, Persia, Portugal, Russia, Siam and the USA—jealously guarded their own financial interests. As the world leaders in the pharmaceutical industry, the Germans were opposed to any restrictions on the sale of cocaine and morphine. The Persians aimed to protect their lucrative poppy-growing industry, and the Dutch, British and Portuguese remained wary of over-regulation of the opium market. Other countries were conspicuous by their absence, not least the great poppy-growing nation of Turkey.

Despite their differences, there was general agreement that opium-smoking was a vice that should be consigned to history. While morphine, cocaine and heroin had legitimate medical uses, opium-smoking had none and so all delegates agreed, with varying degrees of hope and sincerity, to eliminate the habit in their countries and colonies. This commitment offered sufficient promise for the Americans to arrange an international conference with treaty-making powers two years later. Mindful of the unspoken purpose of the Shanghai commission, Wright assured doubters in Washington that the meeting would "be used as oil to smooth the troubled water of our aggressive commercial policy" in China.[58]

The International Opium Conference got underway in the Hague in December 1911 and continued into the new year. With the exception of the absent Austro-Hungary, the list of attendees was the same as in Shanghai. Chaired again by Bishop Brent, and riven with the same mutual suspicions, the twelve nations nevertheless signed an agreement—the International Opium Convention—which committed each party to "the gradual suppression of the abuse of opium, morphine, and cocaine".[59]

The wording of the treaty left ample room for interpretation. The accepted need for opiates in medicine allowed for a loosely regulated international opium trade. The production and distribution of opium was to be "controlled" rather than prohibited. Signatories were expected to "use their best endeavours"[60] to create a system in which opiates were sold only for medical use by responsible and licensed individuals. How they chose to do this was their business, and it would take many years and several more conferences to close all the loopholes, but the fundamental message of the International Opium Convention soon became the unshakeable policy of the twentieth century's global struggle against narcotics. The production, sale and distribution of drugs were taken out of the hands of private individuals and placed in the hands of pharmaceutical companies, doctors and criminals. All that came later were clauses and crackdowns.

The Harrison Act

The War on Drugs is often said to have begun in 1971 when Richard Nixon increased spending on drug enforcement sevenfold and declared narcotics to be America's "public enemy number one". Tempting though it is to blame a failed policy on an unpopular President, the crackdown of the early 1970s was just one in a series of drastic attempts to make good on a commitment made sixty years earlier. Nixon may have been the first President to use the phrase 'war on drugs' but that is largely a matter of semantics. Eisenhower called for "a new war on narcotics"[61] in 1954 as the head of an administration that introduced the death penalty for some drug offences, and many battles had been lost in earlier decades, so it is unfair to saddle Tricky Dicky with all the blame. If a date must be given for the outbreak of the War on Drugs, 1909 is as good as any.

When the Smoking Opium Exclusion Act was made law in 1909, Hamilton Wright declared that a "new era has dawned in the United States."[62] Tragically, he was right. As smoking opium became scarce, prices rocketed. In 1917, when a tin of smoking opium cost $20 elsewhere in the world, it sold for $70 in the USA. By 1924, the price had risen to $200.[63] Faced with limited availability and unaffordable prices, opium-smokers turned to cheaper alternatives.

In California, the Chinese continued to smoke opium if they could find it, but white Americans switched to morphine *en masse*. On the East Coast, there was a huge surge in the use of heroin after 1909 which was further prompted by local laws against morphine and cocaine. In New York City, which had 6,000 opium-smokers according to Hamilton Wright,[64] there was a veritable epidemic of heroin use. By 1920, nine out of ten American heroin addicts could be found within 180 miles of the city.[65]

The drug scene in New York in the wake of the opium-smoking ban gave a taste of what was to become a worldwide phenomenon. For the first time, street-dealers became the dominant source of opiates. No longer was the typical American addict a middle class woman or a Chinese immigrant buying opium or morphine from a grocery store or pharmacist. With doctors reluctant to prescribe morphine, and with opium banned or heavily restricted, the typical addict became the young, working class male. Whereas opium-smokers had once met in an opium den, heroin users gathered in the street. Whereas the opium addict had been viewed as weak-willed but basically harmless, the street junkie was feared as part of a criminal underclass.

Heroin was first developed when the English chemist C. R. Alder Wright mixed morphine with acetic anhydride in an attempt to find a cure for morphine addiction. A study published in 1899, a year after the drug became commercially available, found heroin to be effective in getting habitués off morphine but by 1902 scientists had established that heroin was the most addictive and destructive opiate derivate yet discovered. Because the truth about heroin was recognised within a few years of its appearance, it never enjoyed the same honeymoon in general medical practice as opium, morphine and cocaine. (Cocaine became briefly fashionable in medical practice after 1884 when the fame-hungry Sigmund Freud wrote a starry-eyed article in praise of cocaine injections. By 1890, the dangers of addiction and overdose had become well known and general use was discontinued. Responding to growing anti-drug sentiment, *Coca-Cola* replaced cocaine with caffeine in 1903.)

Heroin was perfectly suited to the age of prohibition. Strong, compact and odourless, it lent itself to smuggling more readily than opium. As a pure white crystal, it could be easily cut with milk powder to extend dealers' profit margins. For the user, heroin had the benefit of being easier to conceal and consume. Whereas opium required an elaborate system of preparation and a conspicuous pipe, heroin could be sniffed and, as the drug war escalated, injected.

In 1914, New York restricted the sale of all "habit-forming drugs" to physicians under strict regulation. The architect of the law was Charles B. Towns, a salesman who had made a career out of selling quack cures for drug addiction. Towns accepted that the ban would have no effect on those who bought habit-forming drugs illicitly but insisted, with considerable naïvety, that "it will, however, cut off the supply of those who in the past have broken no law to obtain drugs."[66] The predictable reality was that those who had previously broken no law became habitual law-breakers as they sought out illicit channels for the opiates they craved. At first this was not so difficult. New Yorkers were still able to buy their drugs in neighbouring states, but Towns soon echoed the cry of the Anti-Saloon League in calling for national legislation to cure a local problem. He did not have to wait long.

In March 1915, the Harrison Narcotics Tax Act came into effect with Hamilton Wright's fingerprints all over it. Wright had been pushing for nationwide prohibition since returning from Shanghai six years earlier. The way Wright told the story, the Americans had gathered twelve countries together to help them put their house in order only to find, upon closer inspection of the figures, that it was Uncle Sam who was the world's biggest consumer of narcotics. It was therefore a matter of urgency for the shame-faced United States to fight the drug war on the home front before they lectured others.

"The history of the opium fight," said Wright, "forms a queer illusion of our national blindness to our own faults and emphasizes our national tendency to see, with an amazing clarity, the sins of others, while remaining blind to our own faults."[67] In many ways this was a perceptive comment. Americans had long condemned the drug use of immigrants and foreigners without recognising their own appetite for opiates, which was considerable, although not quite at the world-beating level claimed by Wright. He insisted that his country was hooked on opiates "to an astonishing extent",[68] but his own figures showed that only 0.18% of the population were regular users and, by 1910, opiate consumption had been falling for fifteen years.[69]

Certainly it was true that Americans tended to blame foreigners for the drug problem and Wright was justified in calling attention to America's self-deception and xenophobia, but the idea that he and Brent had undergone a Damascene conversion in Shanghai is wholly unconvincing. It is hard to imagine either of them tolerating recreational opiate use on any scale and, by 1910, they had devised a scheme for national prohibition that would overcome the obstacle of the American Constitution. Initially, they planned to bury those who dispensed drugs under a mountain of paperwork. It was hoped that a complex system of records, registers and regulation for even the smallest quantity of narcotics would discourage their sale. At the very least, it would make it possible for the government to keep track of the nation's drug consumption and identify which doctors and druggists were oversupplying.

This proposal became the Foster Bill, named after its sponsor, Vermont Congressman David Foster. Wright personally took charge of drafting the legislation and hoped to see it become law in time for the Hague conference of 1911, thereby giving the rest of the world further evidence of America's good intentions. Standing in their way were the many druggists and physicians who found the terms too onerous and the penalties too harsh. Along with the makers of patent medicines, whose businesses would be crippled by a total ban on pick-me-up drugs, they successfully lobbied for its defeat.

After attending the Hague conference empty-handed, Wright spent three years negotiating with the pharmaceutical lobby to find an acceptable compromise while whipping up fear about America's supposed drug epidemic. This time the focus of public hysteria was cocaine use amongst blacks. The ban on opium-smoking, combined with the rising tide of dry legislation, had led to an increase in cocaine's popularity in the

Deep South which had since spread up the East Coast.[70] Although blacks tended to prefer cocaine to opiates, both drugs were disproportionately used by whites.[71] Wright and his fellow travellers nevertheless focused on alleged acts of rape and violence committed by "cocaine-crazed negroes".[72] According to Wright, cocaine was the "creator of criminals" which drove "the humbler negroes all over the country to abnormal crimes."[73] Evidence of these crimes was anecdotal at best and it was patently untrue to claim, as the *New York Times* did,[74] that cocaine made blacks impervious to bullets, or that "most of the attacks upon white women in the South are the direct result of the cocaine-crazed Negro brain."[75] These tales were so similar to the contemporary scare about liquor-soaked blacks on the rampage in the Deep South that it is fair to assume that one set of prohibitionists was borrowing from the other.

Playing on the Southerner's fear of black insurgency was not the only trick the anti-narcotic crusaders copied from the Anti-Saloon League. While the temperance zealots warned that drink was a threat to civilisation, anti-drugs campaigners warned that opiate abuse would lead to the nation "degenerating back into something worse than monkeydom".[76] While the water-drinkers blamed booze for 90% of crime, drug prohibitionists insisted that no less than 40% of crime was due to cocaine and morphine.[77]

By 1913, the opium-smoking ban, combined with numerous statewide prohibitions of drugs and alcohol, had created an environment in which a subterranean drug culture could take root. Prohibitionists insisted that America's embryonic narcotics problem could only be nipped in the bud with national legislation. As the rumbling fear of black cocaine fiends and white junkies grew louder, even those whose livelihoods depended on the sale of drugs accepted the need for much tighter regulation. Respectable physicians held no brief for the 'dope doctors' who handed out opiates indiscriminately and they were falling out of sympathy with opiate habitués who were increasingly being drawn from the dregs of society. When Wright drew up a new bill to restrict narcotic sales in 1913, it was remarkable for how few concessions he felt compelled to make.

Put before Congress by New York Representative Francis Burton Harrison in June 1913, the Harrison Narcotics Tax Bill reduced the amount of paperwork to be filled in upon sale and excluded cannabis, which was not universally regarded as a narcotic and was, in any case, little used. The main exemption was for patent medicines, which were permitted to contain two grains of opium per bottle—a meagre dose. Beyond this, the new proposal remained the same as the Foster Bill. Every manufacturer, importer and supplier of opium, cocaine and their derivatives was required to pay a nominal tax to register with the government and keep a written copy of every prescription. Penalties remained harsh, with violators subject to five years in prison or a $5,000 fine.

Passed into law on 14 December 1914, the Harrison Act was presented as a means of raising tax, but this facade was hard to maintain since the registration fee cost only $1 a year, and tax revenues from the sale of drugs were bound to fall once they were only available on prescription. The tax argument served mainly to obscure the plain truth that the government had prohibited recreational drug use in the United States.

History almost demands that a law as portentous as the Harrison Act should have been the subject of anguished discussion and national controversy. In fact, the Congressional debate lasted only a few minutes and the public, insofar as they cared at all, were overwhelmingly supportive. Drug prohibition was not carried on a wave of popular fervour so much as nodded through on an undulation of indifference. Americans were far more interested in the Congressional debate that took place eight days later when Richmond Hobson beckoned in the Eighteenth Amendment with his histrionic speech 'Alcohol: The Great Destroyer'. Drink, not drugs, was the subject that divided opinion in the 1910s. The Harrison Act was not seen as an epoch-making fork in the road but as, to borrow David Musto's phrase, "a routine slap at a moral evil."[78]

The Harrison Act, which had been supported by the American Medical Association, placed the nation's trust in the doctors and, after 1915, controlling the medical profession became the key to controlling the licit drug supply. Alas, having been handed a virtual monopoly over the opiate trade, many doctors proved to be neither trustworthy nor controllable. With thousands of dedicated potential customers, physicians continued to prescribe opiates on a scale not envisioned by the architects of the Harrison Act. With quacks handing out hard drugs with impunity, the full damage of the Harrison Act was postponed for four years before the narcotics industry was handed to criminals for good.

The final break came in March 1919, when the Supreme Court was required to rule on a key question that the Harrison Act had not addressed. It was unclear whether physicians were permitted to prescribe opiates to otherwise healthy addicts to maintain their addiction. Many reputable doctors argued that a policy of enforced 'cold turkey' was inhumane and impractical, but others argued that prescribing opiates to addicts only served to feed a vice. The Supreme Court ruled in favour of the hard-liners and the maintenance of addiction was outlawed. It was the legal confirmation of an attitude that had been hardening in America for over twenty years—that addiction was not an illness, but a crime. It also left approximately 200,000 habitués without a legal source of drugs. Over the next two decades, the Narcotics Division shut down all of America's drug clinics and arrested 25,000 'dope doctors'.[79] By 1930, a third of America's prison population had been incarcerated for drug violations.[80]

In the same way that the sale of extra-strong liquor such as Jamaica Ginger was incentivised by Prohibition, drug prohibition stimulated the market in the strongest and deadliest narcotics: heroin, cocaine and, much later, crack. Largely thanks to the International Opium Convention, global opium production fell from 42,000 to 8,000 tons a year between 1906 and 1934.[81] As supply dropped, prices roses. In New York City, for example, the price of an ounce of heroin climbed from $6.50 to $100.[82] The only way most addicts in the inner cities could afford narcotics was by becoming drug dealers themselves or engaging in petty thefts and robberies.

For prohibitionists, drug-related crime was seen not as a by-product of suppression but as proof that opiates bred criminality. The loudest proponent of this view was Richmond Hobson who dealt with the dwindling market for anti-saloon soapbox orators in the 1920s by switching his attentions to heroin. By crossing out the word 'alcohol' and substituting 'narcotics', the old sea-dog was able to maintain his tub-thumping, sub-Darwinist rhetoric without missing a beat. The tone of Hobson's anti-drugs polemics in this period is hinted at by the titles of his many books, including *Drug Addiction: a Malignant Racial Cancer* and *Modern Pirates—Exterminate Them*. Now able to speak directly to the nation on the radio, he routinely claimed that there were one million drug addicts in America—a fivefold exaggeration—and it was he who first described opiate habitués as "the living dead". The whole human race was, he said, "in the midst of a life and death struggle with the deadliest foe that has ever menaced its future. Upon the issue hangs the perpetuation of civilization, the destiny of the world and the future of the human race."[83]

Hobson believed that addicts did not commit crime to acquire drugs, rather he believed that drugs made addicts want to commit crime. He was wrong, but it scarcely mattered. The seeds of America's drug-related crime wave had been sown.

The worldwide war on drugs

America's drug war began with a complacent shrug and the global crusade was set in motion with similar nonchalance. Most countries regarded the International Opium Convention, as agreed in the Hague in 1912, as an aspiration rather than a commitment. Although intended to take force in late 1914, this was contingent on thirty-five countries ratifying it in the meantime. Since only twelve nations had bothered to send a representative to the conference in the first place, this was a tall order. Few governments were prepared to lose millions of dollars in tax revenue by acting unilaterally and only seven countries had made any attempt to stamp out drug use by the time the First World War ended in 1918.

But it was the war that allowed matters to be sped along, just as it had for the alcohol prohibitionists. Not only did Germany's defeat mean that the world's leading drug manufacturer was silenced, but the Americans managed to insert a clause into the Versailles Treaty which automatically ratified the International Opium Convention. All the nations that had fought in the war were thereby compelled to restrict and regulate the sale, production and export of opiates. Narcotics control effectively became an issue for the League of Nations—founded in the same year and replaced with the United Nations in 1945 —which put pressure on the neutral countries to sign up to drug prohibition.

The passage of domestic drug laws continued to be characterised by lethargic insouciance. In the UK, the right to consume opiates was one of the many liberties lost under the Defence of the Realm Act during the war. The Versailles Treaty demanded a permanent peacetime solution and the Dangerous Drugs Act (1920) was the result. Largely based on the Harrison Act, it remained the cornerstone of British narcotics legislation for the next fifty years but was debated by just six MPs when it came before Parliament.[84] Five years later, marijuana was added to the Dangerous Drugs Act after a debate lasting less than five minutes.[85]

By the time the Eighteenth Amendment was repealed in 1933, all the fundamental aspects of the War on Drugs had been set in stone. All that remained was to close loopholes and increase enforcement. A series of conferences held in Geneva in the 1920s and 1930s tightened regulations and limited the production of drugs to a level deemed sufficient for the world's legitimate medical needs. New international treaties were drawn up to criminalise possession and ban exports. In the USA, the price of a drug-dispensing tax rose and the number of registered suppliers dwindled. Possession of drugs became a crime in most US states. The manufacture of heroin was banned outright in 1924. Patent medicines were outlawed. Prison sentences got longer.

In 1937, the sale of marijuana was put under the same limitations as cocaine and opiates after a Congressional debate lasting half an hour.[86] Most states had already banned the weed after a wave of hateful propaganda in the Prohibition era. Almost a carbon copy of the moral panic about Chinese opium-smoking and black cocaine use, this time the deviant minority were the Mexicans who were accused of murder, rape and other acts of insanity while under marijuana's baleful influence.

What came next is a whole other story, but a few statistics may suffice. The Harrison Act allocated $150,000 for enforcement of the new drug laws, the equivalent of around $3 million today. In 2009, nearly $10 *billion* was spent in the US for the same purposes. A further $5 billion was spent on treatment and prevention.[87]

In 2008, there were more than a quarter of a million Americans in jail for drug offences, each costing over $20,000 a year to keep.[88] With 5% of the world's population, the United States currently houses 25% of the world's prisoners. In Britain, one in six prisoners were convicted of drug violations and half the money spent on drugs comes from theft.[89] 19% of

Americans living with HIV caught the disease by sharing needles.[90] Worldwide, of the 16 million injecting drug users, more than half are infected with hepatitis C.[91]

The global market for opiates is worth $68 billion a year,[92] with all but $7 billion coming from the sale of its most dangerous derivative—heroin. The cocaine market is worth $85 billion.[93] The heroin market in the US alone is valued at $8 billion.[94] The global turnover of the illicit drugs industry, though difficult to measure, undoubtedly runs into the hundreds of billions of dollars. All of this money, needless to say, is untaxed and lies in the hands of criminals.

Between 1980 and 2009, global opium production rose from 1,000 to 8,000 tons.[95] Afghanistan is currently responsible for farming 90% of the world's opium, with the Taliban receiving $350-650 million from the trade between 2005 and 2008.[96]

Periodic attempts to win the War on Drugs have yielded only temporary gains. Suppression of one drug only stokes demand for another. The crackdown on heroin in the 1950s, for example, led to a rise in methamphetamine use. A subsequent crackdown on methamphetamine in the 1970s led to a rise in cocaine. The overall effect on addiction rates has been negligible. The number of non-medical opiate addicts remained static in the 1920s and 1930s before falling sharply during the Second World War and rising after 1950.[97] Before the Harrison Act, there were believed to be around 200,000 opiate addicts. At the start of the twenty-first century, the Centers for Disease Control estimated that the figure had risen to "at least 980,000".[98]

As before, illicit drug users are only a small part of America's substance abuse problem. Since 1915, the pharmaceutical industry has developed new drugs for the depression, fatigue, sleeplessness and pain that were once treated with laudanum, opium, patent medicines or nothing at all. *Prozac, Vicodin, Zoloft* and many other prescription drugs are used and abused by millions of people to treat ailments that were not even recognised as medical conditions at the start of the twentieth century. By 2008, 11% of American adults were taking some form of anti-depressant[99] and seven million Americans were defined as abusers of prescription drugs.[100] With drug companies also producing heroin substitutes such as methadone and oxycodone to maintain the addiction of opiate habitués, the triumph of pharmaceuticals over nature's remedies was complete. Of all the mood-altering substances that came under attack at the start of the twentieth century, only caffeine, alcohol and nicotine have not been fully medicalised and controlled.

And what of the Philippines, the islands that inadvertently became the cradle of drug prohibition? The prohibition of opiates came into force in March 1908, just as Bishop Brent had planned, and the government's opium monopoly was consigned to history. Before prohibition, the monopolists had used their privileged position to charge high prices and were forbidden from selling to Filipinos. When the monopoly was replaced with prohibition, illicit drug dealers actively solicited trade and competed with one another with lower prices. Under a regulated monopoly, the legal vendors of the drug had been careful to protect their profits by reporting any smuggling to the authorities. Under prohibition, officials from the police to the post office were corrupted with bribes and the country was soon flooded with opium from Borneo.

In 1927, Herbert L. May investigated opium use in the Philippines on behalf of the League of Nations and came to a predictable conclusion:

To students of prohibitory laws as a means of bringing a vice under control it will be no surprise to learn that prohibition of opium-smoking in the Philippines does not in fact prohibit. Anyone who wishes to buy prepared opium can buy it at a moderate price.[101]

The Philippines attained national independence in 1946. Under Ferdinand Marcos's regime (1965-1986) the death penalty was introduced for drug dealers, with one execution broadcast live on television. Capital punishment has since been abolished, but death squads continue to roam the streets killing dozens of suspected drug dealers every year.[102] This brutal policy of suppression has been successful in raising the price of heroin and, as a result, opiate use in the Philippines is low by international standards. Instead, the country has the world's highest per capita consumption of methamphetamine.[103]

The Art of Suppression

4

Snus

If you can, ban

"Prohibition is only feasible if relatively few people use a product."
— Ann McNeill, 1990

A £200,000 government grant to convert a disused clock factory into a smokeless tobacco warehouse unleashed a chain of events that led to one of the strangest and most self-defeating prohibitions in recent history.

In 1985, United States Tobacco Inc. chose the economically depressed Scottish town of East Kilbride as its European base for the manufacture and distribution of *Skoal Bandits,* a brand of smokeless tobacco that had been launched in the United States two years earlier. Looking to expand into Europe and the Middle East, the company selected East Kilbride because of "the valuable incentives provided by the Scottish Economic Planning Board, the available labor force and the plant's proximity to the Company's developing markets." This, it said, "enables US Tobacco to provide the freshest possible product at an affordable price."[1]

Skoal Bandits were not, however, products that everyone wanted to see available at *any* price. The product consisted of moist, fine-cut tobacco contained in what looked like small, rectangular tea-bags. Low in nicotine, sweetly flavoured and with a masked cowboy emblazoned on each container, *Skoal Bandits* were accused of being aimed at teenagers.

Britain, unlike America, had little experience of using chewing and dipping tobacco and the nation's public health campaigners wanted to keep it that way. US Tobacco's arrival in Britain suddenly alerted the guardians of the nation's health to the fact that since *Skoal Bandits* were designed to be neither smoked nor chewed, a legal loophole allowed them to be sold to children.

Under the leadership of the state-funded anti-smoking pressure group Action on Smoking and Health (ASH), and aided by the fleeting fury of the tabloid press, the medical profession campaigned first for a ban on sales to minors and then for the complete prohibition of oral snuff.

In December 1985, the Scottish MP John Home Robertson introduced a private member's bill to ban the sale of all tobacco products to persons under the age of 16. "Would 'all tobacco products' include the infernal *Skoal Bandits*?" enquired fellow Scot Norman Godman MP. Indeed it would, replied Robertson, who described the infernal *Bandits* as "extremely dangerous" and quoted evidence from the United States which showed a link between smokeless tobacco and mouth cancer.[2]

No parliamentarian cared to speak out against Robertson's proposal and the ban on underage sales was passed into law the following year, but not before the Irish had gone a step further and banned *Skoal Bandits* from sale altogether. The Irish health minister described them as "a particularly insidious product which should be effectively banned. It is a particular habit that we are determined should not take root in Irish society."[3]

The *Skoal Bandit* peril remained on the British political radar for the rest of the decade. In February 1988, Edwina

Currie, the controversial junior health minister, announced her intention to introduce a total ban on *Skoal Bandits* because, as she later explained, "they caused a form of mouth and throat cancer which was virulent, which tended to attack young people ... and which was easily prevented by not permitting this product to be sold in the UK."[4] In late 1989, Parliament passed the Oral Snuff (Safety) Regulations which banned the sale of all products consisting of "tobacco in fine cut, ground or particulate form or in any combination of those forms and which are for oral use other than smoking."

The ban was greeted with rapturous applause from the spokesmen and women of public health. With action against cigarettes hitherto limited to gradual tax rises and educational campaigns, oral snuff offered campaigners an opportunity to flex their regulatory muscles. Whilst the prohibition of smoked tobacco remained a distant dream, outlawing one form of tobacco, little used though it was, felt like progress.

The irony of banning a niche smokeless product while keeping its more hazardous combustible cousin on the market was not lost on everyone. "Some find it hard to justify the ban on oral snuff when cigarette smoking, which is undoubtedly more dangerous, is still permitted," wrote Ann McNeill in the *British Journal of Addiction*. She then explained: "The answer is simple. Prohibition is only feasible if relatively few people use a product."[5]

No one disputed that smokeless tobacco was less harmful than cigarettes, but nor did anyone doubt that oral snuff raised the risk of oral cancer. The World Health Organisation and the US Surgeon General had both made this clear, as had Britain's Chief Medical Officer who said: "The habit significantly increases the risk of developing cancer of the mouth, an extremely unpleasant disease which might be difficult to treat and could result in disfigurement or death."[6] With the health risks seemingly established, Ann McNeill wrote that "the UK government should be congratulated for acting now to protect people from this new addictive carcinogenic hazard."[7] Alison Hillhouse of ASH Scotland joined the chorus, saying: "Enough is known about the health effects of oral tobacco use to justify the decision to prevent its introduction."[8]

Few dared raise the question of whether oral snuff might have a role to play in helping people quit cigarettes. Those who saw mass abstinence as a pipe-dream gently suggested that nudging tobacco users towards less harmful products made sense from a public health perspective, but were denounced by Hillhouse for being "pessimistic about the long-term outcome of the campaign against tobacco disease." Such pessimism, she said, was "unacceptable in the context of health education and public policy. Fortunately, this pessimism is not shared by the UK Government, who live in the real world, like the children whose health is at stake."[9]

Judith Mackay of the Asian Consultancy on Tobacco Control was equally dismissive of the perceived defeatists who saw switching to safer products as a valid health strategy. Acknowledging only that the health risks of smokeless tobacco were "likely to be less than those of smoked tobacco", she concluded that the 'harm reduction' strategy was like encouraging sniffing cocaine as a safer alternative to mainlining heroin."[10] In the US, where the Surgeon General had set out his vision of a 'Smoke-free America by 2000 AD', Gregory Connolly of the Office on Smoking and Health asserted that "the fight against the cigarette is a fight against tobacco in all its forms." He congratulated the British government for "denying the industry the ability to control the future" and expressed his hope that the prohibition of oral snuff would "spur the Government to take stronger action against the cigarette."[11]

The EU ban

The Oral Snuff (Safety) Regulations had a profound effect on the UK's one and only manufacturer of oral snuff—US Tobacco Inc.—which found itself criminalised and sent home by the same government that had subsidised and courted it just four years earlier. Having appealed against the new law, the company won a judicial review in December 1990 on the basis that the government had failed to disclose the scientific evidence on which the prohibition hinged. This, however, gave oral snuff only a brief stay of execution before the European Commission took the matter into its own hands.

With *Skoal Bandits* banned in Ireland and with the UK making every effort to follow suit, the European Economic Community (EEC) decided that such unilateral action by member states posed a threat to its internal market. Only by banning oral snuff across the board could the desired level of harmonisation be achieved. On 15 May 1992, Council Directive 92/41/EEC announced that "the only appropriate measure is a total ban" on "new tobacco products for oral use."[12]

Once again, oral cancer was cited as the threat to public health that justified banning these niche products. According to the Directive, *Skoal Bandits* and the like had "particularly large quantities of carcinogenic substances" which "cause cancer of the mouth in particular." In addition to banning "new" smokeless products, the Directive instructed the tobacco industry to add the unambiguous warning 'Causes Cancer' to its range of "traditional" (and therefore still legal) smokeless products.

The 1992 ban was transparently aimed at US Tobacco Inc. and their *Skoal Bandits*. The European Commission made no attempt to explain why traditional oral tobacco products were exempt from the ban, let alone why the more deadly, and vastly more popular, smoked products should go untouched.

Widely perceived as purveyors of candy-flavoured carcinogens, few mourned the departure of US Tobacco Inc.

from European shores. Few even noticed. Oral snuff was only consumed in any quantity in the Nordic countries and, of these, only Denmark was a member of the EEC.

Snus—which rhymes with 'juice' and simply means 'snuff' in Swedish—had been used for two hundred years in Sweden and had inspired the creation of *Skoal Bandits* in the first place; both products consisted of finely cut moist tobacco in a bag which was placed under the top lip. After decades of slow decline, Swedish consumption of snus underwent a revival from the late 1960s as the dangers of smoking pushed people away from cigarettes. Being manifestly similar in design to *Skoal Bandits*, Swedish snus was included in the EEC ban, but since Sweden was not in the EEC, this was of little immediate significance.

Legislators seemed not to notice that Denmark had its own small snus industry, but the Danes favoured loose snus—finely cut tobacco dipped into the mouth without the bag—and were able to exploit the "traditional" clause and continue business as usual. It was only when Sweden prepared to join what was by then the European Union (EU) in 1994, that the ban on snus became a subject of serious discussion. The proportion of Swedish men who were regular snus users was 24% and rising. The rate was higher still in the north of the country where the prospect of a looming ban became a major issue as Sweden's referendum on EU membership approached.

Faced with the real possibility that an arbitrary ban on an otherwise obscure tobacco product could jeopardise Swedish accession, EU officials swiftly abandoned their commitment to a harmonised common market and worked with the Swedish government to negotiate an opt-out.* Swedes would be permitted to continue the manufacture and sale of snus within

---

* With the referendum won by a narrow margin of 52.3% to 46.8%, it is possible that without the exemption for snus, Sweden would not have joined the EU.

their own borders, but be prohibited from exporting it to other member states.[13]

They were also obliged to prominently display the 'Causes Cancer' warning on all snus products. Few who read that warning could have been aware of the paucity of evidence behind it. Whilst it struck many as perfectly believable that an oral tobacco product would increase the risk of oral cancer, in the case of Swedish snus this intuition had long been a substitute for science. It was *assumed* to cause mouth cancer, but no one had ever proved it.

This was in contrast to the coarse, adulterated chewing tobaccos used in Africa and Asia, which had a strong and proven association with oral cancer. Some studies of smokeless tobacco in the United States had also found associations, but most of these involved the powdered, dry snuff that had been used by women since the early nineteenth century and which was little used by the end of the millennium. Powdered, dry snuff was a fundamentally different product to Swedish snus. It differed in form (snus was contained in a pouch), method of application (dry snuff was often kept between gaps in the teeth) and duration of use (dry snuff was often used even whilst asleep).

Above all, powdered, dry snuff contained much higher levels of carcinogens (as did the Asian and African products). Nicotine itself does not cause cancer, but levels of tobacco-specific nitrosamines in dry, powdered snuff could be found at levels well in excess of 1,000 parts per million (ppm), compared to 6.8 ppm in *Skoal Bandits* and just 2.1 ppm in Swedish snus.[14] Although smokeless tobacco products were often lumped together, moist Swedish snus and dry American snuff were poles apart both in the way they were used and in their chemical profile.[15]

Nevertheless, it was a study of elderly women using powdered, dry snuff in the southern states of America that had the most profound influence on legislation against moist snus in Europe. Conducted by Deborah Winn in 1981, the study's most eye-catching finding—that non-black women who use dry, powdered snuff for more than fifty years increase their risk of developing gum and cheek cancer by a factor of 48—continues to be repeated thirty years later.[16] Typically, this very specific finding is reduced to the simplistic message that, to quote the American Cancer Society, "smokeless users are 50 times more likely to develop oral cancer than non-users".[17]

A sober reading of the Winn study leads to a less sensational conclusion. She reported a four-fold increase in the risk of gum and cheek cancer from the use of a smokeless tobacco product that was exceptionally high in carcinogens and that had already fallen out of fashion by the 1970s. Outlier or not, Winn's study was enough to damn all forms of smokeless tobacco by association and it became the cornerstone of efforts to prove that smokeless tobacco caused cancer. It carried the most weight when the International Agency for Research on Cancer (IARC) evaluated the health risks of smokeless tobacco in 1985.[18] The following year, the US Surgeon General described the Winn study as "the most informative body of data on the carcinogenicity of smokeless tobacco in North America" before concluding that smokeless products "can cause cancer".[19]

The 1985 IARC report was the scientific foundation for the 1992 EEC Directive, but in the years that followed, numerous studies of smokeless tobacco showed no increase in risk for any form of oral cancer and no study has *ever* found an association between Swedish snus and oral cancer.[20] In the late 1990s, two studies of Swedish populations found no link between snus and oral cancer.[21] These null findings have been replicated on several occasions in the years since.[22]

In 1999, the EU acknowledged the lack of evidence for the oral cancer theory:

"...scientific opinion no longer supports a strong warning as is currently set out in Directive 92/41/EEC ('Causes Cancer'). It is therefore proposed to replace this warning with a more general one. This will better reflect the established health risks for such products..."[23]

Since the mouth cancer myth had been debunked, and with no suggestion that snus caused any other form of cancer, the European Commission took the unprecedented step of watering down a tobacco warning. In 2001, after another Swedish study concluded that "oesophageal adenocarcinoma was not associated with snuff", 'Causes Cancer' was changed to the more equivocal 'This tobacco product can damage your health and is addictive.'

The revelation that snus did not cause oral cancer undermined the entire public health justification for the EU's ban. Mouth cancer had been the only health threat mentioned by campaigners against *Skoal Bandits* in the 1980s and it was the only type of cancer named in the 1992 Directive. Anti-tobacco campaigners could still complain that snus contained an addictive drug, but this was primarily a moral argument and the same could be said of nicotine patches and gums.

In light of this new information, two smokeless tobacco companies—Swedish Match and Arnold André—challenged the ban in court in 2001 and had their case referred to the European Court of Justice (ECJ) in November 2002. The companies complained that the ban was arbitrary, disproportionate and a restraint of trade. The case would take over two years to be resolved. In the meantime, the public health establishment had to choose between prohibition and harm reduction.

Harm reduction

If, as was by now apparent, the use of moist snuff did not cause disease, the prohibition of snus was not merely arbitrary, it was perversely counter-productive. Estimates varied, but it was certain that many smokers would switch to snus if given the chance, with all the reduction in lung cancer and heart disease that would accompany it.

This was not wishful thinking. Sweden was living proof. In 1976, its male smoking rate had been an unexceptional 40%. Thereafter, snus consumption more than doubled as the hazards of smoking became widely acknowledged. By the end of the century, Sweden's smoking rate was the lowest in Europe. In 2002, the proportion of men who smoked was just 15%. A third of male ex-smokers had used snus as a cessation aid and Sweden was almost unique in having a smoking rate that was higher for women than for men* (snus had traditionally been seen as a masculine product and was mainly used by men).[24]

Confirmation that snus had played a key role in Sweden's plummeting smoking rate came from the North of the country where resistance to the EU's ban had been so vociferous in 1994. There, snus use was extremely common and only one in 10 men smoked, falling to just one in 33 men in the 25-34 year age group.[25] No other European country had smoking rates that were anywhere near as low as this. Consequently, Sweden had roughly half the tobacco-related mortality of other EU countries, despite consuming the same quantity of tobacco.

Strangely, neither the snus manufacturers nor the Swedish medical establishment had noticed the spontaneous experiment in harm reduction that was going on in their backyard. Instead, it was the oral pathologist Brad Rodu, working in the United States, who first observed and documented the 'Swedish

---

* The other nation being the tiny Republic of Nauru in Micronesia (population: 14,000).

experience' in a series of seminal studies beginning in 2002. As the work of Rodu and others filtered through the academic journals, those who worked in public health began to debate whether the Swedish experience could, or should, be exported to other countries.

In 2001, Clive Bates, the director of Action on Smoking and Health (UK), raised the issue of harm reduction on the worldwide tobacco control forum Globalink. Referring to a recent article in the *New Scientist*, he wrote:

It takes the radical line that the public health community and regulators should encourage or mandate products, including tobacco products, that do less damage. I wholeheartedly agree with that approach and think that the alternative proposition of 'quit or die', which some in our community subscribe to, is wrong—totally wrong, unethical and irresponsible.[26]

In 2002, the Royal College of Physicians issued a report which remarked on the "perverse regulatory imbalance" that allowed cigarettes to be sold while "much less hazardous ways of administering nicotine" were banned. It described Sweden's exemption from the ban on oral snuff as "one reason why there is a lower cancer rate in Sweden."[27]

The following year saw Clive Bates and others explicitly call for the EU to legalise and regulate all smokeless tobacco products, and snus in particular. In a paper published in the anti-smoking lobby's house journal *Tobacco Control*, Bates *et al.* reminded colleagues that:

The ultimate purpose of tobacco control campaigning and organisations should be clearly stated: in our view it is to reduce the burden of disease and death, mostly from cancer, cardiovascular disease (CVD), and lung disease, arising from tobacco use. The aim is not *in itself* to campaign against tobacco. [emphasis in the original][28]

The authors described snus as "very substantially less dangerous" than cigarettes, even if one assumed there were negative effects on the cardiovascular system (which, as they said, was unproven). They suggested that snus was a more effective cessation aid than nicotine gums and patches because it delivered a higher dose of nicotine. To the objection that snus could be a "gateway" to smoking for young people, they pointed to the Swedish example and concluded that it was more likely to be a gateway *away* from smoking. Seeing no reason to concede the moral high ground to their prohibitionist opponents, the authors concluded that it was "ethically wrong to deny users the option to reduce their risk."

The Bates paper was a forthright denunciation of a law its signatories described—in a nod to the ongoing Swedish Match court case—as "arbitrary and disproportionate, and impossible to justify". One of the article's co-authors was Ann McNeill who had led the celebrations when the British government announced the ban on oral snuff thirteen years earlier. Back then, she had believed that moist snuff caused oral cancer, and had called the ban "the most positive action on tobacco in Britain for over 20 years"[29], adding that "the case for similar legislation elsewhere is irrefutable."[30] Now, in the light of changing evidence, she was not too proud to change her mind. Like several other anti-smoking campaigners, McNeill described the EU's prohibition of snus as "absurd" and called for it to be repealed.

The alliance against snus

Not everyone was able to change their mind in response to changing evidence. In the same year, the US Surgeon General said: "There is no significant scientific evidence that suggests smokeless tobacco is a safer alternative to cigarettes." This was a worrying sign of scientific illiteracy from the country's foremost authority on health, but the claim that smokeless tobacco was "not safer than cigarettes" was repeated often by government agencies until it was declared scientifically unsupportable under the Data Quality Act in 2004.[31]*

The debate about harm reduction in the USA differed from that in the EU because snus had never been banned in America. The question for reformers across the Atlantic was whether snus use should be actively promoted as a way of quitting cigarettes. Many veteran anti-smoking advocates were vociferously opposed to anything that might help the tobacco industry sell any product. Alan Blum was typical of the old guard. Having founded the anti-smoking lobby group Doctors Ought to Care in the 1970s, Blum called snus as "a true health threat and a gateway to cigarettes". He dismissed the idea that the Swedish experience could be exported and described snus as "almost totally a Swedish custom, like that smelly fish that only Swedes eat."[32] In an e-mail to Scott Tomar, a dentist working in public health, Blum complained that "the scurrilous use of the epithet 'quit or die' to characterize those of us who oppose any collaboration with a tobacco manufacturer is deeply disturbing." He went on to equate people like Clive Bates and Ann McNeill with Japanese prisoners of war, writing: "I think these folks need to see 'The Bridge on the River Kwai' to better understand how one can unwittingly aid the enemy."

If anti-smoking campaigners had ideological reasons to oppose tobacco harm reduction, the pharmaceutical industry was not short of financial motives for wanting snus to be kept off the shelves. Having spent millions developing Nicotine Replacement Therapy (NRT), their share of the smoking-cessation market was suddenly threatened by a simple, old fashioned tobacco product. Nicotine gum had much in common with snus in the way it delivered nicotine and, with oral cancer now discounted as a health threat, it was difficult to argue that one was significantly more dangerous than the other

---

* The Data Quality Act ensures "quality, objectivity, utility, and integrity of information (including statistical information)" from government agencies.

(neither are considered 100% safe because both increase the heart rate).

In many respects, snus was the kind of product the pharmaceutical industry would have loved to make, had the industry not felt obliged to produce something more overtly medicinal. And yet, it was precisely because snus was designed for pleasure and recreation that made it such an effective substitute for cigarettes amongst people who did not see themselves as patients requiring medical intervention. Snus also delivered more nicotine than its pharmaceutical equivalents which, while arguably making it more addictive, brought it closer to the delivery profile of cigarettes and, therefore, made it a better substitute.

By the end of the 1990s, all the pharmaceutical companies who sold or manufactured NRT products had become involved in global anti-tobacco programmes and were consistently the most generous commercial sponsors of anti-smoking groups and conferences. Both the EU and the WHO counted pharmaceutical companies as stake-holders to be consulted over tobacco regulation and the anti-smoking movement was happy to have them and their money on board. Their ideological interests happened to coincide with the pharmaceutical industry's financial interests, as WHO Director-General Gro Harlem Brundtland acknowledged when she launched the European Partnership Project on Tobacco Dependence in 1999:

"Three major pharmaceutical companies have joined this partnership: Glaxo Wellcome, Novartis, and Pharmacia & Upjohn. They all manufacture treatment products against tobacco dependence. Together, these companies will support a common goal that will have a significant impact on public health... And I am happy to welcome other stakeholders—and that includes industry—to join us, because investing in health yields high returns."[33]

With the tobacco control movement divided on the issue of harm reduction, and the Swedish Match court case underway, the Third International Conference on Smokeless Tobacco was held in Stockholm in September 2002. Part-funded by GlaxoSmithKline, Novartis and Pharmacia, this conference represented the first serious effort to make the case against easing the oral snuff ban.

The scene was set with the opening address from the Director General of the Swedish National Institute of Public Health (SNIPH) who began proceedings by stating that there was little evidence that snus had had any effect on Sweden's smoking rate and that SNIPH did not endorse snus as part of a smoking cessation strategy. This message was echoed by his colleague Paul Nordgren, who attributed Sweden's low lung cancer rate to tobacco control policies, such as the ban on advertising, rather than rising snus consumption. Although evidence presented by Brian Wicklin of the Swedish Statistical Bureau showed Sweden's male smoking rate to be significantly lower than other Scandinavian countries (which also had strong tobacco control policies) most delegates were happy to dismiss this as a coincidence.

Two researchers from SNIPH's Karolinska Institute presented evidence that men who used snus to quit smoking were 50% more likely to succeed than those who didn't. Nevertheless, they concluded that "snus is not a necessary component of smoking cessation."

Alan Blum and Scott Tomar were both flown over from the USA to speak out against the harm reduction strategy, while Clive Bates of ASH and David Sweanor of the Canadian Non-Smokers' Rights Association spoke in favour. The conference made no attempt to silence those who were supportive of snus legalisation, but the balance of power lay with the prohibitionists and the official record of the conference states that "there is no intention to consider lifting the EU ban."[34]

It was notable that the loudest voices against snus were coming from within the Swedish public health community. Since many countries hoped to emulate the Swedish experience, it seemed paradoxical that so many physicians in the country were dismissive of snus. In part, this stemmed from the same reservations expressed by Alan Blum. The tobacco industry had long been viewed as "the enemy", and although the snus manufacturers could hardly be described as 'Big Tobacco', there was a reluctance to do anything that might keep them in business.

The prohibitionist mentality also played a part. By the first decade of the new century, anti-smoking campaigners were beginning to talk more openly about abolishing the sale of tobacco within a generation. They knew that this final goal could only be worked towards gradually, but every step had to be in the right direction. With snus already outlawed, any repeal of the EU ban would instinctively feel like a step backwards, even if it turned out to be a progressive move in terms of public health.

There was no realistic prospect of extending the snus ban to Sweden itself, but the least the Swedish anti-tobacco movement could do was hold the ban in place in the rest of the EU. What, after all, would become of their reputations if efforts to export the Swedish experience went awry in some way? Maintaining the *status quo* was preferable to taking the risk of something going wrong for which Sweden might be blamed.

Neither the European Commission nor the Swedish National Institute of Public Health, nor the Karolinska Institute had any desire to see the ban on oral tobacco lifted. And yet there was little scientific evidence to suggest that snus was harmful. The Institute of Medicine had recently concluded that "the long-term experience with nicotine via Swedish snus is reassuring with respect to safety".[35]

There were murmurings about the effect of snus on the cardiovascular system. Two studies in the 1990s had implicated snus as a risk factor for hypertension and cardiovascular problems. Both were conducted by Gunilla Bolinder of the Karolinska Institute, who rather excitedly described her unreplicated findings as "sufficiently impressive to call for action against the use of smokeless tobacco."[36] Two other studies published in the same decade found snus users to be no more likely to suffer a heart attack than were nonsmokers[37-38], and Bolinder stood alone as the only scientist to have found epidemiological evidence to the contrary.

With evidence against snus thin on the ground, an opinion piece appeared in the *European Journal of Cancer Protection* in 2003. Written by the husband and wife team of Harri Vainio and Elizabete Weiderpass—who had previously claimed that snus caused oral cancer—the editorial asserted that "all four published cohort studies which examined snus use found an increased risk for pancreatic cancer".[39] This was news to scientists in the field, as little was known about the effect of snus on the pancreas. Despite explicitly claiming that these studies had been published, Vainio and Weiderpass did not cite the articles by name, but instead referred to a "personal comm-unication" from Olof Nyrén, a scientist at the Karolinska Institute.

In truth, no study linking Swedish snus to pancreatic cancer had ever been published. The nearest anyone had come to making such a claim was in a study of chewers of a Norwegian oral tobacco product in 1983,[40] which had also appeared in a Norwegian journal a year earlier.[41] The same researchers had also presented some findings from an American cohort to a conference in 1982, with an abstract being published in the conference records.[42] This cohort had been revisited in 1993 and the Karolinska Institute would use it again, but to describe this rehashing of evidence as four distinct published studies was highly misleading, especially since none of them involved Swedish snus.[43] Whatever the evidence, Vainio and Weiderpass predicted that it was "likely that pancreatic cancer is the first distant site, outside the site of snus application, where snus use will be shown to increase the risk of cancer in humans."[44]

With no major studies due for imminent release, the European Commission instructed the European Network for

Smoking Prevention (ENSP) to carry out a report on smokeless tobacco to form an evidence base on which to fight the repeal of the ban. The report was funded by the European Commission, the Swedish National Institute of Public Health and the Dutch public health group STIVORO.

Work on the report was co-ordinated by STIVORO, who outsourced much of it to the research company Research voor Beleid. STIVORO delivered a draft version to ENSP in 2003 with the title 'Lifting the ban on oral tobacco'.[45] It was not published for several months, but when it finally appeared it had been rewritten so thoroughly that it left no doubt about the bias against snus amongst representatives of the Swedish National Institute of Public Health and the European Commission.

The report that nearly was

The original version of the ENSP report was by no means an unequivocal endorsement of snus in harm reduction. Instead, it weighed up the evidence and accepted that there were cogent arguments on both sides. It conceded that there were always risks in trying a new approach, but it welcomed "new and fresh ideas" and called for a comprehensive tobacco control strategy which "maximises public health gain while respecting individual self-determination." This balanced approach was evidently not to the ENSP's liking and both the tone and the content were radically altered before publication. Contrasting the final publication (renamed 'ENSP Status Report on Oral Tobacco'[46]) with the version submitted by Research voor Beleid reveals the extent of the rewriting.

Chapter 3 of the original report, for example, was written by the Polish scientist Witold Zatonski and was titled 'The harm reduction capacity of oral tobacco'. In the original document, Zatonski had written:

There can be no doubt that the survival in Sweden of the 19th century custom of using oral tobacco [by] the male population has *contributed significantly* to the fact that the prevalence of smoking in Sweden in the second half of the 20th century was much lower than in many European countries. The relatively low prevalence of smoking is the reason behind a low incidence of lung cancer in Sweden. [emphasis added]

This was changed in the final report to downplay the role of snus in the 'Swedish experience':

It is likely that the surviving 19th century custom of oral tobacco use by Swedish men is *one of the factors* responsible for the lower rates of lung cancer and other tobacco-related diseases in the 20th century among Swedish men, compared to male populations in other European countries... *We must also consider the Swedish tobacco control model*, which is regarded as exemplary in the world. [emphasis added]

Zatonski had originally written that lung cancer rates in Finland and the UK will have dropped to Swedish levels by 2020. That, in itself, was speculation but it was still not optimistic enough for the ENSP who changed it to 2010, a prediction that we now know was way off the mark.

Elsewhere in the original document, it said that "it is not known whether snus may be a gateway into smoking for young people." The final report says: "oral tobacco can be a gateway, particularly for children and youth, to using tobacco in the form of cigarettes."

The original report also told a truth that is rarely spoken, which is that while snus can be accused of giving smokers a way of 'getting round' smoking bans and using nicotine at work, the same was also true of NRT products. The section in question read as follows:

Although 'clean', nicotine replacement products are open to many of the same kind of criticisms as snus. For example, NRT products may be used by smokers to circumvent environmental bans which restrict smoking in certain locations (e.g. the work place) and as such they may reduce any effect which such bans might have upon rates of smoking cessation. Similarly, NRT products may be used by youth, including never-smokers and may act as a gateway into cigarette smoking, as well as having the potential to become habit forming.

That paragraph was deleted in its entirety, as was the following discussion of pharmaceutical nicotine:

The medical view of smoking underpinning NRT sees users of tobacco as 'sick' and NRT the 'cure' for these 'patients'. Many professionals reject this model, and consumers may have similar reservations - not all users of tobacco may see themselves as sick, for example, and many would-be quitters do not respond to NRT.

The closing summary was effectively torn up and rewritten from scratch. The original conclusion stated that "there can be no doubt the current ban on oral tobacco is highly arbitrary". That admission—which was one of the key objections cited in the ECJ court case—was, again, left out of the final report.

Having negotiated all these hurdles, ENSP was able to conclude, in a way that the original report never had, that the snus ban should most certainly not be lifted:

Thus it would appear that Sweden is going to face an oral tobacco problem in the 21st century (especially if the chewing of tobacco will continue to increase in popularity among Swedish children and youth as it has done in the past 20 years). Seen in this way and from the viewpoint of the health of Europeans, arguments for allowing Swedish oral tobacco into the European market in the 21st century are simply unreasonable.

Having been thoroughly revised, the report was sent to the printers, but one final edit awaited. Since it was now widely accepted that Swedish snus did not cause oral cancer, the ENSP had fudged the issue in its rewritten report by conflating other smokeless products with snus and coming to the following conclusion:

An increased frequency of oral cancer has been found among snuff users in North America but not unequivocally in Sweden.

"Not unequivocally" was a huge understatement—there was no increased risk of mouth cancer found amongst snus-using Swedes—but it was still too much for the wary ENSP. When the report was finally released the second half of this sentence was literally Tipp-Exed out so it read:

An increased frequency of oral cancer has been found among snuff users

In the end, however, it was not new evidence, nor even the ENSP's lengthy defence of the ban, but a single press release that sealed the victory for snus's opponents at the European Court of Justice.

In November 2004, with the ECJ ruling due any day, the IARC suddenly announced to the world that there was "sufficient evidence" to link smokeless tobacco with both pancreatic and oral cancer. It didn't single out snus, and that was the problem. Once again, Swedish snus was being lumped in with smokeless products from India and Pakistan which had completely different pharmacological profiles.

The IARC's press release was headlined 'IARC Monographs Programme Finds Smokeless Tobacco is Carcinogenic to Humans'. The monograph in question had not yet been published and would not become available for another three years; the preliminary meetings to discuss the document had only begun a few weeks earlier. But the press release did the IARC's work for them in the meantime. Four weeks after the IARC produced its press release, the European Court of Justice ruled against the smokeless tobacco companies and declared the prohibition of oral tobacco products to be valid.

The EU ban had been saved.

Scientists for prohibition

While the EU and the Swedish health establishment were going to great lengths to prop up the ban on oral snuff, others saw the prohibition as an accident of history which needed putting right.

ASH (UK) had been the main driver behind the campaign to ban oral snuff in the 1980s. Twenty years later, they officially acknowledged that the 1985 IARC report that had been used to justify the ban was "based on studies that were almost exclusively on US and Asian oral tobacco products, not snus."[47] In June 2004, Clive Bates' successor as director of ASH, Deborah Arnott, called for snus to be legalised and regulated, saying:

"ASH believes that there is no logic to the banning of snus, when cigarettes, which are far more deadly, are on general sale."

In the same year, a study in the *European Journal of Epidemiology* estimated that 200,000 lives could be saved if the EU had the same male smoking prevalence as Sweden, which the authors largely attributed to the use of snus.[48] In 2007, the editor of *Tobacco Control* acknowledged that Sweden's exceptionally low smoking rate was "largely because of the major shift that has occurred from smoking to snus use in men."[49] This assertion was supported by numerous studies in the first decade of the twenty-first century.[50]

Around the world, medical authorities with impeccable anti-smoking credentials were endorsing snus as a valid part of tobacco harm reduction. These included the American Association of Public Health Physicians, the European Respiratory Society, the Norwegian Directorate of Health and Britain's Royal College of Physicians.[51-53] The latter published a major report titled *Harm Reduction in Nicotine Addiction: Helping People Who Can't Quit*, which noted that the effectiveness of pharmaceutical nicotine drugs was "disappointing".[54] The RCP concluded that the Swedish experience showed that snus was rarely used as a gateway to cigarettes, and was instead "used among smokers predominantly as a substitute and/or cessation product." In any case, they said, even if snus was only 90% safer than cigarettes—and most scientists believed it to be a good deal safer than that—for every smoker who switched to snus, ten nonsmokers would have to take up the habit to generate an equal public health problem.

The RCP calculated that if snus was marketed in Britain with a warning that accurately reflected its risks, the smoking rate would fall twice as fast as it had been doing and save 25,000 lives in the space of a decade. In the forthright final chapter of this 252 page document, the RCP concluded:

Use of smokeless tobacco products, although substantially less hazardous than smoking, is currently actively discouraged, and in relation to some products in the European Union, prohibited. The fundamental argument of this report is that this current situation is perverse, unjust and acts against the rights and best interests of smokers and the public health.

Two months later, an editorial appeared in the *Financial Times* saying that it was "absurd to stick with a blanket ban."[55] It continued:

Any effort to alter the directive would face difficulty because it would need to be approved by the European parliament, which is likely to be suspicious of anything that smacks of endorsing tobacco. Well, tough. Sometimes you have to choose the lesser of two evils, no matter how compromised it makes you feel. Smoking tobacco is a deadly pastime that no government has yet found an acceptable way to eradicate. If the Swedes have come up with a safer alternative, it behoves other countries to give it a chance.

Two new studies in 2005 confirmed yet again that there was no increased risk of mouth cancer amongst snus users.[56] Any lingering doubts about this popular myth were dispelled by the simple fact that Sweden had the third lowest incidence of oral cancer in the EU.[57]

It was also noticeable that Sweden's rate of pancreatic cancer was the fourth lowest in the EU,[58] but that did not prevent researchers claiming that snus caused this disease as well. As Vainio and Weiderpass had predicted in 2003, pancreatic cancer replaced oral cancer as the new snus-related health peril as the decade wore on. Evidence linking smokeless tobacco (of any sort) to pancreatic cancer had thus far been characterised by studies involving very few cases. The number of nonsmoking smokeless tobacco users with pancreatic cancer in the studies so far carried out had ranged from three to twelve and it was impossible to derive firm conclusions from such limited samples.

This did not change with the heralded arrival of a new study in the *International Journal of Cancer* in 2005. Boffetta *et al.*, (one of the *et al.* being Elisabete Weiderpass) was the third reworking of data collected from a group of Norwegians who used a form of chewing tobacco known as *skrá*, which the researchers considered to be similar enough to snus to make the study of relevance. They announced that snus users had a 67% increased risk of pancreatic cancer. In truth, the study could only identify three snus users with the disease who had no history of smoking, and they appeared to be at no greater risk than those who did not use snus. The researchers only arrived at the 67% figure by including a further 42 individuals who were current or former smokers, thereby making the conclusion far shakier. Furthermore, there was no attempt to control for alcohol consumption. This was a major flaw, since a previous study of the same cohort had found a strong association between drinking and pancreatic cancer.[59]

The study did, however, have the desired impact on public opinion. This report from the Swedish press was representative of the media's lack of comprehension when faced with epidemiological research:

A study carried out by the World Health Organisation and released this week followed 10,000 Norwegians, of whom two-thirds were snus-lovers. The results show that users of the popular chewing tobacco increase their risk of contracting mouth or pancreatic cancer by 67%.[60]

Almost the only accurate piece of reporting in these lines is the size of the sample group (10,000), from which the reader might wrongly assume the number of cases of pancreatic cancer to have been substantial. Snus is not a "chewing tobacco" and the proportion of "snus-lovers" was not two-thirds but less than a third. The study was neither carried out nor funded by the WHO, and although the study found a 67% risk elevation for pancreatic cancer (albeit only for snus-users with a smoking history), there was no association between snus use and oral cancer.

A slew of studies then appeared implicating snus as a risk factor for cardiovascular disease. This was a hypothesis previously associated only with Gunilla Bolinder of the Karolinska Institute who, in the mid-1990s, had looked at incidence of cancer and cardiovascular disease amongst a group of Swedish construction workers. She found snus users to be at no greater risk from cancer but found a 40% increase in cardiovascular disease risk. Bolinder went on to write a report for the Karolinska Institute based on six of her own papers (two of which were unpublished), in which she concluded that smokeless tobacco users were at greater risk of cardiovascular death than non-users.[61]

Bolinder followed this with a more strident paper in 2002 in which she dismissed snus as a factor in Sweden becoming the only country to have met the World Health Organisation's goal of bringing smoking rates under 20%. As evidence, she cited the low smoking rate amongst women, ignoring the fact that the rate for men was—uniquely for a Western country—lower still. She added that there was "absolutely nothing concrete to suggest that doctors should recommend snus as a smoking cessation aid" and attributed the relatively high rate of snus consumption amongst female doctors to them adopting "a more masculine lifestyle".[62]

For all the ink expended on the topic, Bolinder's study of Swedish construction workers remained the only epidemiological evidence suggesting a link between snus and heart disease. All seven of the subsequent studies failed to reproduce her findings[63] and it was suggested that the construction workers were healthier than the general population and therefore an atypical sample, a criticism that Bolinder accepted to some extent.[64-65]

After twelve years of consistent null findings, three studies appeared in quick succession in 2007 and 2008 reporting links between snus and heart attack mortality, hypertension and stroke. All three studies looked at the Swedish construction workers and all were written by Maria-Pia Hergens, a graduate student at the Karolinska Institute.

Hergens had earlier conducted a study that found no association between the use of snus and myocardial infarctions (heart attacks). Now furnished with the construction workers cohort, she produced a doctoral thesis which—while still failing to find an association with heart attack incidence—was able to find a modest association with *fatal* heart attack incidence. She then published a study reporting an association between snus use and hypertension and completed the hat-trick with a study that found no association with stroke but did find a statistically non-significant association with *fatal* stroke.

The stream of studies from the Karolinska Institute became a river when Juhua Luo used the Swedish construction workers data-set for her PhD dissertation which reported that snus use doubled the risk of pancreatic cancer, a finding that was inconsistent with the low incidence of pancreatic cancer amongst Swedish men in the general population. And, perhaps most surprisingly, Kazem Zendehdel—another graduate student at the Karolinska Institute—reported that using snus significantly increased the risk of developing oesophageal cancer.

Yet again, the data came from the Swedish construction workers cohort.

These findings were unusual, not just because they were out of line with the bulk of the scientific literature, but because different methodologies were applied in each case. For example, both Hergens and Luo excluded workers enrolled between 1971 and 1975 because there was inadequate information about smoking status. Since smoking had the potential to seriously skew the results, this seemed reasonable, but the excluded cohort was the very group Bolinder had used in her 1994 study. If Hergens and Luo were right, it cast doubt on Bolinder's claim that snus was a risk factor for cardiovascular disease.[66] In his study, Zendehdel acknowledged "certain weaknesses of the smoking information collected in 1971-75" and admitted that some of the supposed non-smoking snus users may have been smokers, but he used the cohort all the same.[67]

Such inconsistencies in method and outcome were all the more baffling considering how close-knit this group of Karolinska researchers was. Despite rejecting the 'Bolinder cohort' (of subjects enrolled before 1976) Luo was happy to be listed as a co-author of the Zendehdel paper which included it. Zendehdel, meanwhile, was named as a co-author on Luo's paper. And although Hergens and Luo rejected her cohort, Bolinder herself was a co-author on both their papers. Paolo Boffetta and Olof Nyrén were also serial co-authors.

This avalanche of new evidence in 2007-08 was as timely as the IARC's sudden decision to condemn snus by press release in 2005. Just as the IARC helped sway the European Court of Justice, the Karolinska Institute influenced the European Commission's new assessment of the evidence. The EC's Scientific Committee on Emerging and Newly Identified Health Risks (SCENIHR) was in session as the Karolinska studies appeared. When it published its findings in 2008, the committee accepted that snus was unlikely to act as a gateway to smoking, but otherwise cast serious doubt on the product.

The Boffetta and Luo studies were given the most prominence in the discussion about pancreatic cancer, despite most other studies finding no association with smokeless tobacco. Like the IARC, the committee said there was "sufficient evidence" that smokeless tobacco was carcinogenic to humans but now claimed that the pancreas was "a main target organ". They accepted that smokeless tobacco did not increase the risk of heart attack but, largely thanks to the Hergens study, stated that it probably increased the risk of a heart attack being fatal.

The seemingly simple task of clearing snus as a cause of oral cancer was made more difficult by "a recent cohort study from Sweden" which meant the committee could only say that the evidence that snus caused mouth cancer was "less clear" than the evidence implicating Asian and African smokeless products. The study in question was so recent that it was still unpublished when the SCENIHR report went to press. When it finally appeared in print later that year, the study claimed that Swedish snus tripled the risk of oral cancer, although it was based on just eleven cases of the disease. This was an extraordinary finding and its author—Ann Roosaar of the Karolinska Institute—admitted that "the combined previous Scandinavian literature on snus and oral cancer has not shown any association". Only the previous year, Roosaar's colleagues at the Institute had failed to find any such association using the Swedish construction workers cohort (Luo, 2007). Acknowledging that her own study was an obvious outlier, Roosaar could only plead that her findings "should not be categorically dismissed."[68]

The exceptionally prolific output of Karolinska researchers in the advent of the SCENIHR committee's report was a gift to the anti-snus lobby and was difficult to attribute to coincidence. The Institute was, and is, highly respected and the construction workers cohort is sizable (the Bolinder cohort alone contains 135,000 individuals). Nevertheless, there was a suspicion that its PhD students were being encouraged to mine the data for positive associations under the tutelage of long-time supporters of the EU ban.

The Institute did nothing to ease these fears by repeatedly refusing to allow other researchers access to the raw data. After Hergens used the construction workers cohort for the third time, Brad Rodu and two American epidemiologists—Carl Phillips and Karen Heavner—wrote to the journal *Epidemiology*:

In a series of studies, the Bolinder cohort has been subjected repeatedly to a revolving door of inclusion and exclusion by Karolinska investigators, which is unacceptable from a scientific perspective... If these discrepancies cannot be resolved by Karolinska epidemiologists, they must release the data for analysis by independent investigators. In the interim, the results should be considered as potentially unreliable, and unworthy of the certainty that they have been afforded by some European officials.[69]

In July 2008, a formal request from Rodu was turned down by the Karolinska Institute on the basis that disclosing the data would violate the construction workers' privacy. After being assured that identities could be removed from the files with ease, Rodu, Phillips and Heavner travelled to Stockholm to request the data under Swedish freedom of information laws. Still, the Karolinska Institute refused to share them.

Farcical new depths were plumbed in 2010 when the Swedish media reported that snus caused impotence and infertility. The story came directly from Asa Lundquist, the tobacco control project manager for the Swedish National Institute of Public Health, who not only informed a journalist that researchers had made this dramatic discovery in a new study, but personally checked the article before publication. Weary from two decades of similar scare stories, the Swedish public demanded to see the study in question, only to be told by the Karolinska Institute that:

"There is no such study. We have a hypothesis and plan to conduct a study among snus users after the new year."[70]

The following year, thirty scientists published by far the largest study of smokeless tobacco and pancreatic cancer to date. It unequivocally showed that snus was not linked to the disease.[71] As if responding to this compelling research, Maria-Pia Hergens and her colleagues at the Karolinska Institute produced a new study which made the novel suggestion that snus somehow caused men to put on weight.[72] And so it continued.

First, tell the truth

The banning of snus, and the elaborate efforts made by the custodians of public health to maintain the ban, is one of the more baffling prohibitions of the twentieth century.

The disputes over data, the scare stories, the lobbying and the recriminations continue in Sweden, but all of it is ultimately a distraction from the simple issue at stake. What no one denies is that snus is, to quote the World Health Organisation, "considerably less hazardous than cigarettes."[73] For all the wrangling over this study or that study, all that is really being argued over is whether snus is 99% safer, or merely 97% or 95% safer than the world's most commonly used tobacco product.

When the *Skoal Bandits* debate was raging in the 1980s, the tobacco control veteran Judith Mackay acknowledged that the health risks of smokeless tobacco were "likely to be less than those of smoked tobacco", but concluded that harm reduction was like "encouraging sniffing cocaine as a safer alternative to mainlining heroin."[74] Robert West responded to her with another narcotics metaphor, saying that it would be more apt to compare it to "banning coca leaves and allowing the promotion of crack".[75] Considering the relative risk profiles of snus and cigarettes, West's analogy came closest to the truth, but a still better example is the real-life harm reduction policy of substituting methadone for heroin.

Modern, liberal democracies smile on harm reduction when it comes to the illegal pursuits of hard drugs, prostitution and underage sex. An abstinence-only approach is seen as unrealistic in those instances, but nicotine use—which is far more common—has become the subject of what is effectively a harm maximisation approach. The peculiar prohibition of snus has, by accident or design, become the flagship policy of the harm maximisation strategy. It is almost as if the desired goal is to keep those who want to enjoy nicotine using the most dangerous and most highly taxed forms of tobacco.

No one would advocate banning light ales and shandy for fear that they might act as a gateway to stronger, but legal, beverages. Few people could make a robust defence of a drugs policy that banned cannabis but kept heroin on the market. There would, however, be people who could make a coherent moral argument for the criminalisation, or legalisation, of all these substances and, as one of the deleted passages of the ENSP report said, the issue of snus prohibition is not primarily a scientific question, but a philosophical and ethical one.

Veteran anti-smoking campaigners cannot bear to contemplate a scenario in which the tobacco industry becomes part of the solution. For some anti-tobacco fundamentalists, all addictive drugs are vices to be suppressed when the opportunity arises. That the world's least hazardous tobacco product happened to be suppressed before its combustible cousin is, from their perspective, merely an accident of timing. For prohibitionists, it would have been negligent to ignore the window of opportunity that opened with the *Skoal Bandits* panic.

But there are other long-time advocates of tobacco control who joined the movement in the belief that they were fighting for better public health. For those who do not foresee, or do not desire, the prohibition of tobacco in their lifetime, banning snus is a morally unjustifiable infringement of the individual's right to reduce their risk of harm. Forcing tobacco users to maximise the damage to their health for the sake of spiting the tobacco industry or gaining favour with pharmaceutical companies is not what they signed up for. Nor do they consider it reasonable to maintain an arbitrary prohibition on low-risk products for fear of sending out 'the wrong signal' to consumers.

Something has gone seriously askew when honest information becomes viewed as dangerous and telling the truth becomes synonymous with sending out the 'wrong signal'. This was illustrated by a fictional exchange between two doctors, written by a supporter of harm reduction, Dr Lynn Kozlowski:

Dr W: I hope these principles will have small, constructive effects on the dialogue. That we will move closer to true science based policy and that human rights will be respected... I think the ethical physician should be able to discuss smokeless as an option. And I don't think he should fear that the army of anti-tobacco litigators will swoop down on him—because to inform that smokeless is much less deadly than smoking is honest, health relevant information.

Dr. A: You don't get it. You are sabotaging the policies that most of your closest colleagues support.

Dr W: How about instead of 'First, do not harm' you try, 'First, tell the truth'. Just who do *you* think *you* are, to be deciding so much for so many? [76]

At the time of writing, the EU's ban on snus remains in place; a testament to grand bureaucratic folly, stubbornness and vested interests.

5

Narcotic moonshine

Designer drugs and the media

"Ban this killer drug... NOW."
— *Daily Mirror*, 2010

"It is the worst drug ever to hit the shores of Britain," Dave Llewellyn told *The Sun* newspaper in March 2010. "It will make users want to tear out their own eyes. It makes people feel like God himself but really it is the Devil's Powder."

The powder in question was naphyrone, a legal high better known as NRG-1 that was being touted as a replacement for the soon-to-be-banned mephedrone. Mephedrone was itself a substitute for the long since banned Ecstasy. Warning readers that "the horror drug" was made in Chinese factories, *The Sun* claimed that naphyrone was "13 times STRONGER than coke and even more ADDICTIVE than heroin".[1]

Llewellyn seemed like the right man to ask since he ran one of the UK's leading legal high companies.[2] And yet NRG-1 did not make users feel like God, nor did they tear out their own eyes. They just ground their teeth and felt anxious, tired and unwell the next day. Most of them never took it again and when it was banned ten weeks later—following a campaign by *The Sun* —naphyrone went unlamented into the dustbin of designer drug history.

As Llewellyn knew, there is no such thing as bad publicity in the grey market of legal highs. While expressing their moral outrage at 'killer drugs' targeted at 'our children', newspapers helpfully give their readers information about where to buy them, how much to pay and what dose to take.* Sooner or later, this tabloid attention leads to the drug *du jour* being banned, but not before mountains of chemicals have been shifted by mail order.

When the door is slammed shut on one drug, there is an unending stream of new 'research chemicals' to plug the gap. Twenty-four new legal highs were synthesised in 2009, with a further thirty-three appearing in 2010.[3] "Right now, I have enough new chemicals on my books to last for the next 15 years," boasted Llewellyn. "We pro-act and the miserable excuse that we have for politicians overreact, as they are programmed to do."[4]

The next best thing

Designer drugs and second-rate substitutes are as old as prohibition itself. Properly defined, a designer drug is a substance specifically created to replicate the sensation of an illicit drug while being sufficiently different in molecular structure to get around the law. They are the subterranean equivalent of what are known in the pharmaceutical industry as

---

* The same was true of the reporting of opium dens in nineteenth-century San Francisco, as Diana L. Ahmad recounted in her book *The Opium Debate*: "The reporters' aim was probably to dissuade people from visiting the establishments; however, the articles were sufficiently informative to give those with the desire to try opium a place to go to do it, as well as complete instructions in how to smoke the narcotic." (p. 27)

'me-too' drugs—substances which replicate effects without treading on patents.

In the restless pursuit of hedonistic diversions, human beings will try almost any substance if more appealing avenues of pleasure are closed off. From the diethyl ether inhaled in Prohibition-era American to the solvents inhaled by those who cannot acquire drink or drugs today (which are responsible for dozens of deaths in the UK every year), legal highs might not be as good as the real thing, and they are often more dangerous, but at least users don't have to worry about being arrested.

When heroin was banned in America in 1915, users turned to the previously obscure opiate analogues dibenzoylmorphine and acetylpropionyl-morphine before they too were banned in 1930. In 1976, another synthetic opiate, *alpha*-methylfentanyl, or China White,* arrived unnoticed on American streets, only coming to the attention of the government when it was found in the blood of two overdose victims three years later.

The reader will, I trust and hope, not be surprised to hear that the consumption of untested chemicals made in basements by amateur and frequently drug-addled scientists carries a certain degree of risk. In 1976, an attempt to create the synthetic opiate MPPP went tragically awry when chemistry student Barry Kidston overheated the ingredients and inadvertently created MPTP. By accident, Kidson had discovered an entirely new chemical, and neither he nor anyone else could have predicted the result. Just three days after injecting himself with the drug, the young man developed something very similar to Parkinson's disease. A few years later, several drug addicts in northern California arrived in hospital rigid with Parkinsonism. They had been on a three day binge on what they believed to be heroin but was in fact MPTP. Some good came of this

---

* It was neither invented nor manufactured in China, but the nickname helped maintain the American tradition of blaming Orientals for the nation's drug problem.

unsolicited experiment, however, since the discovery of MPTP provided scientists with a means of modelling Parkinson's disease in animals for the first time. Barry Kidston was cured of his Parkinson's symptoms but died of a cocaine overdose in 1982. His autopsy also advanced scientific understanding of the disease.

Everything starts with an E

In the 1990s, the ubiquity of dance music culture and the internet produced a fertile breeding ground for new research chemicals to replace MDMA, otherwise known as Ecstasy.

MDMA (3,4-methylenedioxymethamphetamine) was first synthesised in 1898 and was patented by the German pharmaceutical company Merck sixteen years later. Not designed for any specific purpose, it lay forgotten until the US Army's Chemical Warfare Service tried it out as a potential truth serum in the 1950s. In 1965, the Californian chemist and mescaline devotee Alexander Shulgin synthesised the drug while searching for a new psychedelic experience. MDMA is not, however, a psychedelic but a serotonin-releasing empathogen. Instead of hallucinations and disorientation, it induces empathy and a sense of well-being. It was not exactly what Shulgin was looking for, but he was not disappointed.

In the 1970s, still unknown to the general public, MDMA was quietly passed around a select group of American psychologists, intellectuals and drug connoisseurs who cherished its therapeutic qualities but feared that widespread use would lead to prohibition, as had happened with LSD. Even the great evangelist of psychedelic enlightenment Timothy Leary agreed that MDMA should remain "an elitist experience" to be used only by "sophisticated people who sincerely want to attain a high level of self-understanding".[5]

MDMA's uncanny ability to induce empathy and openness afforded psychiatrists rare insights which they dared not publish lest they drew unwanted attention. "One MDMA-assisted session does more than half a year [of] two weekly sessions," said one shrink.[6] This small clique of psychotherapists knew MDMA by the name of Adam, a near-anagram with undertones of spiritual rebirth. Alexander Shulgin called it "penicillin for the soul". But when it was mass manufactured, quite legally, in the USA in the early 1980s, it was rebranded Ecstasy. "Ecstasy was chosen for obvious reasons," wrote the psychologist Bruce Eisner, who had been an early adopter. "The man who first named it Ecstasy told me that he chose the name 'because it would sell better than calling it Empathy'. Empathy would be more appropriate, but how many people know what it means?"[7]

Everybody knew what Ecstasy meant and when it flooded the colleges and gay clubs of Texas in 1983, MDMA began to lose its therapeutic sheen. It became notoriously popular at Dallas's Southern Methodist University when, in a classic example of unintended consequences, the temperance policy of banning alcohol across campus led students to seek alternative thrills. Wide-eyed college kids partying all night on an exotic substance could not fail to attract the attention of the Drug Enforcement Agency and hopes of keeping MDMA under the legislative radar were dashed.

The press scathingly, and inaccurately, termed MDMA "the yuppie psychedelic". The combination of young people taking an unfamiliar drug while dancing to unusual music set the stage for a moral panic almost identical to the LSD scare of the 1960s. As sociologists have long recognised, moral panics are easier to generate when there is an existing template to work from. Old tales of hallucinogenic depravity were mixed up with horror stories from the recent MPTP debacle, leading to rumours that MDMA was a mentally debilitating, Parkinson's inducing, addictive, psychedelic menace to the nation's youth. A drug with this reputation never stood a chance of remaining legal at the height of Ronald Reagan's War on Drugs and there could only be one outcome. Ecstasy was classified as a Schedule I drug (the equivalent of the British Class A) in July 1985.

By a slice of serendipity, MDMA had been a Class A drug in Britain since 1977 when the Misuse of Drugs Act was updated to include a family of chemicals that were considered suspect. Although MDMA was not listed by name, its chemical structure had been presciently criminalised. This rare example of prohibitionist laws being ahead of the market did nothing to prevent Ecstasy becoming the dominant party drug of the late twentieth century and, as in the USA, scare stories about Ecstasy seldom went beyond reviving the clichés of the Sixties. Some journalists believed, quite wrongly, that the whole movement was fuelled by LSD—a confusion not helped by the associated musical genre being called 'acid house'*—and even the Summer of Love tag was revived in 1988. *The Sun* characteristically tried to have its cake and eat it, railing against the "danger drug that is sweeping discos and ruining lives" one minute and producing its own "acid house fashion guide" the next (the latter was marketed with the lazy and anachronistic tag-line "It's groovy and cool!")[8] The whiff of flower power lingered for several years before the super-clubs took over, the pure MDMA ran dry and the gangsters moved in.

Between 1990 and 1995, MDMA consumption increased by 4,000%, with half a million pills sold in Britain every week.[9] By 2008, it was estimated that up to five million Ecstasy tablets were taken every month. (This apparent rise in consumption was the result of pills becoming weaker and cheaper rather than there being more users.[10]) As house music culture became mainstream and the purity of Ecstasy pills diminished, clubbers

---

* Accounts vary as to how it acquired this name. The most plausible explanation is that it was named after Phuture's influential 1987 record 'Acid Trax'.

began to experiment with research chemicals which, unlike Ecstasy, did not carry a potential fourteen year prison sentence.

Like all drugs, Ecstasy is not without its risks. With over 500,000 annual users,[11] Ecstasy was mentioned on between 8 and 48 death certificates each year in England and Wales between 2006 and 2010.[12] These figures exaggerate the health threat because they include every instance of the drug being found in the bloodstream. In most instances the deceased had taken the drug alongside other substances and/or alcohol. The number of genuine Ecstasy-related deaths is not known but it is much smaller and, contrary to popular belief, there are no documented instances of anyone dying from an allergic reaction brought on by Ecstasy. According to the charity Drugscope, Ecstasy-related deaths are the result of heatstroke, heart failure due to an undiagnosed heart condition or hyponatremia (drinking too much water).[13]

Liberalisers are keen to point out that prohibition exacerbates the dangers because illicit supply leads to adulterated pills and unpredictable doses. Heatstroke and hyponatremia are both preventable and the advice to drink plenty of water may have killed as many Ecstasy users as it has saved; Leah Betts, who remains Britain's most famous casualty of Ecstasy-related hyponatremia, drank seven litres of it prior to her death in 1995.

Liberalisers also argue that the number of Ecstasy-related deaths are dwarfed by the tens of thousands of fatalities attributed to tobacco and alcohol every year. Indeed, one can pick almost any comparison from road traffic accidents and peanut allergies to bee stings and ladder-climbing which make the hazards of Ecstasy look minimal. Unexceptional deaths rarely have a face, however, whereas Ecstasy-related deaths are guaranteed press attention.

A calm look at the numbers reveals that the chances of coming to harm by taking Ecstasy are vanishingly small, but carefully gathered statistics cannot compete with anecdotal evidence and the testimony of bereaved relatives. A study of media coverage in Scotland found that the press reported just one of the 265 paracetamol-related deaths and only ten of the 481 *Valium*-related deaths recorded in the 1990s. The ratio rose sharply when street drugs were studied. One in eight cocaine-related deaths were reported, as were one in five heroin-related deaths. But in the case of Ecstasy—which was responsible for fewer fatalities than any of the other drugs—all but two of the twenty-eight deaths were the subject of media coverage.[14]

There are sound commercial reasons for Ecstasy's over-representation in the popular press. Newspaper readers have a limited appetite for news about overdoses from prescription drugs or the deaths of junkies. The ghoulish appeal of Ecstasy tragedies lies in the apparently random manner in which they strike down middle class youngsters who do not fit the traditional image of wasted addiction.

The sensational and hysterical coverage of Ecstasy in the 1990s set the benchmark for how designer drugs would be presented to the public thereafter. In a typical scenario, grieving parents would swear on a stack of Bibles that not only had their progeny never taken drugs but that they were positively *anti*-drugs. And while it could not be denied that they had taken drugs on this occasion, it had been a one-off experiment that could be blamed on the government's failure to criminalise the substance or, if it was already illegal, to give the drug a high enough classification.

The media would, not unreasonably, report the fatality as 'Every Parent's Worst Nightmare' and, less reasonably, launch a campaign either to ban this "killer drug" (if it was not yet illegal), or to hunt down the drug dealer (if it was).[15] The story would receive extra coverage if the deceased came from a white, middle class family or was an attractive woman. If one of the parents happened to be a policeman or drugs counsellor, this unfortunate irony would be offered as proof that it really could happen to anyone.

In an equally typical scenario, the tragedy would be all but forgotten when, months later, the local press quietly reported the results of the inquest which found that the deceased had either not taken the suspected substance or had done so as part of a cocktail of drink and drugs. A subsequent police investigation would then reveal that the deceased was rather more familiar with the drug scene than had first been believed and the person who sold the drugs would turn out to be a close friend.

"The police and the media get into a vicious circle where they hype each other up into an explosion," says David Nutt, former chairman of the Advisory Council on the Misuse of Drugs. "Cases are brought up of supposed deaths that turn out not to be related to the drug at all but the drug is banned just in case."[16]

Date rape and other nightmares

The first of the legal highs to invade the club scene after the demonisation of Ecstasy were not designer drugs as such, nor did they seem immediately suited to all night dancing. Gamma-hydroxybutyric acid and flunitrazepam are both powerful sedatives which react badly with alcohol. Better known as GHB and Rohypnol, they can induce an unsteady euphoria in small doses. In very large doses they can lead to respiratory failure, unconsciousness and death.

Both drugs have legitimate medical uses. Rohypnol was developed in 1972 to sedate hospital patients. GHB, an amino acid that occurs naturally in the human body, began to be commercially synthesised in the 1960s as an anaesthetic. It has since been found to be effective in treating narcolepsy and alcohol withdrawal.

In the late 1980s, body builders started using GHB as an alternative to steroids before introducing it to the American club scene. After a few ravers began taking GHB as an off-the-shelf alternative to MDMA, and with Rohypnol being used as a post-rave sleeping aid, the Food and Drug Administration withdrew both drugs from sale in 1990. Although taken off the shelves, the drugs were not banned entirely and illicit sales continued, but neither substance had more than a relative handful of users until GHB was rebranded 'liquid Ecstasy' and a blizzard of publicity labelled them both 'date rape drugs'.

Rohypnol may be more infamous, but GHB has long been the more popular recreational drug. "In some ways it's quite similar to Ecstasy," Frank Warburton of Drugscope told the BBC in 2003. "It's pleasant and it slows down body activity, if you take a small amount. It's not unlike a few drinks of alcohol." But, as with all designer drugs, GHB's real appeal lay in its legality: "I think there's the feeling among clubbers that it does not have quite the same effect as Ecstasy, but it's easy to get hold of."[17]

GHB first appeared on the radar of middle America when it was blamed for the death of the supposedly clean-living actor River Phoenix outside a Hollywood nightclub in 1993. In a pattern of misinformation that would become familiar in the years ahead, it later emerged that he had in fact died from a cocktail of heroin, cocaine and diazepam. He had not taken GHB at all.

In the context of the War on Drugs, it was easy to make a case for banning Rohypnol and GHB on their risk profiles alone. The need to mix GHB with water or other liquids left ample room for accidental overdose. This, combined with its unpredictable reaction with alcohol, made it potentially more hazardous than Ecstasy. But it was not the risk of overdose that dominated this chapter of drug prohibition. On this occasion, a more terrifying narrative was constructed.

In 1998, an episode of the *Oprah Winfrey Show* was dedicated to the menace of 'date rape drugs'. Millions of American viewers were confidently informed that "thousands" of women had been raped after being drugged with GHB and Rohypnol. This was baseless nonsense and no serious evidence was presented to suggest otherwise, but it appealed to subconscious fears about the dark side of youth culture and it was enough to bring about fresh legislation.

When it comes to naming new laws, American politicians have a fondness for emotional blackmail. What kind of traitor, for example, could disagree with something called the 'Patriot Act'? What kind of monster could oppose 'Megan's Law' or the 'Saving Kids from Dangerous Drugs Act'? The 'Hillory J. Farias and Samantha Reid Date-Rape Drug Prohibition Act' of 2000 maintained this ignoble tradition. Few politicians have lost votes by voicing their disapproval of drugs and rape. When Rohypnol imports were banned in 1996, the *New York Times* ran the sneeringly apt headline: 'Clinton relishes signing bills no one could possibly hate'.[18] The same newspaper once said that "the surest way to pass a law is to name it after someone, ideally a girl or woman".[19]

Hillory Farias and Samantha Reid were not just girls, they were white, middle class teenagers who had died after taking GHB at parties. Farias had a congenital heart condition and there are significant doubts over whether her death can be attributed to GHB at all. Having died from a blood clot, her death was not blamed on 'liquid Ecstasy' until small traces were found in her body two months later. There was less uncertainty in the case of fifteen year old Samantha Reid who died after having her drink spiked with a large quantity of GHB at a house party by some 'friends' who then failed to call an ambulance when she became ill.

Whatever the circumstances of these two deaths, there was one fact upon which everyone was agreed: at no point had there been any attempt at sexual assault. It therefore seemed wholly inappropriate to immortalise Farias and Reed's names alongside the words 'date rape'. And yet, on the back of this innuendo, the Hillory J. Farias and Samantha Reid Date-Rape Drug

Prohibition Act made GHB, which had been freely available until 1990, a Schedule I substance with first offences for possession punishable with a twenty year prison sentence. For good measure, the Act also placed ketamine in Schedule III on the basis that it was "used by rapists to incapacitate their victims".[20] Ketamine, a synthetic anaesthetic which had been used to sedate animals in veterinary practice since the 1970s, had gained a cult following on the US gay scene and began to be taken by a small minority of clubbers in the early 1990s. There were no confirmed cases of it being involved in sexual assaults.

Was it really likely that all three of the new party drugs were being used to rape women? It seemed an improbable coincidence. The DEA had twice refused to support a ban on ketamine in the past and even the Act's chief advocate in Congress conceded that there was "little evidence" linking ketamine to rape.[21-22] A more realistic proposition is that the moral panic over Rohypnol was being used as a blueprint for the demonisation of other legal highs. Having created a narrative of widespread drink-spiking and sexual assaults, prohibitionists were able to push a series of drugs out of the door on the basis of minimal anecdotal evidence.

The drink-spiking panic reached the UK in 1997 when the Roofie Foundation was formed by a concerned citizen named Graham Rhodes to campaign for a ban on Rohypnol. There had never been a confirmed case of the sedative being used in a sexual assault in the UK and it had long been a tightly controlled prescription drug. Nevertheless, Rohypnol was banned outright in April 1998 and by the turn of the century Rohypnol and GHB had become synonymous with date rape.

How serious is the risk of drug-assisted sexual assault? The Roofie Foundation says that it receives hundreds of calls to its help-line every year. A survey by the British women's magazine *More* found that a quarter of its readers believed they had been victims of drink-spiking and two-thirds believed drink-spiking had happened to a friend.[23] *The Guardian* reported in 2004 that "one in four young women who regularly go to clubs and pubs had their drinks spiked last year."[24] Another survey found that women were more worried about being sexually assaulted after having their drink spiked with drugs than the prospect of being the victim of a mugger, drink-driver or burglar.[25]

There is little doubt that drink-spiking is perceived as a serious threat to women in the towns and campuses of Britain, and yet numerous scientific studies have shown that this heightened sense of fear has little empirical basis. A toxicological examination of 1,014 alleged victims of drug-facilitated sexual assaults found that only 2% had traces of unexplained sedative drugs in their body. The researchers found no evidence of a single Rohyphol-related sexual assault in the UK during their study's three year duration.[26] Another study conducted by six British police forces found evidence of 'date rape' drugs in just two out of 120 cases of alleged drug facilitated rape,[27] and a further study of 75 individuals who had been admitted to hospital after alleged drink-spiking did not find traces of Rohypnol or GHB in any of them.[28]

Studies from the USA have also failed to support the idea of widespread drink-spiking. Hindmarch and Brinkmann (1999) found traces of unexplained sedatives in only six of 1,033 alleged drug facilitated rape victims, and four of these had also taken alcohol, cocaine and/or morphine.[29] In a similar study of 1,077 cases, Mullins (1999) found traces of Rohypnol in just two.[30]

Finally, in a large study of over 3,000 alleged drug facilitated sexual assaults, Hindmarch (2001) concluded:

Detailed examination of the testing results does not support the contention that any single drug, apart from alcohol, can be particularly identified as a 'date rape' drug. Rather, the alleged sexual assaults may often take place against a background of licit or recreational alcohol or drug use, where alcohol and other drugs are frequently taken together. The extensive forensic database examined here does not support the concept of a commonly occurring 'date rape' scenario, in which the victim's drink is covertly 'spiked' with a tablet, capsule or powder containing a sedative-hypnotic.[31]

None of this should be taken to mean that these women are lying about their experiences, nor should it be inferred that date rape itself has been exaggerated as a problem. (We can only speculate as to whether the press attention given to these otherwise obscure drugs has planted ideas in the minds of rapists.) Whether taken knowingly or not, Rohypnol and GHB can facilitate sexual assault by lowering defences and incapacitating victims, but the same can be said of many substances. As Hindmarch says, if anything should be described as a 'date rape drug' it is alcohol itself. Study after study has found that fewer than 5% of women who claim to have been drugged have unexplained sedatives in their bodies. Rohypnol is typically identified in between 0% and 1% of cases while GHB —a more common recreational drug—is found in no more than 5%. Alcohol, however, is invariably found in the majority of cases.

The media's focus on drink-spiking, buttressed by expensive advertising campaigns urging women to take their drink to the toilet with them, to buy bottles rather than glasses and to take their own alcohol to parties, has led women to overlook the dangers of the alcohol in their glass. As Julie Bentley, chief executive of the Suzy Lamplugh Trust, a British charity that works to raise awareness about personal safety, says:

"As far as I am aware, there has never been a case of Rohypnol in this country found *ever*. We ask women when they are out to look after themselves and they say 'I always put my finger over the bottle so it can't be spiked.' I want to tear my hair out because what is in the bottle is what's lethal!"

Drug-induced date rape is, as Adam Burgess points out in an academic paper on the subject, "improbable as a widespread crime, involving as it does a stranger extracting an individual from her social group unnoticed, precisely controlling drug effects, administering a substance undetected, and reliably erasing memory of the experience."[32]

It is the fiendish degree of planning and the impeccable execution that makes drink-spiking so appealing as a newspaper story. Readers can relate to the concept from spy novels and thrillers where the hero is knocked unconscious by a spiked drink as a plot device. In the real world, however, such events are extremely rare. Burgess found "a stark contrast between heightened perceptions of risk associated with drink spiking and a lack of any evidence that this is indeed a widespread threat."

Commenting on Burgess's article, Nick Ross of the Jill Dando Institute of Crime Science, said:

"There is no evidence of widespread use of hypnotics in sexual assault, let alone Rohypnol, despite many attempts to prove the contrary. During thousands of blood and alcohol tests lots of judgement-impairing compounds were discovered, but they were mostly street drugs or prescription pharmaceuticals taken by the victims themselves, and above all alcohol was the common theme. As Dr Burgess observes, it is not scientific evidence which keeps the drug rape myth alive but the fact that it serves so many useful functions."[33]

'Myth' is probably too strong a word. There have been documented cases of drug-facilitated rapes occurring, although they typically occur in the home rather than in the less controlled setting of a club or bar. The media-driven image of an *epidemic* of drug rapes can, however, be fairly described as a myth. What function could such a myth serve? For the individual who has overestimated their alcohol tolerance, drink-spiking absolves them from blame. For those who have taken recreational drugs and landed in hospital or prison, it absolves them from guilt. For wider society, the lurking evil of the lone drug-rapist appeals to our deepest fears of what might be going on in an alien youth culture of which we have no personal knowledge.

There is a parallel with the fear of drunk black men raping white women in the American Deep South ninety years earlier.

That moral panic—based on a single documented case—helped turn the South dry from 1908. With alcohol condemned, the anti-drugs campaigner Hamilton Wright leapt on the scare and was soon making the remarkably similar claim that "cocaine is often the direct incentive to the crime of rape by the Negroes of the South".[34] This baseless rumour eased the passage of the Harrison Narcotics Tax Act in 1914. The twist in the 1990s was that it was the victim rather than the perpetrator who was under the influence.

"After taking..."

By the time GHB was banned in Britain in 2003, the internet had become a bountiful source of mood-altering chemicals for punters who would normally baulk at the idea of giving their credit card details to a drug dealer. Chat rooms and internet forums allowed anonymous users to swap notes and share experiences about a host of research chemicals masquerading as room odourisers, plant foods, dietary supplements and pond cleaners.

Over the next five years, the average MDMA content of Ecstasy pills plummeted from 67% to 33%[35] and the market was hungry for legal replacements. Ketamine, which acquired a peculiarly specific reputation in Britain as a horse tranquiliser, was foremost amongst them. A survey conducted in 2004 by the house music magazine *Mixmag* found that 43% of its readers had taken 'Special K', to give it its most appealing nickname, or 'techno smack' to give it its least. The idea that ketamine was a date rape drug never caught on as it had in America but it was banned on health grounds in 2006 all the same.

GHB's place was soon taken by *gamma*-Butyrolactone (GBL), which the body naturally converts to GHB after ingestion. Being essentially the same drug, it received essentially the same coverage. Variously described as a 'Coma in a bottle' (*Daily Mail*) and a 'lethal but legal drug' (*The Independent*), GBL's days as a licit high were clearly numbered. *The Independent*'s report ran as follows:

Amid the sweat and adrenaline fuelled by the pounding music and swirling lights of the dance culture, a new menace has emerged. In clubs around Britain, the use of recreational drugs is on the increase, and, as a result of the reclassification of GHB, users are changing to a new drug—GBL. Experts claim that GBL is also growing in popularity as a date-rape drug.

The only "experts" quoted by *The Independent* were Graham Rhodes of the Roofie Foundation, who had never come across the drug before, and a criminal lawyer who was concerned that the 'liquid Ecstasy' tag would lead Ecstasy users to experiment with what he melodramatically described as "a loaded pistol pointed at people's heads".[36] In an implicit denunciation of the drug laws, the lawyer's main concern was that the use of the word Ecstasy would encourage savvy pill-poppers to assume that GBL was equally benign.

The implied message was that Ecstasy was safer than many research chemicals. This was echoed by the Canadian Mounted Police when they warned their countrymen that batches of what appeared to be Ecstasy pills were actually benzylpiperazine (BZP), a legal, low-grade amphetamine substitute. "The colours, the stamps and the logos on it, are strictly marketing," said Sgt. Lorne Adamitz, "and as a consequence when you take this substance you're playing Russian roulette."[37]

It had come to something when even the police were suggesting that Ecstasy was the blank chamber in the gun, but BZP did not fit any reasonable definition of a killer drug either. Having been popular for years in New Zealand's relatively liberal legal high market, BZP began to be shipped into Britain in the Noughties. Known as 'herbal Ecstasy', there were no documented cases of it killing anybody despite five million doses being consumed each year in New Zealand alone.[38] Inevitably, the drug had shown up in the blood of several people who perished after taking a cocktail of alcohol and drugs, and yet even these cases could be counted on the fingers of one hand. But since one of the casualties had been British, the writing was on the wall for BZP. It was banned in 2009, along with GBL, the 'date rape drug' that had never been linked to a single date rape.

All the chemicals so far mentioned can cause death from overdose. Since illicit drugs vary in potency and do not come with instructions from the manufacturer, the risks of adverse reactions and overdose are real, though small. But there are other drugs which pose no realistic threat of poisoning or overdose because they are smoked—users fall asleep or run out of energy before they can attain a toxic dose.

When there is no plausible reason to believe that a substance can kill by overdose, prohibitionists turn to a more tenuous definition of a 'killer drug'. It is always possible to find someone in a large population who has committed suicide or died in an accident after taking a drug. Several benign recreational substances have been banned after campaigners willfully mistook correlation for causation in this way.

Salvia divinorum is a herb from the mint family that produces brief psychoactive effects when smoked or chewed. Salvia is no designer drug. It has been used for centuries in Mexico by the Mazatec shamans and has never been known to kill any of its users. Westerners have been aware of the herb since the 1930s but its hallucinogenic properties were too feeble and fleeting to compete with LSD, and the salvia high could not compete with marijuana. As with all legal highs, it crept into the market when all else was banned.

Non-toxic and non-addictive, salvia is an unlikely candidate for a 'killer drug' but in 2006, after 1.8 million Americans had tried it, a Delaware teenager named Brett Chidester committed suicide by sitting in a tent with a burning charcoal grill. After his death, his parents found an essay the seventeen year old had written on his computer which included the words "our existence in general is pointless when compared with everything else there is in existence". Since he was a known smoker of salvia—although not under its influence at the time of his death—his grief-stricken parents concluded that the Mexican herb had killed him and successfully campaigned for 'Brett's law' which banned the use of salvia throughout Delaware. "My hope and goal is to have salvia regulated across the US," said his mother. "It's my son's legacy and I will not end my fight until this happens."[39]

Even by the standards of knee-jerk prohibitions, the case against salvia was remarkably weak. Blaming a suicide on a drug someone had taken in the past on the basis that it *may* have led to dark thoughts raised serious questions about causality. The same rationale would ban any number of films, books and songs. Nevertheless, this isolated tragedy was sufficient to get salvia categorised alongside heroin and crack as a Category I drug in thirteen US states. Five uneventful years later, a twenty-one year old died after falling out of a fifteenth floor window in New York. He had smoked salvia with his ex-girlfriend shortly before this apparent suicide and *post hoc ergo propter hoc* logic dictated that the herb had driven him to it. Again, the parents campaigned for a ban.[40]

It is normal for the grief-stricken to seek an explanation for the suicide of a loved one, just as it is understandable for relatives to want some good to come out of a tragedy. But while no one wins friends by disparaging the views of bereaved parents, having a son who killed himself does not make someone an expert on drug regulation. Males aged between 16 and 25 have the highest rates of suicide and the highest rates of drug use of any group in the population. It would be remarkable if the two never coincided. Neither the Drug Enforcement Agency nor the Food and Drug Administration have ever found evidence to justify a ban on salvia and these two incidents—five years apart—remain the only deaths that have been even tangentially linked to salvia anywhere in the world. This, in a country where the herb is believed to be used recreationally by a million people every year.

A similar situation emerged with a synthetic cannabis substitute sold under the name of Spice or K2. Like cannabis, it has mild psychoactive properties and poses no risk of overdose. And like most designer drugs, it was a second rate replacement for the real thing. "I would use K2 if I only had access to low-grade marijuana," wrote one pot-smoking reviewer.[41]

In July 2010, a twenty-eight year old woman died in Middletown, Indiana. A bag of Spice was found in her room and the media reported it as the first recorded death due to synthetic cannabis. The woman was known to have smoked marijuana in the past but it was believed that she had never before used Spice. A fatal poisoning as a result of taking such a drug defied science, but the story of an otherwise healthy young woman dropping dead after taking a substance for the first time fit the well-worn narrative of a killer drug striking at random. Politicians pledged to ban the drug after the dead woman's mother laid down the gauntlet, asking: "How many people is it going to have to kill before they'll do anything about it?"[42]

The answer was none. A month later, a coroner ruled that the woman had died from an overdose of prescription drugs.[43] The following year, a ban on Spice was passed by Indiana's House of Representatives by 93 votes to 0.

DJ Nutt

In Britain, salvia escaped the prohibitionist noose, at least temporarily. Spice did not. In July 2009, the Advisory Council on the Misuse of Drugs (ACMD) informed the Home Secretary that the hazards of synthetic cannabis drugs were "broadly commensurate with those of cannabis and that they should be classified accordingly".[44] This was an ambiguous comment. The ACMD had been in an acrimonious dispute with the government over the classification of cannabis for some time. The agency had first urged the government to downgrade the drug from Class B to Class C in 1978 but had been rebuffed. Liberalisation was unthinkable in the subsequent years of Conservative government when American rhetoric about the War on Drugs was amplified by scaremongering advertising campaigns and bumptious, grand-standing Tory ministers.

In 1999, with Labour now in power, the Police Foundation called for the downgrading of cannabis. This would have meant the *de facto* decriminalisation of small quantities of ganja. Although possession of a Class C drug carried a maximum sentence of two years in prison, this was largely theoretical and the average pot-smoker was more likely to receive a verbal warning and have his cannabis confiscated. The "seize and warn" approach offered the police respite from the time-consuming charade of treating minor drug offences as serious crimes.

In 2002, Tony Blair's government, with the support of the ACMD and the Association of Chief Police Officers, announced that cannabis would indeed be downgraded. It was the first time a British government had so much as flirted with drug liberalisation since the Misuse of Drugs Act had replaced the Dangerous Drugs Act in 1971 and it provoked a predictable howl from right-wing journalists and politicians. The *Daily Mail* columnist Melanie Phillips accused the government of being manipulated by a "liberal elite" and warned of a "co-ordinated international effort to disband the world's anti-drug laws by stealth".[45] Oliver Letwin, the shadow Home Secretary, predicted that the downgrading would lead to "open season for drug peddlers"[46] while the Conservative leader Michael Howard complained that the reclassification was sending out a "confused and muddled signal."[47]

Opposition to this sliver of liberalisation emphasised the supposed inability of the lumpen proletariat to understand that cannabis remained illegal and was not being endorsed by the government. While the chairman of the ACMD said that it was "logically stupid" for marijuana to be grouped in with amphetamines, he was outnumbered by those who wanted the government to send out a "clear message" rather than one that reflected cannabis's lower risk profile. "It sends a confusing message to youngsters that in some way drugs are acceptable", opined *The Sun,* under the dire headline 'Law change: Pot a joke!'[48] The government's 'drug tsar' Keith Hellawell, a moustachioed police chief from the old school and a torch-bearer for the War on Drugs, resigned in protest, complaining that the government was "giving out the wrong message."[49]

The downgrading of cannabis lasted just five years. From the moment of its implementation in January 2004, a barrage of negative publicity was unleashed in the press. Opponents of liberalisation seized on the popularity of skunk—the strongest form of marijuana—and a possible link between cannabis use and mental illness. This was not new information. Skunk had been around for many years and the potential association between cannabis and psychosis had been around longer still; it had been acknowledged by the ACMD in successive reports. The government had known all this when it made the decision to downgrade, but drug warriors treated this old news as if it was a game changer.

Press coverage made no allowance for the possibility that users would smoke less of the stronger and pricier skunk weed to achieve the same high, nor did journalists acknowledge that there were doubts about whether the connection with schizophrenia was truly causal (rather than being the result of the mentally ill self-medicating with cannabis, as they did with tobacco.)

Rather than accepting that the possible link with mental illness was one reason why cannabis was to remain an illegal drug, albeit one in a lower category, the tabloid press reported scientific studies with absurd exaggeration. 'Smoking just one cannabis joint raises danger of mental illness by 40%' ran one *Daily Mail* headline. Newspapers variously reported that cannabis was addictive, caused violence and was on the rise thanks to lax drug laws. None of these claims were true. Cannabis consumption actually fell after it was downgraded and one had to go back to the 1930s to find anyone who seriously believed that marijuana caused violence. That bygone age was recalled by some of the headlines of the mid-2000s, including such sensational claims as 'Cannabis downgrading blamed for psychotic killer gangs by vicar' (*Daily Mail*), 'Soldier in cannabis frenzy killed father of best friend' (*Daily Mail*) and 'My son died due to skunk habit' (*The Sun*).

The departure of Tony Blair from government in June 2007 sounded the death knell for cannabis's Class C status. His successor, Gordon Brown, had never portrayed himself as a child of the Sixties and spat out the word 'liberal' with contempt. The son of a Presbyterian minister of the Church of Scotland, Brown announced a review of cannabis's legal status within days of taking office. The review was conducted by the ACMD and was published in April 2008. They found no evidence that marijuana, including skunk, was more physically harmful than any other Class C drug; they regarded the link with psychotic illness as "probable, but weak"; they found that cases of schizophrenia had declined in the period when skunk became popular; they were "unconvinced" by the claim that it led to anxiety or depression; they found no link with acquisitive crime or anti-social behaviour, and they found no substantial risk of users progressing to harder drugs (the 'gateway' hypothesis). In conclusion, they said: "Cannabis should remain a Class C drug."[50]

The new Prime Minister ignored every word of it. Within hours of its publication, Brown ignorantly claimed that skunk was "now of a lethal quality." On the gateway effect that the ACMD had just dismissed, he said: "If people start with cannabis and then move on to other drugs that is also a big problem." Once again, the clarity of the message was paramount: "We really have got to send out a message to young people that this is not acceptable."[51] A fortnight later, he announced that cannabis would be returning to Class B.

That might have been the end of the rift between the scientists and the ministers were it not for Professor David Nutt taking over as chairman of the ACMD in May 2008. *The Sun* wasted no time in welcoming the relatively obscure psycho-pharmacologist into the debate by digging out something Nutt had said in a committee meeting two years earlier:

Drug Czar's plea to downgrade 'E'

Britain's new drug Czar wants to DOWNGRADE mind-bending ecstasy and LSD, it was revealed last night.

Nutt made no claim to be a 'drug czar' and his "plea to downgrade 'E'" consisted of him saying "I think LSD and Ecstasy probably shouldn't be Class A",[52] but it was enough to make him a marked man in the eyes of the press. It was a role that Nutt soon became accustomed to and even relished.

In January 2009, Nutt wrote an article in the *Journal of Psychopharmacology* which could not fail to unleash the wrath of politicians and newspaper editors alike. It discussed an addiction called 'Equasy' that kills ten people a year, causes brain damage and has been linked to the early onset of Parkinson's disease. It releases endorphins, can create dependence and is responsible for over 100 road traffic accidents every year. 'Equasy', Nutt revealed, stood for Equine Addiction Syndrome—otherwise known as horse-riding. Horse-riding, he explained, caused acute harm to the individual in one in 350 episodes. This made it much more risky than taking Ecstasy, where the ratio was one in 10,000. Judged on their relative risks, the clear implication was that either horse-rising should be banned or Ecstasy should be legalised.[53]

Nutt's article raised a question that is often asked by both prohibitionists and libertarians. Why are some risky activities socially acceptable while others are illegal? The answer, surely, lies in the value that society places on the activity. Cultural norms dictate that horse-riding and mountaineering have an inherent value that outweigh the risks, while taking Ecstasy and marijuana do not. That these norms change over time and vary from country to country demonstrates that social acceptability is a moveable feast, sensitive to prejudice, hype and accidents of history. If the cultural baggage is put to one side, and activities are assessed on the basis of mortality rather than morality, there are glaring inconsistencies in the way the law deals with different hazards.

Unsurprisingly, the tabloid press did not leap at the chance to discuss the finer points of legal philosophy. At best, Nutt was portrayed as being too clever by half; at worst, he was accused of peddling a killer drug. Under the headline 'Drugs no worse than horse-riding? The folly of these "experts" simply beggars belief', Melanie Phillips described the comparison with horse-riding as "simply ridiculous" and called for Nutt to be sacked.[54] A Conservative MP said "he might be appropriately named but he's in the wrong job" while the Home Secretary, Jacqui Smith, accused Nutt of "trivialising" the dangers of Ecstasy and of "insensitivity to the families of victims."[55]

Days later, the ACMD published a report on Ecstasy which recommended the drug be downgraded to Class B. This came as a surprise to the government because they had not asked the agency to investigate the issue. Nutt had done so anyway, telling the Home Secretary that he believed the report was "timely".[56] If the professor was not behaving impishly, he was being breathtakingly naïve. Coming hot on the heels of the Equasy controversy, the timing could scarcely have been worse and the Home Office summarily dismissed the report's findings.

An unrepentant Nutt reappeared in the news in October when he wrote an editorial for *The Guardian* reviving the previous year's dispute over cannabis. He disparaged concerns about high-strength cannabis as "the skunk scare", strongly implied that the government was not telling the public the truth and declared—accurately, but provocatively for a man in his position—that "we have to accept that young people like to experiment." This, together with the implication that the government had "distorted" and "devalued" the scientific evidence, was the final straw for the new Home Secretary, Alan Johnson, who had grown tired of this turbulent scientist and his apparent thirst for publicity.[57] On October 30, Johnson told Nutt that he had created "public confusion between scientific advice and policy" and told him to stand down. Nutt did so, but five members of the ACMD followed him out of the door in protest.

Without question, the government was yielding to the tabloids, but Nutt's well-publicised martyrdom obscured the fact that the fiercely contested issue at stake was, in practical terms, immaterial. Neither Nutt, nor anyone at the ACMD, was arguing for an end to drug prohibition. The only item up for discussion was whether a couple of illegal drugs should be given a higher or lower classification. In theory, changing the classification could mean the difference between a seven, five or two year stretch in prison for those caught in possession, but since every casual drug user was well aware that custodial sentences were rarely imposed for possession of *any* drug, this had a negligible effect as a deterrent.

Nutt and his colleagues insisted that the degree of harm should be the sole factor to be considered in drug classification. From their perspective, it was plainly wrong that MDMA was grouped in with crack and heroin. The politicians, meanwhile, did not want the public to infer that the downgrading of a drug meant the government was giving a nod and a wink to users of the least hazardous substances.

In their own ways, both the scientists and the politicians wanted to send a message to the public. The ACMD wanted the message to be that drug laws were based on solid evidence. The politicians wanted to make an unequivocal statement about the harmfulness of all drugs. Gordon Brown articulated the politicians' position when he defended the sacking of Nutt in November 2009.

"We cannot send out a message to young people that it's OK to experiment with drugs and to move on to hard drugs. We have to send out a message to young people that it's simply not acceptable."[58]

This can be dismissed as fatuous gesture politics, but the scientists were no less obsessed with sending out the right message, as they made clear in a letter they wrote to *The Guardian* supporting cannabis's Class C status:

The classification system must be credible—reclassification would send out an ambiguous message about the dangers of current class B drugs.[59]

What neither side appeared to grasp during the pantomime of 2009 was that drug classification, whether arbitrary or evidence-based, has not the slightest impact on patterns of drug consumption, nor do drug users have any interest in whether the system that criminalises them is "credible". Politicians and advisors alike flatter themselves by believing that bureaucratic discussions about the finer points of the Misuse of Drugs Act have consequences for real-world behaviour. In truth, once a drug is made illegal, classification has no effect on consumption because price, supply and changing tastes are the driving forces. Fixated with sending messages, neither faction bothered to ask whether the public was in the mood to listen.

If downgrading a drug to Class C tacitly encouraged use, as the politicians believed, cannabis consumption should have risen after 2004. In fact, the percentage of adults using cannabis peaked at 10.9% in 2003 and went into steady decline during the Class C years, falling to 7.6% in 2008. By 2010, the rate had fallen further still—to 6.6%—but neither its downgrading nor its subsequent upgrading (in January 2009) had any effect on the long-term decline in marijuana's popularity.* Meanwhile, the Class A drug cocaine saw a quadrupling of use between 1996 and 2010 (from 0.6% to 2.4%) and the use of Class B amphetamines dropped by two-thirds.[60]

The only Class A drugs to have seen a fall in consumption in Britain in the last fifteen years are LSD and magic mushrooms, reflecting the preference for stimulants over traditional hallucinogens. The number of people using ketamine, on the other hand, doubled in the two years after it was banned in 2006. Every piece of evidence points to the fact that drug classification simply does not matter. The tears, tantrums, recriminations and resignations of the Nutt saga obscured the truth that this was a squabble between two sets of prohibitionists over an issue that was supremely inconsequential.

---

* In their letter to *The Guardian*, the scientists attributed the 2004-08 decline in cannabis use to the downgrading and implied that a return to Class B would reverse this decline: "Cannabis use has fallen in recent years, especially following its downgrading to class C in 2004, and it is obviously unwise to risk reversing that trend." This blatant case of mistaking correlation for causation showed that the liberalisers could be as credulous as the politicians when they found evidence that suited their case. So flawed was some of their logic that the letter was republished as a case study in a book on critical thinking. The book describes the argument mentioned above as "almost definitely unsound" and says the scientists' claim that upgrading cannabis would undermine the credibility of the classification system was "of doubtful soundness and unpersuasive." I can only concur. (*Critical Thinking: A Concise Guide,* T. Bowell & G. Kemp, Routledge, 2010; pp. 188-90)

'Meow Meow'

If the spat between David Nutt and Alan Johnson showed anything, it was that the government's tabloid-pleasing precautionary approach had made evidence-based drug policy impossible. By the end of 2009, the cycle of panic and misinformation that characterised Britain's war on narcotic moonshine was playing out once more as the euphoric stimulant mephedrone became the nation's fourth most used drug. Mephedrone is an Ecstasy-like drug derived from cathinone, a compound found naturally in the plant khat. This provided two sources for cat puns which somehow evolved into the truly ridiculous street name Meow Meow.

A survey of mephedrone users in Slovenia found that the majority of them used the drug because of "the absence of MDMA and/or bad quality of cocaine and amphetamines."[61] British users were no doubt driven by the same motivation. A 2009 survey of British clubbers found that 42% had taken mephedrone in their lives and 33% had taken it in the last month.[62]

As with most other legal highs, UK law forbade the sale of mephedrone for human consumption and it was instead sold as plant fertiliser. British teenagers proved to be surprisingly green-fingered. "I sell strictly for horticultural use," one supplier told *The Guardian* with a heavy wink. "A lot of orders are for just a few grams, so this is obviously intended for the customer's own garden."[63]

With vendors legally obliged to withhold advice on how much to take, users were left vulnerable to overdosing. With designer drugs coming and going through a revolving door in Britain, users were dangerously ignorant of what constituted a safe dose. Naphyrone (NRG-1) for example, is active at just 20 milligrams while mephedrone is active at 200 milligrams. Since naphyrone was billed by the media as "the new Meow Meow" when it appeared in 2010, users who were accustomed to mephedrone might easily have taken ten times the recommended dose. Even this was unlikely to be fatal—no deaths have ever been attributed to naphyrone—but Dave Llewellyn's warning that "they will feel worse than they ever have in their lives" was eminently possible.[64]

Acting on the fringes of prohibition, some dealers attempted to provide coded health warnings, such as this for the 'pond cleaner' that was naphyrone:

NOT FOR HUMAN CONSUMPTION

Directions for use: Add 20mg to your pond for best results. DO NOT add more than 20mg to any pond within 24 hours due to possible strong adverse effects for your pond life.

Naphyrone never caught on but mephedrone was soon regarded as one of the more euphoric research chemicals and, by the beginning of 2010, it trailed only cannabis, cocaine and Ecstasy as the nation's most popular recreational drug.[65] Despite the thousands of kilograms being consumed, there was no more evidence that anyone had died from snorting mephedrone than there was that its users ever seriously referred to it as 'Meow Meow'. It was widely reported that a fourteen year old girl had died at a party in Brighton "after taking" mephedrone but it was later reported—much less widely—that she had actually died as a result of broncho-pneumonia.[66]

An eighteen year old man in Hertfordshire was speculatively reported to have died "after taking" mephedrone. In fact he had overdosed on morphine,[67] a fact that did not deter the *Daily Mail* from using the story to announce that: "Children across the UK are taking this legal drug in lunch breaks and on the way to school" (under the headline 'Legal but lethal: The drug snorted by school kids which is sweeping Britain').[68]

The clincher came when two young men collapsed and died at home after a night out in Scunthorpe. Friends told police the pair had been taking mephedrone. The grieving parents insisted that their sons would still be alive had the drug been illegal and called on the government to ban it. Insistent that his son was not a "druggie", one of the fathers said: "I assume that because it's a legal drug he thought it was safe to take. I am convinced he took it because it was legal, why would anyone assume it could kill you?"[69]

By this time, even the normally sober *Times* was producing headlines like 'Meow Meow sank its claws into my mind'[70] and, with the death toll apparently mounting, the government rushed to judgement. Business secretary Peter Mandelson admitted to never having heard of mephedrone but nevertheless promised to "take any action that is needed ... to avert such tragic consequences in the future."[71] This time, the Nutt-free ACMD played ball with the government, taking just a fortnight to produce a draft report advising that mephedrone be made a Class B drug. The ACMD's decision came at the cost of another resignation at the troubled agency—the eighth unexpected departure in six months—when Eric Carlin walked out complaining of being "unduly pressured by media and politicians to make a quick, tough decision to classify."[72]

The prohibition of mephedrone came into force three weeks later, with the *Daily Mail* lamenting the police's admission that they would not be arresting users and with the *Lancet* complaining of a "collapse in integrity of scientific advice."[73] Two days later, *The Guardian* reported that a new synthetic chemical called MDAI "has already emerged as a successor to the drug mephedrone".[74] *The Mirror* heralded the arrival of this "new danger" with the headline 'Danger drug meow meow's successor MDAI could flood Britain'. Only the dates on the calendar changed.

On April 19, the *Daily Mail* ran news of another tragic death with the headline 'Is Carmen, 17, the latest victim of killer drug meow meow?'[75] The answer, once again, turned out to be no. An inquest later concluded that the teenager had not taken mephedrone at all but had died from an overdose of the pharmaceutical heroin substitute buprenorphine.[76] The following month, toxicology tests on the two men from Scunthorpe showed that they too had not taken mephedrone but had died from a combination of alcohol and the similarly named methadone. At the inquest, the police chief responsible for the original briefing could only say that there was evidence that the deceased men might have tried to buy mephedrone at some point during the fateful night.[77]

NRG-1—"the Devil's Powder"—quickly joined mephedrone on the Class B list, but within a year a surge in ketamine use was being blamed on the demise of the Meow Meow industry. It mattered not that one was a stimulant and the other was a depressant. "People started using ketamine because it was cheap, but then they went on to mephedrone, which was legal," said Laurie Yearley of the drug charity Addaction, "but when mephedrone was made illegal they went back to ketamine because they said it was a milder form of mephedrone, which has pretty harsh side effects."[78] And for those who found that ketamine disagreed with them, there was always the newly launched methoxetamine which was marketed as being similar to ketamine but "with none of the shambolic lurching".[79]

In this game of snakes and ladders, illicit chemists remain always one step ahead of legislation. The near-impossibility of lawmakers keeping up with innovation is hinted at by this typical paragraph from the 2009 revision of the Misuse of Drugs Act.

Any compound structurally derived from 3–(1–naphthoyl)indole or 1*H*–indol–3–yl–(1–naphthyl)methane by substitution at the nitrogen atom of the indole ring by alkyl, alkenyl, cycloalkylmethyl, cycloalkylethyl or 2–(4–morpholinyl)ethyl, whether or not further substituted in the indole ring to any extent and whether or not substituted in the naphthyl ring to any extent.[80]

Some campaigners have called for Britain to introduce a law similar to the USA's Federal Analog Act which automatically bans drugs which are "substantially similar" to banned substances. It seems a simple solution, but this Nixon-era legislation is gesture politics. In practice, the Act is too vague to be legally useful and has rarely been invoked.

And so the carousel keeps spinning while the public balances risk against benefits and legality against price. In the fifteen years since the Ecstasy scare peaked, there has been no change in overall drug consumption in the UK. The demand for passports from reality remains as unquenchable as the inventiveness of illicit scientists is endless. In this most recent chapter in the story of prohibition, an unprecedented number of research chemicals have been born, demonised and criminalised in short order. For all the immense effort involved in regulating and monitoring the market for designer drugs, the net effect on the consumption of party drugs—and the risks associated with them—has been zero.

Whether Meow Meow is a killer or not, its similarities to MDMA, both in its chemical structure and in its effects, make it difficult to argue that it should remain legal while MDMA is banned. What is easier to maintain is that people would not be taking these dubious substitutes at all if MDMA was available as a regulated drug in a controlled environment. While MDMA originally came to prominence as a therapeutic love drug crossed with a truth serum, BZP was used as a worming tablet for cattle until it was discontinued after it was found to cause epileptic fits. Ketamine was a veterinary drug which has been linked to bladder cancer in humans. GBL was a superglue remover. In all likelihood, this is what they would have remained had less unpleasant drugs not been banned.

The outcome of the war on designer drugs has been an ever-widening menu of narcotics, many of which are more dangerous than the chemicals they are designed to mimic. If we could see through the fog of hysteria that obscures all reasoned debate, we might ask whether it would not just be easier to make MDMA—a drug which induces "a state of empathy where the feeling is that the self, the other, and the world is basically good"[81]—legal.

6

The Art of Suppression

"The people never give up their liberties
except under some delusion."
— Edmund Burke

History has not been kind to the architects of America's Noble Experiment. In 1928, a year after his death, Wayne Wheeler was the subject of a scathing biography, written by a close colleague, which painted the 'dry boss' as a megalomaniac who "desired to be pictured as a dictator."[1] The following year, Herbert Asbury published a biography of Carry Nation which portrayed the long-dead prohibitionist as a monstrous, sour-faced lunatic endowed with Herculean strength. After the collapse of Prohibition, Wheeler was virtually erased from the American consciousness while a cartoon caricature of Nation became the enduring symbol of an era in which the USA lost its mind.[2] A drinking fountain dedicated to her memory stood in Wichita, Kansas until one day in 1945 when, as if settling a score for all the saloons Christ's bulldog had smashed decades earlier, a beer truck careered off the road and knocked it down.[3]

In the years following repeal, the story of Prohibition was written by wet historians who were only kicking the corpse to make sure it was dead. When the wine and whisky flowed freely again in mid-century, the dry years were remembered as a scarcely believable orgy of utopianism brought about by cranks and screwballs who exploited American idealism to further their own obsessive agenda. The rich comic potential of the ultimate lost cause is at the heart of the classic accounts of the period, such as Herbert Asbury's *The Great Illusion* (1950) and Andrew Sinclair's *Era of Excess* (1962)—a literary tradition splendidly revived by Daniel Okrent in *Last Call* (2010).

Today, Prohibition lives on in the nation's collective memory as a bizarre aberration; a freakish event created by the madness of the mob which was always doomed to failure. This version of events contains more than a grain of truth, but it is a crude rendering which lets the American people off the hook and fails to explain how such a project ever received widespread support. Historians are naturally uncomfortable with the concept of anomalous events and inevitable failures, and as the archives were plundered in the 1960s, a more nuanced picture began to emerge. Much of this later research has been incorporated into the first chapter of this book, but two strains of revisionism deserve particular attention.

The first of these sought to rehabilitate the reputation of the prohibitionists to some extent. The traditional narrative of religious maniacs beguiling the population with an unworkable wheeze was clearly unsatisfactory when so many intelligent people supported the dry cause. Historians on the political left began to realise that many of the prohibitionists came from a reform tradition much like their own. "I was looking for a good liberal story to tell, the overcoming of a reactionary movement by progressives, when I decided to research repeal," said David Kyvig, author of *Repealing National Prohibition*. "And lo and behold, the farther I got into the tale, the more I discovered that the real advocates of Prohibition were the social progressives, and the opponents were the conservatives."[4] Earlier historians had underplayed the relationship between the Drys and the political left. Since the prohibitionists had been predominantly rural Protestants, it was easy to assume that they had a conservative mindset. In truth, the Drys saw nothing reactionary about their cause and nor did many of their contemporaries. Prohibition was widely viewed as a progressive measure that would propel the United States into a new age of science and reason. Had they succeeded in abolishing the drinks industry for good, we might still view it as their crowning achievement. Instead, and with the hindsight that comes from witnessing the soaking wet twentieth century, Prohibition looks like the reactionary's last swipe at modernity. In the end, history decides what is progressive.

The paradox of liberals pushing for illiberal laws no longer seems as counterintuitive as it did in the 1960s, when the concept of liberalism was more clearly defined. With the word 'liberal' now claimed by an assortment of libertarians, free marketeers, social democrats, Classical liberals, socialists and conservatives, practically the only political activists who do not hide under this umbrella are the Maoists and fascists. In the 1960s, however, liberalism and personal freedom were more transparently aligned and contemporary historians were surprised to find the same breed of reformer who had campaigned for votes for women and the abolition of slavery—and, later, for civil rights and gay liberation—at the heart of the campaign for alcohol suppression. Prohibition was the first instance of progressives harnessing the force of law to limit the freedom of the individual. Although they borrowed heavily from the anti-slavery campaign by targeting the drinks *trade* and using the rhetoric of emancipation (from drunkenness), Prohibition was fundamentally an assault on personal freedom and it was an assault which disproportionately hit the working class, because the more affluent Americans could make their own cider and afford speakeasy prices. As such, it was a watershed for the progressive movement. After years of attacking corrupt institutions and denouncing discriminatory laws, Prohibition marked the moment when liberals resorted to using coercion to reform ordinary Americans.

The realisation that many water-drinkers fought for political causes which are not usually associated with reactionaries allowed some historians to cast prohibitionists in a more sympathetic light. The progressives might have been wrong on the drink question, they implied, but their hearts were in the right place. Whether or not this is true is essentially a moral question which cannot be answered with empirical evidence. Certainly the prohibitionists were idealists, and there is no suggestion that they set out to harm the United States, but they nevertheless compelled millions of Americans to live under a law which many found intolerable. It is questionable whether such behaviour can ever be considered well-intentioned, and the Drys' endemic lying, bullying and racism, as well as their liking for eugenics and their links to the Ku Klux Klan, make them improbable heroes.

The second strain of historical revisionism began in 1968 when John C. Burnham published a controversial paper arguing that Prohibition was a popular cause which had been betrayed by successive presidents who refused to police it. Even the Anti-Saloon League, he said, was too scared of public opinion to demand proper enforcement. The Noble Experiment could have succeeded, he claimed, if it had not been for the Wets taking control of the media and persuading Americans that Prohibition had caused the Depression.

Burnham described the belief that there was a crime wave in the 1920s as a "myth" fostered by unreliable anecdotes. Using data from New York hospitals, he showed that incidence of alcohol psychosis fell sharply in the dry era. Most importantly, he provided sound evidence that alcohol consumption fell dramatically in 1920 and although it soon rose again, the amount drunk in the early 1930s remained lower than the pre-

Prohibition level. Since drinking declined and crime did not rise, the young historian concluded that Prohibition "can more easily be considered a success than a failure."[5]

Burnham's paper provided a valuable corrective to the popular belief that "everyone drank" during Prohibition. Several early accounts had depicted America as being awash with booze in the 1920s when it would have been more accurate to say that America was awash with booze *considering booze was illegal*. This clarification aside, Burnham's argument was unconvincing. If Prohibition was so popular, it is difficult to explain why so many politicians, presidents and even many Anti-Saloon League members were reluctant to enforce it. The answer, surely, is that a very great number of Americans did not believe in Prohibition, even in theory, and tougher enforcement risked turning simmering resentment into open revolt. Burnham's claim that there was no crime wave looks shaky in the light of America's murder rate which rose by a third during Prohibition, peaked in 1933 and then fell by half in the first decade of repeal. And while cases of alcohol psychosis did indeed fall in 1920, subsequent research has shown that they increased thereafter, as did arrests for drunkenness. Any gains made in terms of mental health were dwarfed by the upsurge in deaths from poisoning and homicide.[6]

Burnham remains a prominent apologist for Prohibition and is a keen supporter of anti-drug laws. "The myth [that Prohibition failed] came from the repeal forces," he said in 1988, "it's right out of their propaganda. We see the same myth was used by the marijuana people about fifteen years ago when they said everyone is smoking pot and the prohibition against pot doesn't work."[7] In his book *Bad Habits*, Burnham laments America's descent into "minor vices" which, he argues, began with the repeal of Prohibition and has continued thanks to the influence of wealthy corporations—the "vice-industrial complex"—and their exploitation of otherwise wholesome Americans. His pining for Prohibition is not a mainstream view amongst historians, but his basic argument—that Prohibition could have worked and, in many respects, *did* work—has found supporters. Some have said the experiment would have succeeded if the Drys had compromised and permitted beer to be sold.[8] Others have made the opposite case, saying that Prohibition was too soft and could only have worked if the consumption of alcohol had been criminalised along with its manufacture and sale, or if the law had been more rigorously enforced.[9]

The idea that permitting beer to be sold would have eliminated the worst of the damage sounds plausible and yet Norway's experiment with banning strong liquor between 1916 and 1926 led to the same health and social problems that accompanied alcohol prohibition elsewhere in the world. The alternative view—that Prohibition was too lenient—was widely held by prohibitionists at the time and many advocates of the War on Drugs entertain similar beliefs today. The journalist Peter Hitchens, an ardent supporter of marijuana prohibition, has argued that "[Drug] 'Prohibition' has not failed because 'Prohibition' has not been tried, at least not in the sense that the druggie lobby mean it."[10] By this, he means that police and magistrates do not enforce laws against the consumption of soft drugs with enough vigour. Upton Sinclair concluded his temperance novel *The Wet Parade,* published in 1931, with almost exactly the same words:

PROHIBITION HAS NOT FAILED!
PROHIBITION HAS NOT BEEN TRIED!
TRY IT.[11]

Could Prohibition have worked if people had been banned from drinking? The question is academic since Congress would never have passed a law banning consumption, but America's failure to suppress marijuana despite tough laws against possession suggests that Prohibition would have been no more successful had it been more draconian. A zero-tolerance approach would, in all probability, have inflicted still greater damage on society and hastened repeal. Similarly, only by reaching for the full apparatus of a police state, and thus creating a society in which few would choose to live, could any government come close to eradicating drug use.

The cornerstone of the revisionists' belief that "Prohibition worked"—a view that is by no means confined to John C. Burnham[12]—is the fact that drinking declined after 1920 and did not return to pre-Prohibition levels for another fifty years. The generally accepted estimate is that alcohol consumption fell by two-thirds in the first years of Prohibition before rising again and settling at 60-70% of the 1919 level.[13]

The public health benefits of the decline in drinking were relatively slight. Rates of liver cirrhosis fell by around 15%,[14] while alcohol psychosis and arrests for drunkenness fell at first before returning to normal as the decade wore on.[15] If this is to the credit of the Eighteenth Amendment, the debit must include a rising murder rate and numerous fatal and non-fatal poisonings, including those who were left crippled and blind. This is surely not what the anti-saloon preacher Billy Sunday had in mind when he conducted a mock funeral for alcohol on January 16 1920 and declared that "Hell will be forever for rent."

And yet in some ways Prohibition *did* succeed. American drinking habits were altered for a generation. The rough old saloon where women feared to tread died in 1920 and was never resurrected. When legitimate drinking establishments reopened in 1933, they took the form of respectable bars, taverns and hotel lounges which accommodated women drinkers (one effect of the speakeasies was to normalise mixed-sex drinking). Fifteen states banned saloons after repeal, many regions remained dry (some still are) and brewers were forbidden from owning licensed premises throughout the country. The word 'saloon' passed into history and so, in the most literal sense, the Anti-Saloon League won. As one of Prohibition's more sympathetic scholars wrote in the *American Journal of Public Health*:

> To wipe out a long-established and well-entrenched industry, to change drinking habits on a large scale, and to sweep away such a central urban and rural social institution as the saloon are no small achievements.[16]

Per capita alcohol consumption did not return to the heights of the 1910s until the early 1970s, although the sobering legacy of Prohibition is not as pronounced as is sometimes suggested (see Figure 1).[17] Nor can changes in drinking patterns be attributed entirely to Prohibition. British trends in alcohol consumption closely mirror those of the United States, with both countries seeing a collapse between 1916 and 1920 and a recovery after 1960. Both saw a prolonged lull during the economically

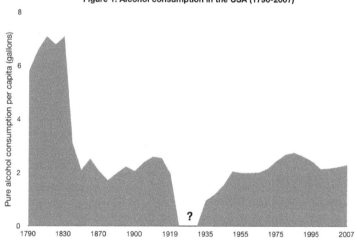

Figure 1. Alcohol consumption in the USA (1790-2007)

depressed 1930s which continued through the Second World War and into the early postwar period. Each experienced their initial slump for different reasons, with the USA banning spirits and then enacting Prohibition, while the British endured high taxes and severe restrictions during the First World War. As unpopular as Britain's wartime measures were, they fell a long way short of total suppression and yet the result was the same— a huge fall in alcohol use and less drinking for decades to come. Prohibition doubtless had some effect on America's long-term drinking patterns, but it must be remembered that other countries achieved the same outcome without having to resort to such extremism.

Ultimately, the problem with the idea that "Prohibition worked" is that it measures success by a very different yardstick to that used by the prohibitionists. No one in the Anti-Saloon League kidded themselves that the Eighteenth Amendment would eradicate drinking entirely, but even their most pessimistic members must have expected alcohol consumption to at least have halved after a decade's suppression. Richmond Hobson, "Pussyfoot" Johnson, John D. Rockefeller and all the other Drys who gave up on Prohibition in its final years evidently did not believe that the experiment had "worked", nor did the representatives of the thirty-eight states who lined up to repeal it. To claim otherwise requires a threshold of success that would be unrecognisable to anyone then alive.

Prohibition was not a failure because some drinking continued (nobody expected the habit to be wiped out), but nor was it a success because drinking was reduced somewhat. Prohibition was a failure because drinking continued on a grand and growing scale without fulfilling the promise of better health, higher morals and less crime. On the contrary, it led to worse health, lower morals and more crime. It dealt the temperance movement a crushing blow, but—as we shall see—it was not a fatal one.

From prohibition to control

The Anti-Saloon League did not slink off into the sunset in 1933. Nearly bankrupt and deprived of its leading players, it changed its name to the Temperance League in 1948 and then to the National Temperance League two years later. In 1964, it dropped all reference to temperance and became the American Council on Alcohol Problems. It survives to this day as a total abstinence society with pretensions of being a public·health group. The once-mighty *American Issue* continues to be published every three months, but it has been reduced to a modest six-page newsletter.

The Woman's Christian Temperance Union also outlived Prohibition and can still be found opposing gay marriage, medical marijuana and pornography in the American heartland. Children can still fill out WCTU pledge cards promising to abstain from alcohol and drugs—or, as the WCTU is always careful to put it, "alcohol and *other* drugs".

Even the Prohibition Party survives; the third oldest party in American politics took all of 643 votes in the 2008 presidential election.

In Britain, the United Kingdom Alliance for the Suppression of the Traffic in all Intoxicating Liquors became the slightly pithier United Kingdom Temperance Alliance in 1942 before rebranding itself as the Alliance House Foundation in 2003. With an annual budget of £10 million coming from rent on its six-storey office block in Westminster—the afore-mentioned Alliance House—this incarnation of the UK Alliance keeps a low public profile while influencing opinion-makers through its "educational charity", the Institute of Alcohol Studies.

The Institute of Alcohol Studies presents itself as an "independent voice on alcohol policy" which "does not have a view on whether individuals should drink or should not drink"[18] —a remarkable display of independence from an organisation that receives nearly all its income from the Alliance House Foundation, whose stated objective is "to spread the principles of total abstinence from alcoholic drinks."[19] A trawl through back issues of the Institute's two journals—*Alcohol Alert* and *The Globe*—failed to unearth a single article that painted alcohol in a favourable light.

Since the 1980s, new temperance groups have emerged, most notably the National Center on Addiction and Substance Abuse in the USA and Alcohol Concern in Britain. The former is funded by the Robert Wood Johnson Foundation, the philanthropic arm of the pharmaceutical company Johnson & Johnson, America's most generous private donor to the anti-drink and anti-tobacco causes. Alcohol Concern was formed by the British government in 1985 and is principally funded by the Department of Health. The short-term aims of these neo-temperance groups are the abolition of all forms of alcohol advertising, progressively higher drink prices, tougher licensing laws and an increase in the age at which alcohol can be bought. Their demands for shorter opening hours echo those of the early teetotal societies but, unlike their forebears, 'alcohol control' groups are not in the business of moral suasion, nor do they rely on donations from the public. Instead, they are overtly political lobby groups run by a small number of media-savvy professionals campaigning for what might be called 'little prohibitions'—bans and regulations to limit the sale, marketing and availability of alcohol. As before, these temperance campaigners believe that only the 'liquor trust', now known as Big Alcohol, stands in their way. Now, as then, the desires of millions of drinkers are scarcely acknowledged.

'Alcohol control' borrows liberally from the blueprint of incremental legislation that has been tried and tested by 'tobacco control'. The rise of the cigarette did not go unnoticed at the turn of the last century, but early successes in banning the product fell by the wayside when reformers were forced to devote all their attentions to alcohol. By the time cigarettes were shown to be a genuine health hazard in the 1950s, the smoking habit had long been ingrained in Western society and reformers had a mountain to climb.* The new wave of anti-smoking activists who emerged in the 1970s vehemently denied seeking to outlaw tobacco even as they raised prices, limited availability and banned advertising. Once again, the industry was viewed as the source of the contagion and while prohibition was always the logical outcome of the anti-smoking push, it has only been very recently that campaigners have made this goal explicit.[20]

In 2004, the tobacco prohibitionists scored their first bulls-eye of the modern era when the tiny kingdom of Bhutan banned the sale of tobacco and dished out lengthy prison sentences to several monks caught in possession of small quantities of chewing tobacco. The prohibition was welcomed by some public health advocates, but when the *International Journal of Drug Policy* evaluated its success in 2011, a familiar picture emerged.

...a thriving black market and significant and increasing tobacco smuggling... tobacco use for adults has not ended or is even close to ending ... 23.7% of students had used any tobacco products (not limited to cigarettes) in the last 30 days ... The results of this study provide an important lesson learned for health practitioners and advocates considering or advocating, albeit a gradual, total cigarette ban as a public policy.[21]

Despite this "lesson learned", the cigarette remains the most likely candidate for legal suppression in many countries, with the most zealous anti-smoking activists looking beyond the 'coffin nails' and seeking to ban all nicotine-containing products, except 'nicotine replacement therapy'. In 2010, the pharmaceutical giant Pfizer called on the European Union to not only maintain the ban on snus, but to ban all forms of smokeless tobacco.[22] Several countries, including Australia, have banned

---

* Cigarettes were banned in more than a dozen US states in the early twentieth century. See my book *Velvet Glove, Iron Fist: A History of Anti-Smoking* for a full account of tobacco prohibition.

the battery-powered electronic cigarette, a device which contains no tobacco and whose greatest crime is to physically resemble the hated 'cancer stick'.

Anti-smoking campaigners benefit from having one trump card that the temperance lobby has always lacked: cigarettes have no medicinal properties and moderate use is not beneficial to health.* Modern temperance campaigners have to deal with the uncomfortable fact that moderate drinkers outlive teetotallers. Hundreds of studies carried out over several decades have shown the health benefits of drinking, particularly in regard to cardiovascular disease, thereby making it difficult for 'alcohol control' to repeat the old WCTU mantra: "Use *is* abuse". Faced with these facts, the anti-alcohol lobby has responded in the same way as their nineteenth century counterparts—with misinformation. Ignoring the weight of evidence, they latched onto an old debate in the scientific literature and used it to create doubt in the public's mind.

At one time, it was suspected that teetotallers had shorter life-spans than drinkers because they had underlying health problems. This was a valid consideration. If abstainers had given up drink because they were former alcoholics or chronically ill, their odds of suffering an early death would shorten, but this would not be the direct result of their teetotalism. Aware of this possible conflation of correlation with causation, epidemiologists conducted further studies in which they controlled for their subjects' former drinking habits. Others avoided the problem by only studying healthy, lifelong teetotallers. The results remained the same: abstainers had a higher mortality rate than moderate drinkers. No matter which confounding factors were brought into the equation, and irrespective of whether researchers studied men or women, young or old, the relationship between

---

* Or, more precisely, cigarettes have no medicinal properties that outweigh the hazards of long-term use. There is evidence that nicotine helps prevent weight gain, Alzheimer's disease and Parkinson's disease.

mortality and alcohol consumption appeared on a graph in a U-shape. Drinkers have to consume large amounts of alcohol before their life expectancy falls to that of a teetotaller.[23]

In spite of this extensive research, the myth that the U-shaped curve is itself a myth continues to be repeated by those who should know better.[24] For example, here is a representative of Australia's National Drug and Research Institute speaking in July 2011:

"The so-called protective effect of alcohol on cardiovascular disease has been over-stated and the reason for that is because the underlying studies themselves, the epidemiology, is flawed, have been biased... What a lot of these studies do is when they define somebody who doesn't drink, an abstainer, who seems to be worse off for not drinking, in terms of heart disease, they include in those groups a whole bunch of people who were drinkers but stop drinking because they became unwell. Laughable, but it's extremely common for researchers to do that, not only for heart disease but for a whole range of other conditions that have recently been reported to be protected by alcohol."[25]

In the same year, an article in *The Guardian* attacked "the myth of a safe level of drinking". Appearing in print shortly after the *British Medical Journal* had reviewed 84 studies and found overwhelming evidence that alcohol reduced the risk of cardiovascular disease, the article's author dismissed the evidence and imposed an impossible burden of proof on future researchers. What was needed, he said, was "a randomised trial where part of this group drink no alcohol, others drink in small amounts and others more heavily. Until this experiment has been done we don't have proof that alcohol has health benefits."[26] Such an experiment could never be conducted, as it would require random people to be forced to drink set amounts of alcohol for many years. It was reminiscent of the tobacco industry's old argument that the link between smoking and lung cancer was merely "statistical" and had never been proven in a "real" experiment. True, but nor could it.

The article went on to regurgitate a list of claims that were uncannily similar to those made in the Scientific Temperance Instruction textbooks endorsed by the WCTU in the 1880s. Mary Hanchett Hunt's distorted view of physiology dictated that alcohol was a poison that was instantly addictive and could never be consumed safely, even in moderation. Having insisted that moderate drinking was not healthy, the author of the *Guardian* article went on to say that alcohol is a poison:

Alcohol is a toxin that kills cells such as microorganisms, which is why we use it to preserve food and sterilise skin, needles etc.

That alcohol is instantly addictive:

I have seen many people who have experienced a strong liking of alcohol from their very first exposure and then gone on to become addicted to it

And that alcohol can never be consumed safely:

We must not allow apologists for this toxic industry to pull the wool over our eyes with their myth of a safe alcohol dose

The resurrection of prohibitionist myths in the British national press was all the more remarkable for having been penned by Professor David Nutt, a man who had been mistaken for a libertarian only a year earlier. After being sacked as chairman of the Advisory Council on the Misuse of Drugs, Nutt openly came out in favour of the decriminalisation of cannabis, but became increasingly preoccupied with clamping down on drink. He published a study in the *Lancet* which ranked alcohol as the most dangerous drug in society, and suggested that an evidence-based policy would put alcohol in Class A of the Misuse of Drugs Act.*

---

* Ironically, in the light of the contretemps that got him sacked, Nutt's system would have left cannabis in Class B.

This kind of rhetoric had long been used by cannabis users to highlight the absurdity of their relatively harmless drug being illegal when alcohol, which kills many thousands every year, remained freely available—but the same argument could be also used to justify the prohibition of alcohol. When Nutt said "if alcohol was discovered today it would be controlled as an illegal drug alongside similar sedatives such as GHB and GBL",[27] he was not recommending the legalisation of GHB. Instead, he moved deeper into temperance territory, calling for the price of alcohol to be *tripled*, for the drinking age to be raised to twenty-one, for drinking games and pub crawls to be banned in universities, for graphic health warnings to be placed on bottles and for a total ban on alcohol advertising. Nutt was not alone. At the same time, Alcohol Concern was calling on the government to place a minimum price on every unit of alcohol sold and the British Medical Association announced that "we have to start denormalising alcohol".[28] (The term "denormalisation" was coined by the tobacco control movement in the 1990s in reference to smoking.)

If this represents the revival of the temperance movement, it is clearly still in its early stages. Outside of the Islamic world, alcohol remains immune from suppression, largely because drinkers are in the majority and because alcohol, unlike tobacco and narcotics, is disproportionately consumed by the middle class—not least by politicians. This gives wine and beer a measure of protection that opiates did not have in the 1920s and tobacco does not have today, as David Courtwright notes:

It may well be that today's growing intolerance of smoking is related to the fact that proportionately more members of the middle and professional classes are kicking the habit, leaving a residue of poorer and less future-oriented smokers ... it would certainly have been more difficult to deny drugs and mete out sentences if, in the 1920s and 1930s, the addict population still had been largely composed of ailing ladies and crippled war veterans.[29]

As important as class prejudice has been in prohibition's history, an evidence-based policy should be based on facts alone, and Nutt is right when he says that alcohol remains legal by virtue of little more than historical accident. Those who support the prohibition of drugs and tobacco on public health grounds are entirely inconsistent if they do not also endorse the banning of alcohol. From the perspective of the medical establishment, tobacco and alcohol have slipped through a loophole that needs to be closed. Not with full prohibition, perhaps, but certainly with severe regulation.

But, as David Nutt found out, drugs policy is not based solely on the health risks and nor should it be. It is natural for the medical establishment to see recreational substances only in terms of health and addiction, but their users do not. For the consumers of all but the strongest drugs, addiction and disease are not major concerns. Only a small minority of drinkers struggle with alcoholism and most drug users experiment for a few years without doing themselves any harm. Nutt's anguished search for an 'evidence-based drugs policy', though laudable in many respects, epitomised the myopic vision of a public health movement which demands that all issues be seen through the eyes of doctors. To suggest, as Nutt has, that alcohol should be a Class A drug while LSD and Ecstasy should be in a yet-to-be-invented Class D is not only politically unpalatable, but willfully ignores the social context of substance use. It may be true that alcohol has a greater destructive potential to health than LSD or ketamine, but one need only imagine a wedding reception or business lunch conducted under the influence of psychedelic hallucinogens and heavy sedatives to see that it is no fluke that alcohol is legal.

It may also be true that alcohol would be a Class A drug if it was discovered today, but this is more a reflection of the risk-averse times we live in than an indictment of alcohol itself. What, one might ask, would *not* be banned if it was invented today? Tobacco, butter, chocolate, caffeine, hamburgers and

Coca-Cola would struggle on health grounds. Coal, oil, the internal combustion engine and aeroplanes would never get past the climate change lobby, while guns, motorcars and—certainly —motorbikes would be turned down on safety grounds. To argue for greater control over alcohol on the basis that other drugs are illegal is to accept the logic of prohibition. The medical establishment *does* accept that logic. Although it takes the more humane view that drug addicts should be seen as patients rather than criminals, it rarely questions the need for prohibition itself. Liberalisers will find little support from a public health movement which not only accepts the fundamentals of drug prohibition, but wishes to extend suppression to all mood-altering substances.

There is a more optimistic lesson that could be learned from Western society's more relaxed treatment of alcohol. For all the hazards of drinking, including the aggression and violence, it has become a largely cherished part of civilisation and there is little appetite for its abolition. Most would agree that alcohol, as a relaxant and social lubricant, has benefits which outweigh its costs. If society can adapt to this drug, it is surely conceivable that less harmful substances could also be tolerated.

"Intoxication," as Richard Davenport-Hines noted, "is not unnatural or deviant. Absolute sobriety is not a natural or primary human state."[30] Prohibition flounders because it is doubly unnatural. Not only does it wage war on plants that grow in the soil, but it denies the human urge for intoxication. Whether we call this urge the "restless search for bliss"[31] or the "pursuit of oblivion",[32] it is an innate characteristic of our species which the law cannot suppress.*

The most prohibition can realistically hope to do is divert the pleasure-seeker from one habit to another. The shift from opium to heroin after 1909 and the rise of marijuana during

---

* And not just our species. Monkeys, bears, elk and other animals acquire a taste for alcohol, and wallabies, deer and sheep have been known to seek out opium in fields and get "as high as a kite".[33]

Prohibition are just two of many examples. There is evidence that the decline in smoking since 1970 has led to greater obesity, with nonsmokers twice as likely to be obese than smokers.[34] Eating, like smoking, drugs and sex, releases dopamine in the brain thus producing the sensation we know as pleasure. Over-eating is what happens when we pursue that pleasure to excess, and obesity, which some regard as a greater threat to public health than either smoking or drug-taking, is the result. The story of designer drugs shows that when the law cuts off one avenue of pleasure, new sources are invariably found. As one doctor said in the 1960s: "The government line is that the use of marijuana leads to more dangerous drugs. The fact is that the *lack* of marijuana leads to more dangerous drugs."[35]

In most Western countries today, the natural human thirst for artificial highs can only be slaked with alcohol, and whilst alcohol serves society well most of the time, it is not for everybody, nor, as David Nutt is keen to stress, is it the least hazardous option. It would be better for society if those who react badly to alcohol searched for pleasure through more placid drugs such as marijuana or MDMA. And it would be better for the health of those prone to addiction to be habituated to cannabis or opium than to whisky. To put it bluntly, the problem is not that there are too many drugs available, but too few.

The case for prohibition

The modern case for prohibition rests on two assumptions: that legalisation will increase consumption and that increased consumption will lead to greater physical and mental harm. If either of these assumptions is false, suppression cannot be justified.

The idea that legalisation will lead to greater consumption cannot be lightly dismissed. It is essentially the same argument as saying "Prohibition worked"; if a ban reduces consumption, then legalisation must increase it. Basic economics dictates that if the disincentive of prosecution is removed and prices are allowed to fall, consumption will rise. Some liberalisers have suggested that drugs are already so freely available that everyone who wants them can get them, but this is an exaggeration.[36] Prohibition may have failed, but it has not failed so utterly that the market for drugs is saturated.

So many years have passed since the Harrison Act and the Dangerous Drugs Act that we cannot guess what a 'natural' level of drug use would be in a free market. We know that opium consumption in the USA tapered off in the 1890s when a fraction of one percent of Americans were regular users. David Musto has speculated that "opiates had nearly saturated the market for such drugs: that is, those who were environmentally or biochemically disposed to opiates had been fairly well located by the marketers and the consumption curve levelled off as the demand was met."[37] If modern consumption returned to this peak, it would be no upheaval at all, rather it would represent a decline in opiate use.

But this is not the 1890s and if opium was to return, it would be as a purely recreational drug. Some people who are currently deterred by the criminal nature of the act would doubtless experiment, but perhaps not so many. The threat of arrest is not a major deterrent when it comes the consumption of intoxicants. Bans on the sale of alcohol in the

USA "had little effect on limiting consumption outside of their effect on price", according to the economists Miron and Zwiebel. In their study of drinking patterns in Prohibition-era America, they suggested that the same may be true of drug prohibition today.

Social pressure and respect for the law did not go far in reducing consumption during Prohibition. We speculate that this is likely to be true as well with illegal drugs today, and therefore claims based on such arguments exaggerate the extent to which drug consumption would increase upon legalization.[38]

When the Netherlands decriminalised cannabis in 1976, critics predicted that the country would be overrun with dope fiends, but while Amsterdam attracts its fair share of drug tourists, there has been no surge in marijuana use amongst the Dutch. Today, it has fewer cannabis smokers than its neighbour Germany, and far fewer than countries like Spain, Canada and Australia. A British teenager is twice as likely to have tried cannabis, and *twenty* times as likely to have tried heroin, than a Dutch teenager.[39]

Portugal went further in 2001 when it decriminalised the consumption of all drugs, including cocaine and heroin. As Joao Goulao, president of the Portuguese Drug Institute, explains, the rise in drug use forecast by conservatives never materialised:

"The rightist parties at the time were saying: 'Portugal will become a paradise for addicts all over the world, planes from everywhere to come and use drugs freely.' In fact, nothing like this happened. The statistics show that drug use has fallen among youngsters since 2001 ... AIDS and HIV problems fell dramatically and drug related deaths have fallen."[40]

Since liberalising the market, Portugal has seen a fall in drug use amongst young people and the number of drug users seeking treatment for addiction has doubled.[41] Ten years after the decriminalisation began, neither public nor politicians have expressed much of an appetite for a return to prohibition.

If the failure of the Portuguese to embark on a frenzy of drug abuse seems surprising, it is only because a century of prohibition has fostered the belief that people are protected from their own bestial instincts by the force of law. But the latent savagery of the lumpenproletariat has been much exaggerated. Portugal no more became a nation of junkies after 2001 than the Netherlands became a nation of pot-heads in 1976, or the British became a nation of alcoholics after the so-called '24 hour drinking' law of 2005. The prohibitionist's fallacy of mistaking availability for demand is as enduring as it is wrong-headed.

One cautious note should be sounded, however. Decriminalisation is a different proposition to legalisation (the former makes possession of small quantities of drugs legal, the latter legalises their sale and import). Under a legalised system, it would be an inevitable—and quite intended—consequence for prices to fall below those charged on the black market. This, more than the lack of criminal sanctions, might increase drug use, as one study of the 'Dutch experience' implied:

> Almost all previous reviews on this issue reach the same conclusion: decriminalization of cannabis does not lead to a substantial increase in cannabis consumption rates. One of the many possible explanations for this finding might be that decriminalization is not associated with reduced prices.[42]

As legalisation would certainly lower prices, an upsurge in use cannot be discounted, at least in the short-term. In a country obsessed with low-fat foods and sugar-free drinks, it is difficult to believe there is a huge untapped demand for the intravenous injection of notoriously addictive drugs, but there will surely be some who abandon alcohol for MDMA or cocaine. Having conceded that possibility, the second question is whether more drug use equals more harm.

For a number of the most popular drugs, the question is barely relevant, since they are neither clinically addictive nor particularly dangerous. There is a strong case for saying that marijuana, MDMA and mephedrone, for example, do not carry sufficient health risks to justify prohibition in the first place. There is some evidence that cannabis, especially in its stronger form of skunk, may increase the risk of schizophrenia in people who are genetically predisposed to the illness,* but since skunk is produced primarily for the benefit of dealers and growers rather than users—because it is stronger and takes up less space—its consumption can be expected to decline in a legal market. Just as bootlegging hard liquor was more profitable for Al Capone than shipping beer, so the War on Drugs has driven up the supply of stronger narcotics. The repeal of Prohibition did not help the sale of strong spirits; on the contrary, drinkers returned to beer while 80% proof concoctions such as Jamaica Ginger faded away. Only the most brutal substances rely on the desperation borne of prohibition to survive.

---

* The link between cannabis and mental illness provides another example of liberalisers displaying as much bias in the face of evidence as the prohibitionists. After the ACMD found that cannabis users had a 158% increased risk of psychotic disorders, David Nutt went to some lengths to downplay the finding.[43] He referred to the "paradox" that "schizophrenia seems to be disappearing (from the general population), even though cannabis use has increased markedly in the last 30 years".[44] It is true that hospital admissions for schizophrenia fell from 36,000 to 24,000 between 2000 and 2008 but to say the disease was "disappearing" was a great exaggeration.[45]

Nutt then cast doubt on the epidemiology which found a 158% increase in risk, saying: "To put that figure into proportion, you are 20 times [ie. 2,000%] more likely to get lung cancer if you smoke tobacco than if you don't." True, but the link between smoking and lung cancer is one of the strongest in epidemiology and almost all other risks pale by comparison. By modern standards, 158% is a substantial risk. Nutt has expressed less scepticism about much weaker epidemiological findings when they appear to support his view that there is "no safe level" of alcohol use. The link between alcohol use and breast cancer, for example, is in the range of 10-30% and questions could be raised about whether the relationship is truly causal.

There are good reasons to question whether cannabis use really does increase the risk of psychosis,[46] but some of those used by Nutt—admittedly to a lay audience in *The Guardian*—are not compelling.

As with alcohol, so it is with drugs. Narcotics suppression invariably favours the most dangerous derivatives and this is especially true of intravenous heroin use, which is the leading cause of accidental overdose. It is wrong to suggest, as some liberalisers do, that the Harrison Act was solely responsible for the rise of heroin, and it is wishful thinking to believe that repeal would eliminate the use of syringes or make heroin, morphine and crack cocaine disappear. Some users will always be inclined towards the strongest substances and the combination of criminalisation and science has opened a Pandora's Box that cannot easily be shut.

So long as opiates and syringes exist, fatal overdoses will occur. The cost of legalisation, as Aleister Crowley coldly put it, is the death of "a few score wasters too stupid to know when to stop."[47] But this is also the cost of prohibition and, while Crowley's words were unfeeling, they were no more callous than Wayne Wheeler's opinion that a man who violated the Eighteenth Amendment "should be free to commit suicide in his own way."[48] Drug warriors have never emulated Wheeler's deliberate poisoning of the alcohol supply, but their methods have led to a vastly higher death-count than anything seen in Prohibition-era America. This is not to absolve drug users from responsibility—ultimately the decision to engage in risky and illegal behaviour is theirs alone—but it is a pitiless man who calls Russian roulette a fool's game and then puts more bullets in the revolver.

The War on Drugs loads the pistol by rigging the illicit market in favour of the most addictive and dangerous chemicals while ensuring a total lack of quality control. Even the hardest drugs can be safely injected for decades if the doses remain controlled and stable. None of the opiates is inherently lethal; they only become so as a result of adulteration, contamination and sudden changes in purity. Addicts who have become accustomed to low-grade street heroin, which has been cut so many times that it might contain less than 10% of the drug, are liable to drop dead if they encounter a batch of the pure Afghan product. The purity of street drugs is always erratic and since users can never be sure of what they have bought, they are far more likely to overdose than if they had obtained a regulated product. Intravenous users are at greater risk of being killed by taking heroin which is unexpectedly pure than by taking drugs which have been deliberately contaminated.*

No less serious is the risk of catching diseases from shared syringes. As well as making addiction more powerful, intravenous injections lead to abscesses, artery damage and several blood-borne diseases. Of the 40 million people living with HIV, 4 million were infected as a result of intravenous drug use.[49] No less than a third of all HIV sufferers outside sub-Saharan Africa caught the disease by sharing a needle with an infected drug user.[50] Of the world's 16 million intravenous drug users, 10 million are infected with hepatitis C and 1.3 million are infected with hepatitis B.[51] Syringes are, in other words, more dangerous than the drugs they contain. They are also largely a product of prohibition.

The criminalisation of drugs exacerbates health risks in more subtle ways. Addicts are at particular risk of overdose after coming out of prison when, assuming they have been unable to find heroin on the inside, their tolerance is low. There is no knowing how many drug users have died because they or others have failed to contact the emergency services for fear of prosecution, but the numbers are unlikely to be trifling. Unable

---

* Although batches of drugs are cut with all sorts of powders, the popular belief that dealers contaminate their products with broken glass, rat poison and brick dust has "no foundation in forensic evidence", according to Drugscope. Chemical analyses of street drugs have not found deadly chemicals added to the mix and this urban legend most likely stems from a desire to further scare people off drugs and demonise those who sell them. Although drug dealers are hardly pillars of the community, they have no incentive to kill their customers and typically cut their products with milk powder, sugar, caffeine and paracetamol.

to seek reliable advice on dosage, and sceptical of government warnings which so often misrepresent the real risks, all drug use is essentially experimentation.

The public health case against drug prohibition cannot be concluded without mentioning the many thousands of murders and extra-judicial killings committed by drug barons, smugglers, dealers and policemen from the backstreets of Bogotá to the fields of Burma. Unable to settle disputes in a court of law, the illicit traders swiftly resort to violence. This is a world designed for psychopaths, and drug prohibition rewards some of the planet's most vicious thugs with unimaginable wealth. In the heyday of Pablo Escobar's cocaine empire, which made him the world's seventh richest man, Colombia was the homicide capital of the world.[52] Mexico's current orgy of drug-related gang violence has claimed over 30,000 lives since it began in December 2006. An unregulated narcotics market is a recipe for corruption and lawlessness which infects the whole of society.

These unintended consequences are not unique to drug prohibition. In all the examples given in this book, political attempts to suppress recreational substances have led to greater harm being inflicted on the user, and to society, than would otherwise be the case. The suppression of alcohol pushed drinkers towards unregulated, high-voltage moonshine of dubious origin; the suppression of MDMA pushed users towards substances which have higher risk profiles; the suppression of naturally occurring narcotics has driven users towards the most drastic, degrading and dangerous methods of consumption. The banning of snus is different only insofar as the unintended consequences remain unseen, but it has nonetheless given nicotine users little choice but to continue consuming the drug in its deadliest form.

In every case, criminalisation exacerbates damage and spreads ill-health. It turns benign substances into health hazards and makes risky products lethal. Legalisation does not offer a utopia, nor can it be denied that many drugs pose inherent dangers that no form of regulation can erase, but, as Miron and Zwiebel note, it would lead to the "elimination of the violent drug culture that results from the battle for illegal profits, a reduction in overdoses from impure drugs, a reduction in robberies and burglaries committed by addicts who pay inflated drug prices, the stabilization of Latin American regimes fighting control battles with drug lords, the ability to combat the spread of AIDS from needle exchanges more effectively, and an unclogging of the criminal justice system."[53] From the perspective of public health, it would take an enormous and unprecedented rise in overall drug consumption before a legalised system came close to wreaking the havoc that has for years been taken for granted under the War on Drugs.

A modest proposal

Any alternative to drug prohibition must aim to reduce intravenous use, keep drugs out of the hands of children and dampen demand for the most damaging derivatives of crack cocaine, heroin and morphine—all the things that prohibition has singularly failed to achieve. It would restore the right of consenting adults to take stimulants, narcotics, empathogens and hallucinogens for recreational and medical use while reducing drug-related crime to a level that has been unimaginable for much of the last hundred years.

The optimal system would take the narcotics industry out of the hands of criminals, regulate purity and quality, and collect the many billions in taxes that have been lost to the government. This money would then be used to pay for treatment and rehabilitation services for those struggling with addiction, as well as financing the agencies that would enforce licensing regulations and control minors' access to drugs. These services could be offered at a world-class standard and still leave huge sums left over for governments to spend on other projects. The optimal system would, in other words, be closer to legalisation than decriminalisation.

For practical reasons, liberalisation should be introduced gradually. No one alive remembers what it was like to walk into a shop and buy laudanum or cocaine. After a century of systematic infantilisation, treating the public as adults might prove disorientating at first, but if the muscles of self-reliance and personal responsibility have been weakened through underuse, they can quickly be restored. One useful side-effect of the War on Drugs has been to leave several generations with an exaggerated sense of the risks of substance use which should help prevent a reckless binge when the clock strikes midnight.

A pragmatic legal market would allow licensed bars, coffee shops and private members' clubs to sell opium and cannabis for smoking on the premises. Nightclubs and some bars would be permitted to sell pure MDMA. Pills, powders and tinctures containing amphetamine, cocaine and opium would be available from registered pharmacists with appropriate warnings and directions for use. Specialised licensed shops, equivalent to tobacconists or 'head shops', would be permitted to sell cannabis cigarettes, MDMA, smoking opium and hallucinogens for sale off the premises. In all cases, sales would be limited to those over the age of eighteen.

This would not be an entirely free market. Pure heroin and morphine would not be available except under doctor's prescription for chronic disease, terminal illness and the maintenance of addiction, both under medical supervision and, in the latter case, subject to the patient accepting treatment for addiction. Marijuana would be available on prescription for sufferers of multiple sclerosis, glaucoma and other diseases where science has established proof of efficacy. Crack cocaine, methamphetamine and, perhaps, skunk would not be sold commercially, although it would be fruitless to try to stop individuals manufacturing or growing these drugs privately.

THC levels in marijuana could be limited by law in the same way as tar levels are limited in cigarettes.

Regulation would be much tighter than for any other legal product. In the short-term, some variation of the Swedish Bratt System for alcohol (see Chapter Two) might be appropriate, limiting the number of purchases that could be made within a certain period of time and forbidding sales to certain persons. Recovering addicts could enrol in a voluntary self-exclusion scheme based on the system which allows compulsive gamblers to ban themselves from casinos.[54] Local authorities might choose to limit the sale of drugs to premises which do not also sell alcohol, but any regulation must be careful not to be so restrictive as to resurrect the illicit trade.

In the tradition of the bootleggers uniting with the Baptists, the big-time drug dealers can be expected to join the prohibitionists in opposing legalisation. It is quite possible that elements of the criminal underworld will shift their attention to other illegal activities once the narcotics gold mine is closed off to them, but legalisation would also free up enormous police resources to detect real crime. In any case, it is not the responsibility of government to provide lucrative openings for organised criminals.

It is possible that a black market will emerge purveying the most dangerous derivatives, but the illicit drug dealer will find the odds stacked against him in several ways. Under legalisation, even the most punitively taxed substances will cost less than half the price charged under prohibition. Addicts would receive their prescriptions free of charge and the legal availability of high quality opium and opium-containing tinctures should soften the demand for illicit heroin, morphine and methadone. These drugs, along with crack cocaine and skunk, are products of prohibition by virtue of their potency. Recreational users have historically preferred to take these drugs in their more natural, less hazardous forms and, under legalisation, the appeal of the strongest derivatives will be lost, except to the most hardened addict. Although it is highly improbable that these drugs will fall into disuse, especially in the first years of repeal, the availability of other options, combined with a well-financed harm reduction agency, should alleviate the worst of the damage.

The illicit dealer will also face a police force that is no longer hamstrung by the War on Drugs. The authorities will be able to direct their drug enforcement agencies at a greatly depleted black market serving a small minority of hardcore addicts and underage users. The illicit industry will be relatively impoverished and socially isolated while the police will be able to rebuild trust with otherwise law-abiding drug users who had previously viewed them with suspicion and fear. The legal vendors of drugs will have an incentive to inform the police about illicit sales, just as the Philippines' opium monopolists did prior to 1908.

Liberalisation would allow some of the world's poorest countries to grow their native crops and trade them openly on the international market. The poppy growers of Afghanistan and the coca growers of South America would continue their work without fear of intimidation and arrest. The manufacturers and smugglers could use their skills and contacts in the new legal industry, just as the illicit casino owners did after Britain's gambling laws were relaxed in the 1960s. The small time drug dealers would find themselves unemployed, but since most of them only sell drugs to feed their own costly addictions, this would be no loss to anyone. Likewise, those who commit petty crime or become prostitutes to feed their addictions would no longer have to do so.

Driving under the influence of drugs would continue to be treated as seriously as drunk-driving, and intoxication from drugs (or drink) would not be viewed as a mitigating factor for any criminal offence. Upon repeal, prisoners convicted for the possession of drugs would receive a pardon and be released.

The triumph of the moral entrepreneur

The scenario described above will delight some and appal others. The appalled can console themselves with the knowledge that there is not the slightest chance of such a system being put in place in their grandchildren's lifetimes, let alone their own. One needs only to consider the many laws against smoking tobacco in bars to be reminded of how fantastically improbable is the prospect of opium dens being allowed to open. Any hope that the legalisation of MDMA is even a distant possibility crashes on the rocks of mephedrone's swift and eager prohibition. At a time when campaigners demand bans on everything from sunbeds to circumcision, the idea that marijuana and cocaine could be sold over the counter is laughable. We live in prohibitionist times and although the past is no guide to the future, there is little to suggest that we will not continue down the path of suppression for many years to come.

There is an irony in the most highly educated and prosperous people that have ever lived not being trusted to make decisions that have not troubled earlier generations, but society has never been more risk-averse and governments have never felt more responsibility for the transgressions of their citizens. It is unthinkable in such an environment that products with known health hazards could be reintroduced to the market.

Ian Oliver, a former British Chief Constable, said: "Inevitably, if you legalise something, it sends out the message that it can't be very harmful. They think 'if the government says it's okay to take these then I'm going to take them.'"[55] Herein lies much of the problem. Decades of legislation aimed at eliminating risk have eroded self-reliance to such an extent that the mere legality of an activity implies government approval. So much is prohibited that what remains is assumed to be desirable, if not compulsory. No meaningful reform of drugs policy is possible until the public understands that free societies tolerate risky and even foolish behaviour without making it a crime.

As the story of designer drugs shows, politicians cannot resist the illusory belief that they are saving lives when they make the decision to ban. That the deaths ascribed to drug use could be more readily blamed on prohibition itself barely registers. Fatal overdoses of heroin addicts are so common that they come to be seen as part of the natural order, whereas a death from a legal high is seen as the fault of government. There is little that can break through this wall of self-deluding irrationality. The political thinking which keeps the War on Drugs in place might be described thus: people die under the present system, but they do so having broken the law. Whilst those deaths are regrettable, for them to have died within the law would have been intolerable.

The fundamental change in political thinking that would acknowledge the human capacity for self-restraint and personal responsibility has never seemed further away. We are patently not on the brink of legalisation, nor anything close to it. Much more likely is the continuing wave of fresh restrictions and little prohibitions that chip away at the remaining 'vices'. After a century of prohibition, the range of legally available mood-enhancers has been reduced to caffeine, nicotine and alcohol, of which only the latter is an intoxicant. All three have been banned at one time or another in various parts of the world, but they now stand as the lone survivors from the days before the First World War when stimulants and intoxicants were freely bought and sold. It is not unthinkable that this trio may one day join the others under some form of prohibition. They all have the potential to become medicalised: caffeine is already available in pill form, pharmaceutical companies have found ways of selling nicotine as a pleasureless drug, and none other than David Nutt is attempting to develop a synthetic form of alcohol. The professor has created a prototype alcohol substitute to be taken as a tablet or injection which creates a "pleasant state of mild intoxication" without leading to hangovers or liver damage.

"Modern science can now provide a safer way for us to have fun," Nutt told *The Times*.[56]

If the day comes when all stimulants and intoxicants are medicalised and classified, it would be the logical outcome of the War on Drugs, which is based on the fundamental principle that mood-altering chemicals must be controlled because recreational use is illegitimate. Use *is* abuse. It would also be the logical conclusion of a process which began in 1868 when the Pharmacy Act transferred the control of drugs from ordinary citizens to licensed doctors and pharmacists. Even during Prohibition, doctors were permitted to prescribe alcohol and, in many ways, this book has been the story of how recreational substances have been taken out of the hands of the people and entrusted to the medical establishment and pharmaceutical industry.

The inability of the authorities to suppress the illicit drug trade has made this transfer of power far less smooth than might have been anticipated, but there is no doubt that doctors and chemists have seen their prestige and profits greatly enhanced since they became the sole (legal) vendors of nature's remedies. So impressive has the victory of the medical and pharmaceutical industries been that some have accused them of being the invisible hand behind prohibition from the outset.[57] As early as 1915, it was suspected that the medical establishment desired a "monopoly on all narcotic sales to the public and wanted a fee for every citizen's head cold.".[58]

Like most theories which begin with the question '*cui bono?*', this theory has something of the conspiracy about it. The historical facts do not fit. The pharmaceutical industry strongly opposed drug prohibition for many years and stood to gain nothing from the suppression of opium and coca derivatives. As the leading producer of heroin and cocaine, Germany would certainly have opposed the early drug treaties had it not been silenced into submission by the First World War. The American-led crusade against narcotics severely limited the industry's customer base, and while it is true that the pharmaceutical companies developed new drugs thereafter, many of these were subsequently banned or tightly controlled.

It is unlikely that drug companies had the foresight to instigate prohibition at its outset, but there is no doubt they used it to their advantage in the years that followed. The idea that the War on Drugs has reduced the ranks of the stupefied and addicted is belied by the millions of people habituated to tranquilisers, pain-killers, synthetic opiates and amphetamines. The world is awash with mood-altering prescription drugs and, as the story of snus illustrates, the pharmaceutical industry will resist any reform that would weaken its stranglehold on the market.

As always, those who profit from prohibition are aided by the moral reformers who seek suppression for ideological reasons. Like most prohibitionists, Frances Willard and Bishop Brent were sincere in their convictions, but, also like most prohibitionists, they suffered from an extreme form of self-righteousness that precluded empathy, combined with a naïve idealism that obscured reality. These are the classic traits of the moral entrepreneur. Typically, he appears on the scene several decades after his *bête noire* has reached its historic peak and is already waning. It is notable that drinking, opiate use and smoking had all declined significantly before their respective crusaders demanded draconian action.* It is notable, too, that only after the middle classes began to abstain from these vices was forceful suppression deemed appropriate.

---

* In the USA, alcohol consumption peaked fifty years before the Women's Crusade and opium consumption peaked twenty years before the Harrison Act. The smoking rate peaked in the 1950s, but it was not until the 1990s that the anti-smoking movement lurched towards extremism. The contemporary scare about designer drugs essentially rehashes a moral panic from the 1980s which, in turn, was an echo of the LSD panic of the 1960s.

Once the vice has been associated with the poor and the undesirable, the prohibitionist can strike. He gets his ban and it does not take long for the unintended consequences to manifest themselves, but his faith in the power of law remains unshakeable. He is "fuelled by optimism unguided by reason or memory".[59] Rather than admit that his policies are wrong-headed, he tells himself that if only more money was spent, if only punishments were made tougher, if only more bans were put in place, then human nature would be tamed and Hell would be forever for rent. No amount of failure can sway him from believing in the righteousness of his cause. As Prohibition floundered, the egregious Wayne Wheeler declared: "The very fact that the law is difficult to enforce is the clearest proof of the need for its existence."[60] The prohibitionist thrives on crisis, real or imagined, and would be out of work if his cure was successful. This leaves him in a quandary. As Stanley Cohen noted, "the unique dilemma of the moral entrepreneur [is] to defend the success of his methods and at the same time contend that the problem is getting worse."[61]

The moral entrepreneur sells fear, and fear is the mid-wife of prohibition. Time after time, we have encountered some variant of the moral panic: fear of the Chinese; fear of the immigrant; fear of the urban masses; fear of the date rapist; fear of racial degeneration; fear of the juvenile delinquent. Most of these moral panics have long since been discredited. Science has shown that opiates do not alter brain chemistry to create criminality; alcohol does not lead to racial degeneracy; snus does not cause mouth cancer; cocaine does not make African-Americans invincible, and there is not an epidemic of drug-related date rapes. The pseudo-science has been debunked. The religious arguments are not as powerful as they once were. The racism and xenophobia have largely disappeared. And yet, with the lone exception of the Eighteenth Amendment, all the prohibitions in this book remain in force and more are on their way. Why?

The answer is that new fears have emerged to justify prohibition's continued advance. Once the prohibitionist's snake-oil has been bought and swallowed, he returns with new nightmares to take our minds off the burning in our stomachs. At first, the prohibitionist exploits existing fears of the Chinaman, the Mexican, the Negro, the homosexual, the juvenile delinquent—often because he is intimidated by these "folk devils" himself. When traditional prejudices have been bled dry or fallen into disrepute, he creates deviants in the general population—the scrounger, the filthy smoker, the selfish glutton, the 'binge-drinker'.

The prohibitionist takes a problem and calls it an emergency. Then, through his own actions, he creates a genuine crisis which he insists can only be treated with more of his medicine. After a century of the same old snake-oil, we might have become weary of the prohibitionist by now. Some might even have lynched him. But, in the end, fear is more intoxicating than hope.

Notes

Introduction

1. Genesis, chapter 2, verses 16-17
2. 'Avoid gold teeth, says Turkmen leader', BBC, 07.04.04
3. Preventative Health Taskforce, *Technical Report No 2, Tobacco Control in Australia: making smoking history*, Parliament of the Commonwealth of Australia, 2008; p. vi
4. 'New York bans most trans fats in restaurants', *New York Times*, T. Lueck & K. Severson, 06.12.06
5. As the Liberal Democrat MP Chris Huhne called it. See 'Labour's 3,600 new ways of making you a criminal', *Daily Mail*, 05.09.08
6. 'Fifty Commandments of New Labour', *Spectator*, Brendan O'Neill, 24.04.10; pp. 22-23 (Brown managed thirty-three laws a month.)
7. Foreword of *Prohibitions* (ed. John Meadowcroft), Institute of Economic Affairs, 2008; p. 17
8. Nick Clegg, 08.09.10, http://yourfreedom.hmg.gov.uk/
9. Franklin, F., *What Prohibition Has Done to America*, Harcourt, Brace & Company, 1922; p. 48
10. *Ibid.*, p. 49
11. Sir Henry Lytton's version of W. S. Gilbert and A. Sullivan's *The Mikado* (1926)
12. Becker, H., *Outsiders: Studies in sociology of deviance*, The Free Press, 1963; pp. 147-8

Chapter One: Bone dry forever

1. Okrent, D., *Last Call: The rise and fall of Prohibition*, Scribner, 2010; p. 13
2. Willard, F., *Glimpses of Fifty Years: The autobiography of an American woman*, Source Book Press, 1889; p. 338
3. *Ibid.*, p. 341
4. Gordon, E. P., *Women Torch-Bearers: The story of the Woman's Christian Temperance Union*, WCTU Press, 1924; p. 14
5. *Ibid.*, p. 13
6. Franklin, F., *What Prohibition Has Done to America*, Harcourt, Brace & Company, 1922; p. 76
7. Sinclair, A., *Prohibition: The Era of Excess*, Little, Brown, 1962; p. 16
8. Billings *et al.*, *Physiological Aspects of the Liquor Problem* (vol. 1), Houghton, Mifflin and company, 1903; p. xix
9. Russell, J., *An Adequate Remedy for a National Evil*, Prohibition Party, 1872; p. 3
10. *Statistics on Alcohol: England*, 2009, NHS; p. 8
11. Rush, B., *Inquiry into the Effects of Ardent Spirits upon the Human Body and Mind*, James Loring, Boston, 1823 (orig. 1785); pp. 5-6
12. Rorabaugh, W. J., *The Alcoholic Republic: An American Tradition*, OUP, 1979

13. Behr, E., *Prohibition: Thirteen years that changed America*, Penguin, 1998; p. 18
14. Gusfield, J., *Symbolic Crusade*, University of Illinois Press, 1963; p. 111
15. *Ibid.*
16. Gordon; p. 15
17. Willard; p. 334
18. 'Among the coal-miners', *Missionary Review*, Margaret Blake Robinson, vol. 25, 1902; pp. 835-839
19. 'A notable woman', *New York Times*, 11.05.1913
20. 'Death of Miss Willard', *New York Times*, 18.02.1898
21. Willard; p. 475
22. *Ibid.*
23. Zimmerman, J., 'The Queen of the Lobby: Mary Hunt, scientific temperance, and the dilemma of democratic education in America, 1879-1906', *History of Education Quarterly*, 32, 1992; pp. 5-6
24. *Science Temperance Monthly Advices,* March 1892; p.4
25. Billings; p. 23
26. Sinclair; p. 45
27. *Union Series*, No. 2, p. 33 (cited in Billings, p. 12)
28. Levine, H. G., 'The Committee of Fifty and the origins of alcohol control', *Journal of Drug Issues*, Winter 1983; pp. 95-116
29. Billings; p. 44
30. Billings; p. xxi
31. Billings; p. 32
32. Sinclair; p. 43-44
33. Woolley, J. G., *Prohibition: With the people behind it,* American Issue Publishing Company, 1911; p. 1
34. Cherrington, E., *The Evolution of Prohibition in the United States of America*, American Issue Press, 1920; p. 251
35. Woolley; p. 22
36. Storms, R. C., *Partisan Prophets: A History of the Prohibition Party*, National Prohibition Foundation, 1972; p. 7
37. Russell; p. 12
38. 'Miss Willard hopeful', *New York Times*, 19.04.1896
39. 'War in the Iowa WCTU', *New York Times*, 22.05.1890
40. 'Anti-Saloon', *Time*, 06.06.27
41. Kerr, K. A., *Organized for Prohibition,* Yale University Press, 1985
42. Lamme, M. O., 'Alcoholic dogs and glory for all: The Anti-Saloon League and public relations, 1913', *Social History of Alcohol and Drugs*, vol. 21 (2), Spring 2007; p. 140
43. Sinclair; p. 5
44. 'Women's social reforms', *New York Times*, 20.06.1885
45. Kerr; p. 95-6
46. Lamme; p. 140
47. Cherrington (1920); p. 62
48. *Ibid.*
49. *Ibid.*, p. 277
50. Cherrington, E., *History of the Anti-Saloon League*, American Issue Press, 1913; p. 63

51. Behr; p. 79
52. Cherrington (1913); p. 9
53. Franklin; pp. 39-40
54. Wightman, L., *The Menace of Prohibition*, Los Angeles Printing Press, 1916; pp. 18-19. Also reprinted in *Oswego Daily Palladium*, 14.03.18; p. 8
55. 'Prohibition in Kansas', *New York Times*, 31.08.1891
56. Nation, C. A., *The Use and Need of the Life of Carry A. Nation*, F. M. Steves & Sons, 1909; p. 130
57. *Ibid.* (Kiowa may have been on Nation's mind as the place where a young woman had recently shot dead her saloon-owning fiancé as revenge for postponing their wedding. Nation's sympathies were all with the woman, whom she befriended while working as a jail evangelist.)
58. 'Mrs. Nation begins her crusade anew', *New York Times*, 22.01.1901
59. *Ibid.*
60. 'Mrs. Nation Horsewhipped', *New York Times*, 25.01.1901
61. 'A "Second Carrie Nation"', *New York Times,* 17.02.1901
62. 'The Mrs. Nation Craze', *New York Times*, 05.04.1901
63. Nation; p. 140
64. Grace, F., *Carry A. Nation: Retelling the Life*, Indiana University Press, 2001; p. 194
65. *Ibid.*, p. 203
66. 'Mrs. Nation paid a visit to New York', *New York Times*, 29.08.1901
67. Grace; p. 274
68. 'Glasgow in Jest or Earnest?', *New York Times*, 16.12.1908
69. *Ibid.*
70. Towne, C. H., *The Rise and Fall of Prohibition*, Macmillan, 1923; p. 1
71. *Ibid.*, p. 2
72. Cherrington (1913), pp. 91-92
73. Stockham, G. H., *Temperance and Prohibition*, 1888; p. 82
74. *Ibid.*, p. 83
75. Franklin; p. 73. (In 1914, the *New York Times* noted that many Southerners would miss having a drink in a bar but that "a large portion of the intelligent whites were ready to make this sacrifice if by doing so they could eliminate the drunken negro." (8/02/14))
76. 'Prohibition denounced', *New York Times*, 23.01.1909
77. 'Liquor men want reforms', *New York Times*, 04.10.1908
78. Sinclair; p. 77
79. Kerr; p. 170
80. Cherrington (1920); p. 320
81. Sinclair; p. 19
82. Lamme; p. 145
83. Lamme; p. 150
84. Thompson, G. B., *The Shadow of the Bottle*, Review & Herald Publishing Association, 1915; p. 64
85. *Ibid.*, p. 22
86. Booth, M., *Opium: A History*, Simon & Schuster, 1996; p. 202

87. Davenport-Hines, R., *The Pursuit of Oblivion: A Global History of Narcotics 1500-2000*, Weidenfeld & Nicolson, 2001; p. 184
88. Musto, D., *The American Disease*, OUP, 1999; p. 327
89. 'He warns women against cocktails', *New York Times*, 22.11.1910
90. Kerr, K. A., *The Politics of Moral Behavior: Prohibition and Drug Abuse*, Addison-Wesley, 1973; pp. 97-102
91. Wightman; p. 28
92. 'For National Prohibition', *New York Times*, 09.11.17
93. Behr; p. 57
94. Sinclair; p. 97
95. Sinclair; p. 37
96. Blocker, Tyrell & Fahey (eds), *Alcohol and Temperance in Modern History, vol. 1*, ABC-CLIO, 2003; p. 296
97. Musto; p. 67
98. Windle, C. A. (ed), *The Anti-Prohibition Manual*, National Association of Distillers and Wholesale Dealers, Cincinnati, 1918; p. 11
99. Sinclair; p. 111
100. Windle; p. 11
101. Kerr; p. 179
102. Windle; p. 11
103. Windle; p. 19
104. Windle; p. 11
105. Thompson; p. 64
106. Cherrington (1920); p. 175
107. Sinclair; p. 120
108. 'Argue for prohibition', *New York Times*, 19.06.18
109. 'For National Prohibition', *New York Times*, 09.11.17
110. 'Argue for prohibition', *New York Times*, 19.06.18
111. Sinclair; p. 20
112. Sinclair; p. 157
113. Franklin; p. 37-8
114. Stockham; p. 80
115. Windle; p. 3
116. 'Nation voted dry; 38 States adopt the Amendment', *New York Times*, 17.01.19

Chapter Two: Prohibition averted

1. 'Now for another world war, waged against demon rum', *New York Times*, 04.01.20
2. Cherrington, E., *America and the World Liquor Problem*, American Issue Press, 1922; p. 65
3. Blocker *et al.*; p. 340
4. Tyrell, I., 'Prohibition, American Cultural Expansion, and the New Hegemony in the 1920s: An Interpretation', *Social History*, vol. 27 (54), 1994; p. 422
5. 'Now for another world war, waged against demon rum', *New York Times*, 04.01.20

Notes

6. Harrison, B., *Drink and the Victorians*, Keele University Press, 1998; p. 66
7. Haydon, P., *The English Pub*, Robert Hale, 1994; p. 196
8. *Ibid.*, p. 69
9. *Ibid.*
10. Smith, S., *A Memoir of the Reverend Sydney Smith*, Harper & Bros., 1855; p. 295
11. 'British drinking from the nineteenth century to the present', James Kneale, April 2009; http://www.publications.parliament.uk/pa/cm200910/cmselect/cmhealth/151/151we16.htm
12. Gately, I., *Drink: A cultural history of alcohol*, Gotham Books, 2009; p. 248
13. Harrison; p. 313
14. Harrison; p. 120
15. Harrison; p. 124
16. Harrison; p. 116
17. Dingle, A. E., *The Campaign for Prohibition in Victorian England*, Rutgers, 1980; p. 23
18. Haydon; p. 216
19. Okrent; p. 172
20. Harrison; p. 188
21. Blocker *et al.*; p. 287
22. Thompson, F. M. L.,'Social control in Victorian Britain', *Economic History Review*, vol. 34 (2), May 1981; p. 202
23. Towne; p. 202
24. Haydon; p. 239
25. Samuel Smith, president of the Liverpool Chamber of Commerce. Quoted in 'Drink and working class living standards in Britain, 1870-1914', Dingle, A. E., *Economic History Review*, Vol. 25 (4), Nov. 1972; p. 615
26. Gately; p. 364
27. Blocker *et al.*; p. 340
28. 'Mob "Pussyfoot" in London Streets', *New York Times*, 14.11.19
29. 'Dry world by 1950, Pussyfoot predicts', *New York Times*, 24.12.21
30. 'Sees a dry world soon', *New York Times*, 15.04.21
31. Eriksen, S., 'Drunken Danes and Sober Swedes?', in *Language and the Construction of Class Identities* (ed. Bo Stråth), Gothenburg University Press, 1990; pp. 55-94
32. Tyrell; p. 425
33. 'Sweden will hold plebiscite on prohibition', *New York Times*, 08.04.22
34. Spence, B. & Nicholson, S., *International Convention: The World League Against Alcoholism*, American Issue Press, 1923; p. 111
35. 'A jovial dry', *New York Times*, 24.04.20
36. Okrent; p. 2
37. Behr; p. 88
38. Towne; p. 5
39. 'Pussyfoot Johnson in New Zealand', *New York Times*, 26.11.22
40. Andreasson, B. D., 'Stuck in the bottle: Vodka in Russia 1863-1925', *Lethbridge Undergraduate Research Journal*, vol. 1 (1), 2006
41. 'Norway: Prohibition repeal?', *Time*, 31.12.23

42. 'Prohibition's failure in Norway', *Canadian Medical Association Journal*, vol. 16 (12), Dec. 1926; p. 1521

43. Cherrington (1922); pp. 49-50

44. Tyrell, 1994; p. 420

45. 'Merry Xmas from Uncle Sam: poison rum', *Daily News*, Jay Maeder, 28.03.00

46. 'National Affairs: Poison', *Time*, 10.01.27

47. 'The Chemist's War', *Slate*, Deborah Blum, 19.02.10

48. 'Prohibition: To make a better country', *Time*, 19.12.27

49. Smith, M. C., 'Much more than prohibition: an overview of differences in attitudes and policy toward alcohol in Finland and the United States', North American Studies Inauguration Ceremony, 15.12.10

50. Levine, H. G., 'Temperance Cultures: Alcohol as a Problem in Nordic and English-Speaking Cultures' in Lader, M., Edwards, G. and Drummon, D. C., (eds) *The Nature of Alcohol and Drug-Related Problems*, Oxford University Press, 1993

Chapter Three: Opium

1. Musto, D., *The American Disease: Origins of Narcotic Control*, OUP, 1999; pp. 98-101

2. De Quincey, T., *Confessions of an English Opium-Eater*, Riverside Press, 1879; p. 82

3. Booth, M., *Opium: A History*, Simon & Schuster, 1996; p. 112

4. Booth; pp. 109-10

5. Booth; pp. 110-15 (From 1,000 chests of opium in 1767 to over 30,000 chests in the mid-1830s.)

6. Gerritsen, J., *The Control of Fuddle and Flash*, Brill, 2000; p. 60

7. Rowntree, J., *The Imperial Drug Trade*, Methuen, 1905; p. 71

8. Booth; p. 135

9. Gerritsen; p. 62

10. Booth; pp. 109-10

11. Davenport-Hines, R., *The Pursuit of Oblivion: A Global History of Narcotics 1500-2000*, Weidenfeld & Nicolson, 2001; p. 53

12. Booth; p. 11

13. Brown, R. H., *Forbidden Substances*, unfinished manuscript, Chapter 2, www.richardharveybrown.com

14. De Quincey; pp. 56-57

15. Berridge, V. & Edwards, G., *Opium and the People: Opiate Use in Nineteenth Century England*, Palgrave Macmillan, 1982 (Chapter 3)

16. Booth; p. 64

17. Berridge, Chapter 9

18. Berridge, Appendix (table 4)

19. Corsini, C. & Viazzo, P. (eds), *The Decline in Infant Mortality In Europe 1800-1950*, UNICEF, 1993; p. 37

20. See Berridge (1982) and Booth (1996)

21. Harrison, B., *Drink and the Victorians*, Faber & Faber, 1971; p. 174

22. Berridge, Appendix (table 3)

Notes

23. Berridge, Chapter 14
24. Richards, J. F., 'Opium and the British Indian Empire: The Royal Commission of 1895', *Modern Asia Studies*, 36, 2002; pp. 375-420
25. *Ibid.*
26. Rowntree, p. 116. (Joshua Rowntree, a teetotal Quaker, was unconvinced by the Commission's belief in the innate human hunger for intoxication, saying: "It was evidently a comfort for the framers of the Report to think so.")
27. Parssinen, T., 'Review of *Opium and the People*', *Medical History*, 26 (4), Oct. 1982; p. 459
28. Parssinen, T., *Secret Passions, Secret Remedies: Narcotic Drugs in British Society*, Manchester University Press; p. 53
29. Ahmad, D., *The Opium Debate and Chinese Exclusion Laws in the Nineteenth-Century American West*, University of Nevada Press, 2007; p. 12
30. Booth; p. 194
31. Ahmad; p. 27
32. American Federation of Labor, *Some Reasons for Chinese Exclusion: American Manhood against Asiatic Coolieism*, Government Printing Office, 1902; p. 22
33. Gerritsen, J., *The Control of Fuddle and Flash*, Brill, 2000; p. 81
34. Musto; p. 37
35. *Ibid.*, p. 17
36. Davenport-Hines; p. 88
37. Courtwright, D., *Dark Paradise*, Harvard University Press, 2001; p. 71
38. The Public Health Service estimated 200,000 addicts in 1902 (Musto, p. 17). Figures from 1909 suggest an addict population of 175,000 (Musto, p. 314). Higher and lower estimates have been made but all figures, official and unofficial, are suspect. Certainly, as Courtwright says, the number of opiate addicts was "never more than 313,000 in America prior to 1914" (*Dark Paradise*, p. 9).
39. Davenport-Hines; p. 68
40. Davenport-Hines; p. 84
41. Courtwright; p. 91
42. Larson, J. L., 'The 1905 anti-American boycott as a transnational Chinese movement', *Chinese America: History and Perspective*, January 2007
43. Musto; p. 313
44. Gavit, J. P., *Opium*, unknown pressing, 1925; p. 26
45. Musto; p. 11
46. 'Dr. Wilbur F. Crafts, crusader, dies at 73', *New York Times*, 28.12.22
47. Musto; p. 26
48. C. H. Brent's letter to James Smith, July 6 1903
49. Bureau of Insular Affairs, *Report of the committee appointed by the Philippine commission to investigate the use of opium and the traffic therein*, 1905; p. 44
50. C. H. Brent's letter to James Smith, July 6 1903
51. C. H. Brent's letter to Theodore Roosevelt, July 24 1906
52. McKee, D. L., 'The Chinese boycott of 1905-06 reconsidered: the role of Chinese Americans', *Pacific Historical Review*, Vol. 55 (2), May 1986; p. 165
53. Rowntree; p. 113
54. 'Uncle Sam is the worst drug fiend in the world', *New York Times*, 12/3/1911

55. Gerritsen; p. 83
56. Musto; p. 34
57. Musto; p. 36
58. Musto; p. 39
59. International Opium Convention, Translation No. 222, January 23 1912
60. *Ibid.*
61. Davenport-Hines; p. 287
62. Courtwright; p. 81
63. *Ibid.*, p. 82
64. '6,000 opium users here', *New York Times*, 01.08.1908
65. Courtwright; p. 87
66. 'New anti-drug law is in effect today', *New York Times*, 01.07.14
67. Musto; p. 314
68. 'Uncle Sam is the worst drug fiend in the world', *New York Times*, 12.03.1911
69. Musto; p. 314
70. Thornton, M., *The Economics of Prohibition*, University of Utah Press, 1991; p. 61
71. Musto; pp. 98-101
72. 'Negro cocaine "fiends" new Southern menace', *New York Times*, 08.02.14
73. Carstairs, C., '"The most dangerous drug": images of African-Americans and cocaine use in the progressive era', *Left History*, vol. 7 (1), 2000; p. 53
74. 'Negro cocaine "fiends" new Southern menace', *New York Times*, 08.02.14 (The *NYT* was presumably repeating contemporary folk tales.)
75. Musto; p. 302
76. 'Say drug habit grips the nation', *New York Times*, 05.12.13
77. 'Great dangers of heroin', *New York Times*, 22.01.14
78. Musto; p. 65
79. Booth; p. 198
80. Booth; p. 202
81. Booth; p. 184
82. Musto; p. 107
83. Booth; p. 198
84. Davenport-Hines; p. 175
85. Davenport-Hines; p. 189
86. Davenport-Hines; p. 277
87. National Drug Control Strategy, *FY2010 Budget Summary*, 2010; p. 13
88. West, H. *et al.*, 'Prisoners in 2009', Bureau of Justice Statistics, Dec. 2010; p. 7
89. 'Searching for a fix: drug use, crime and the criminal justice system', Rethink.org.uk, June 2004; p. 2
90. Centers for Disease Control and Prevention, *HIV in the United States*, July 2010
91. United Nations Office on Drugs and Crime, *World Drug Report 2011*; p. 30
92. *Ibid.*, p. 16
93. *Ibid.*, p. 17
94. *Ibid.*, p. 84
95. United Nations Office on Drugs and Crime, *World Drug Report 2010*; p. 31
96. *Ibid.*
97. Courtwright; p. 113

98. Centers for Disease Control, *Methadone maintenance treatment*, Feb. 2002; p. 1

99. Centers for Disease Control and Prevention, NCHS Data Brief, No. 42, September 2010

100.'Dangerous diversions: Specter of prescription drug abuse creates tough balancing act for doctors', *American Medical News*, A. J. Landers, 17.03.08

101.May, H. L., *Survey of Smoking Opium Conditions in the Far East*, Opium Research Committee, 1927; p. 21

102.Human Rights Watch, *Philippines: You can die any time—death squad killings in Mindanao*, 2009; p. 12

103.United Nations Office on Drugs and Crime, *2007 World Drug Report*, 2007; p. 151

Chapter Four: Snus

1. *U.S. Tobacco Review*, vol. 1 (1), First Quarter 1985; p. 14

2. Tobacco Products (Sales Restriction) Bill, *Hansard*, 31.1.86, vol. 90, pp. 1235-46

3. 'The smokeless Scottish connection', *New Scientist*, 23.01.86; p. 31

4. Letter from Mrs Edwina Currie MP to the Parliamentary Commissioner for Standards, 29.01.97

5. 'Bandits on the run: the oral snuff debate', *British Journal of Addiction*, 1990 (85); p. 1096

6. McNeill, A., 'Restricting the sale of Skoal Bandits', *British Medical Journal*, vol. 292, 15.2.86

7. 'Bandits on the run: the oral snuff debate', *British Journal of Addiction*, 1990 (85); p. 1096

8. Hillhouse, A., 'Why oral snuff did not take off in the UK', *British Journal of Addiction*, 1990 (85); pp. 1104-05

9. *Ibid.*

10. Mackay, J., 'Why smokeless tobacco should be banned', *British Journal of Addiction*, 1990 (85); p. 1100

11. Connolly, G., 'Back to the future with snuff', *British Journal of Addiction*, 1990 (85), pp. 1102-03

12. 'Council Directive 92/41/EEC of 15 May 1992 amending Directive 89/622/EEC on the approximation of the laws, regulations and administrative provisions of the Member States concerning the labelling of tobacco products', EEC, 1992

13. Article 151 of the Act of Accession of Austria, Finland and Sweden

14. Rodu, B & Jansson, C., 'Smokeless tobacco and oral cancer: A review of the risks and determinants', *Critical Reviews in Oral Biology and Medicine*, vol. 15 (5), Sept. 2004); pp. 252-63

15. Rodu, B. *et al.*, 'Smokeless tobacco use and cancer of the upper respiratory tract', *Oral Surgery, Oral Medicine, Oral Pathology*, vol. 93 (5), May 2002; pp. 511-15

16. Winn *et al.*, 'Snuff dipping and oral cancer among women in the Southern United States', *New England Journal of Medicine*, vol. 304 (13), March 1981. Winn wrote

that "among chronic users the risk approached 50-fold for cancers of the gum and buccal mucosa".

17. 'Committee examines athletes' use of smokeless tobacco and its influences— Statement by American Cancer Society Cancer Action Network', 14.04.10 (press release)

18. 'IARC Monographs on the Evaluation of the Carcinogenic Risk of Chemicals to Humans', IARC, vol. 37, 1985

19. 'The Health Consequences of Using Smokeless Tobacco', US Department of Health and Human Services; p. 35

20. Zahm (1992) found a trebling in risk of oral cancer amongst a group of army veterans, although the results may have been confounded by drinking and smoking. Further studies by Marshall (1992), Mashberg (1993), Spitz (1993), Muscat (1996) and Schwartz (1998) failed to replicate Zahm's finding. Both Blot (1989) and Kabat (1994) found an elevated risk for women but not for men, thereby supporting the view that dry snuff is a genuine risk factor but other Western smokeless products are not. Studies have also consistently found positive associations between oral cancer and the smokeless products used India and Pakistan. These products, like the dry snuff used by the women in the Winn study, typically have tobacco-specific nitrosamine levels in excess of 1,000 parts per million. See *Smokeless Tobacco and Some Tobacco-specific N-Nitrosamines*, IARC, vol, 89, 2007; pp. 170-8

21. Lewin (1998) and Schildt (1999)

22. See Rosenquist (2005), Wickholm (2004) and Boffetta (2005)

23. 'Proposal for a Directive of the European Parliament and of the Council on the approximation of the laws, regulations and administrative provisions of the Member States concerning the manufacture, presentation and sale of tobacco products (recast version)', 1999/0244 (COD), 16.11.99; pp. 43-51

24. Foulds, J. *et al.*, 'Effects of smokeless tobacco (snus) on smoking and public health in Sweden', *Tobacco Control*, 12, 2003; pp. 349-359

25. Stegmayr *et al.*, 'The decline of smoking in Northern Sweden', *Scandinavian Journal of Public Health*, 33, 2005; pp. 321-4

26. 'Re:[GLOBALINK] New Scientist on harm reduction', Clive Bates, 8.11.01 (http://tobaccodocuments.org/blum_oral/001_34A_0002.html)

27. 'Protecting smokers, saving lives: the case for a tobacco and nicotine regulatory authority', Royal College of Physicians, 2002

28. Bates *et al.*, 'European Union policy on smokeless tobacco: a statement in favour of evidence based regulation for public health', *Tobacco Control*, 12, 2003; pp. 360-7

29. Raw, M. & McNeill, A., 'Britain bans oral snuff', *British Medical Journal*, 13.01.90

30. 'Bandits on the run: the oral snuff debate', *British Journal of Addiction*, 1990 (85); p. 1096

31. 'News you can't use', *Washington Times*, Brad Rodu, 09.06.03; p. A21. 'Snus ruse', *Reason*, Jacob Sullum, 24.12.04

32. 'E-mails between Alan and Scott Tomar RE: Snus' http://tobaccodocuments.org/blum_oral/001_47A_0006.html

Notes

33. 'Health for the 21st century', G. H. Brundtland (speech), World Economic Forum, 30.01.99

34. Gilljam, H., 'The 3rd International Conference on Smokeless Tobacco: Final Technical Report'

35. 'Clearing the smoke: The science base for Tobacco Harm Reduction', Institute of Medicine, 2001; pp. 9-21

36. Bolinder, G., 'Smokeless tobacco use and increased cardiovascular mortality among Swedish construction workers', *American Journal of Public Health*, March 1994, vol. 84 (3); p. 404

37. Huhtasaari, F. *et al.*, 'Tobacco and myocardial infarction: is snuff less dangerous than cigarettes?', *British Medical Journal*, 21.11.92; pp. 1252-6

38. Huhtasaari, F. *et al.*, 'Smokeless tobacco as a possible risk factor for myocardial infarction: A population-based study in middle-aged men', *Journal of the American College of Cardiology*, vol. 34 (6), 1999

39. Vainio, H. & Weiderpass, E., 'Smokeless tobacco: harm reduction or nicotine overload?', *European Journal of Cancer Prevention*, 2003 (12); pp. 89-92

40. Heuch, I. *et al.*, 'Use of alcohol, tobacco and coffee, and risk of pancreatic cancer', *British Journal of Cancer*, 1983 (48); pp. 637-43

41. 'The use of dietary data in the analysis of cancer incidence and mortality, and in a case-control study of cancer of the ventricle and the intestines', *Var Foda*, 34 (Supplement 4), p. 277

42. 'Chewing of tobacco and use of snuff: Relationships to cancer of the pancreas and other sites in two prospective studies', *Proceedings of the 13th International Cancer Congress*; p. 207

43. Zheng (1993). When the ENSP reviewed the evidence for pancreatic cancer in 2005, it reported that "the evidence with regard to Scandinavian snus is limited and based on repeat analyses that use the same cohort." (*Health risks of Swedish snus*, ENSP, 2005) Olof Nyrén may have been referring to any of these studies or the as-yet released Boffetta study.

44. Vainio, H., & Weiderpass, E., 'Smokeless tobacco: harm reduction or nicotine overload?', *European Journal of Cancer Prevention*, vol. 12 (2), 2003; pp. 89-92

45. 'Lifting the ban on oral tobacco: Overview of the possible effects of lifting the ban', Jochem van der Veen, Research voor Beleid, 23.06.03. (This version of the report was temporarily available on the Research voor Beleid website but has since been removed.)

46. 'ENSP Status Report on Oral Tobacco', Trudy Prins, ENSP, 2003

47. 'Will Europe life ban on oral snuff?', ASH press release, 03.06.04

48. Rodu, B & Cole, P., 'The Burden of Mortality from Smoking: Comparing Sweden with Other Countries in the European Union', *European Journal of Epidemiology*, 2004 (19): pp. 129-131.

49. Chapman, S., 'Falling prevalence of smoking: how low can we go?', *Tobacco Control*, 2007 (16); pp. 145-147

50. Foulds (2003), Stegmayr (2005), Furberg (2005, 2008), Rodu (2003, 2009), Stenbeck (2009)

51. 'The Case for Harm Reduction', American Association of Public Health Physicians, 26.10.08

52. 'SCENIHR Opinion on the Health Effects of Smokeless Tobacco Products: Results from the public consultation', pp. 71-74 (http://ec.europa.eu/health/ph_risk/committees/04_scenihr/docs/scenihr_stp_comments.pdf)

53. Lund, K., 'A tobacco-free society or tobacco harm reduction?', SIRUS-Report no. 6/2009, Norwegian Institute for Alcohol and Drug Research, 2009; p. 74

54. *Harm Reduction in Nicotine Addiction: Helping People Who Can't Quit*, Royal College of Physicians, 2007

55. 'How Europe can help snuff out smoking', *Financial Times*, 04.01.08

56. Boffetta (2005) and Rosenquist (2005)

57. 'Cancer incidence, mortality and prevalence worldwide', IARC, GLOBOCAN, 2002

58. 'Estimated incidence and mortality: men, 2008', European Cancer Observatory (http://eu-cancer.iarc.fr)

59. Heuch, I. *et al.*, 'Use of alcohol, tobacco and coffee, and risk of pancreatic cancer', *British Journal of Cancer*, 1983 (48); p. 639

60. 'Major study links 'snus' to cancer', L. Sizoo, *The Local*, 18.11.04

61. Bolinder, G., *Long-term use of smokeless tobacco*, Karolinska Institute, 1997

62. 'Swedish doctors - smoking prevalence lowest in the world', *Läkartidningen*, vol. 99, 2002; pp. 30-32

63. For a review of the literature as of 2005, see Roth, H. D. *et al.*, 'Health risks of smoking compared to Swedish snus', *Inhalation Toxicology*, 2005. After that report was published, four other studies found no statistically significant elevation in risk for cardiovascular disease: Hergens (2005), Johansson (2005), Wennberg (2007), Haglund (2007)

64. Rodu, B. & Cole, P., 'Excess mortality in smokeless tobacco users not meaningful', *American Journal of Public Health*, January 1995, vol. 85 (1)

65. "In the studies on construction workers, it is important to consider that the high physical demands in these professions imply that, in the older age groups, only very healthy individuals will be employable. The findings of more pronounced excess risks of cardiovascular mortality in the younger tobacco users in the construction industry, compared with tobacco users in the older groups, is probably due to this healthy worker effect." (Bolinder, G., *Long-term use of smokeless tobacco*, Karolinska Institute, 1997; pp. 40-41)

66. 'Snus and risk of cancer of the mouth, lung, and pancreas' (letter), B. Rodu, *The Lancet*, 06.10.07

67. Letter from Brad Rodu to Henrik Grönberg, 21.11.08

68. Roosaar, A. *et al.*, 'Cancer and mortality among users and nonusers of snus', *International Journal of Cancer* (123), 2008; pp. 168-173

69. 'Snuff use and stroke' (letter), B. Rodu, K. Heavner and C. Phillips, *Epidemiology*, vol. 20 (3), May 2009; pp. 468-469

70. 'FHI backar om snus och potens', *DN*, A. Carlsson, 29.11.10

71. Boffetta, P. *et al.*, 'Cigar and pipe smoking, smokeless tobacco use and pancreatic cancer: an analysis from the International Pancreatic Cancer Case-Control

Consortium (PanC4)', *Annals of Oncology*, vol. 22 (6), June 2011; pp. 1420-1426 (Although dated June 2011, the study was actually published in January.)

72. Hansson, J. *et al.*, 'Weight gain and incident obesity among male snus users', *BMC Public Health*, vol. 11 (371), 2011

73. 'The Scientific Basis of Tobacco Product Regulation', Special report of a WHO study group, 2008; p. 273

74. Mackay, J., 'Why smokeless tobacco should be banned', *British Journal of Addiction*, 1990 (85), p. 1100

75. West, R., 'Oral tobacco: reprise', *British Journal of Addiction*, 1990 (85), p. 1105

76. Kozlowski, L. T., 'First, tell the truth: a dialogue on human rights, deception, and the use of smokeless tobacco as a substitute for cigarettes', *Tobacco Control*, 2003, (12); pp. 34-36

Chapter Five: Narcotic moonshine

1. 'NRG-1 is 25p a hit and will kill many more than meow', *The Sun*, V. Wheeler, 31.03.10

2. 'In quest for 'legal high', chemists outfox law', *Wall Street Journal*, J. Whalen, 30.10.10

3. Svagelj, M., 'New trends and patterns of drug use: mephedrone and prescribed opioids', International Harm Reduction Conference, Beirut, April 2011

4. 'Scot vows to flood UK with strong legal highs', *Press & Journal*, R. Crighton, 16.07.10

5. Collin, M., *Altered State: The Story of Ecstasy Culture and Acid House*, Serpent's Tail, 1997; p. 28

6. Fromberg, F., 'MDMA: Penicillin for the soul or destroyer of young souls?', Netherlands Institute for Alcohol and Drugs, presented at the A.I.S.E.L. conference, Varese, Italy, 24.06.94

7. Eisner, B., *Ecstasy—the MDMA Story*, Ronin Publishing, 1989; p. 6

8. Collin; p. 77

9. Holland, J. (ed), *Ecstasy: The Complete Guide*, Park Street Press, 2001; p. 1

10. Advisory Council on the Misuse of Drugs, *Annual Report 2008-09*

11. Home Office, 'Drug Misuse Declared: Findings from the 2009/10 British Crime Survey'; p. 8. (This survey showed that 500,000 16-59 year olds had taken Ecstasy in the past year. Since the Association of Chief Police Officers estimates that 2.5 to 5 million tablets are taken each *month*, this suggests that each user consumes 60 to 120 pills a year. Whilst this is not impossible, it does seem improbable and it may be that the BCS underestimates the number of users. The survey relies on self-reported evidence and its compilers acknowledge that this is likely to lead to under-reporting.

12. Office of National Statistics, 'Deaths related to drug poisoning in England and Wales 2010', August 2011; p. 10

13. Drugscope, 'Why do people die after taking ecstasy?'

14. Forsyth, A., 'Distorted? A quantitative exploration of drug fatality reports in the popular press', *International Journal of Drug Policy*, 12, 2001; p. 435

15. For example see: 'Every parent's worst nightmare: how ketamine killed our daughter', *The Observer*, L. O'Kelly, 17.04.11

16. *Howard Marks on Drugs* (film), Current UK, 2010

17. 'GHB: Unpredictable club drug', BBC, D. Walker, 29.06.03

18. *New York Times*, 15.10.96

19. 'Mourning in America', *New York Times*, J. Tierney, 10.06.06

20. 'Controlled and uncontrolled substances used to commit date rape hearing before the subcommittee on crime', 105th Congress, Second Session, July 30 1998; p. 86

21. *Ibid.*, p. 86

22. *Ibid.*, p. 9

23. Burgess, A., Donovan, P. and Moore, S., 'Embodying Uncertainty? Understanding Heightened Perception of Drink "Spiking"', *British Journal of Criminology*, vol. 49 (6), 2009; pp. 848-62

24. 'One in four "had drinks spiked"', *The Guardian*, L. Glendinning & M. O'Kane, 09.09.04

25. Burgess (2009)

26. Scott-Ham, M. and Burton, F., 'Toxicological Findings in Cases of Alleged Drug Facilitated Sexual Assault in the United Kingdom over a 3-year period', *Journal of Clinical Forensic Medicines*, 12 (4), Aug. 2005; pp. 175-86.

27. Association of Chief Police Officers, *Operation Matisse: investigating drug facilitated sexual assault*, November 2006

28. Hughes, H. *et al.*, 'A study of patients presenting to an emergency department having had a "spiked drink"', *Emergency Medical Journal*, 24, 2007; pp. 89-91

29. Hindmarch, I., & Brinkmann, R., 'Trends in the use of alcohol and other drugs in cases of sexual assault', *Human Psychopharmacology: Clinical and Experimental*, 14, 1999; pp. 225-231

30. Mullins, M., 'Laboratory confirmation of flunitrazepam in alleged cases of date rape', *Academic Emergency Medicine*, vol. 6 (9), Sept. 1999; pp. 966-968

31. Hindmarch, I. *et al.,* 'Forensic urinalysis of drug use in cases of alleged sexual assault', *Journal of Clinical Forensic Medicine*, vol. 8 (4), December 2001; pp. 197-205

32. Burgess (2009)

33. 'Date-rape drink spiking "an urban legend"', *The Telegraph*, S. Adams, 27.10.09

34. Dvorak, R., 'Cracking the code: "Decoding" colorblind slurs during the Congressional crack cocaine debates', *Michigan Journal of Race & Law*, Spring 2000

35. Davie, C. (ed), *United Kingdom Drug Situation*, UK Focal Point on Drugs, Department of Health, 2001; p. 166

36. 'One in four "had drinks spiked"', *The Guardian*, L. Glendinning and M. O'Kane, 09.09.04

37. 'RCMP issue warning about party drug BZP', *Global BC News*, 03.05.11

38. Gee, P. & Foundatin, J., 'Party on? BZP party pills in New Zealand', *New Zealand Medical Journal*, vol. 120 (1249), Feb. 2007

39. 'The salvia ban wagon', *Reason*, J. Sullum, Dec. 2009

Notes

40. 'We must outlaw salvia, says father of student who jumped to his death after smoking drug', *Daily Mail*, 08.03.11

41. 'Product review: will K2 synthetic marijuana get you high?', *Follow That Story*, 09.11.09

42. 'Mother dies after smoking spice', *Fox 59 News*, H. MacWilliams, 04.08.10

43. 'Middletown woman's death not from Spice', *Herald Bulletin*, D. Stafford, 31.08.10

44. Letter from David Nutt to Alan Johnson, 16.07.09

45. 'How the liberal elite made a dope of Blunkett', *Daily Mail*, M. Phillips, 28.04.04

46. 'Blunkett opens up drug laws', *The Guardian*, A. Travis, 11.07.02

47. 'Tories would reverse cannabis reform', BBC, 22.01.04

48. 'Blunkett decision defies all logic', *The Sun*, 23.01.04

49. 'Britain's biggest drugs reform in decades', *The Scotsman*, A. Hardie, 11.07.02

50. Advisory Council on the Misuse of Drugs, *Cannabis: Classification and Public Health*, Home Office, April 2008

51. 'Gordon Brown to make cannabis class B drug', *The Telegraph*, S. Peck, 29.04.08

52. 'Drug Czar's plea to downgrade "E"', *The Sun*, C. Hartley, 20.05.08

53. Nutt, D., 'Equasy—a harmful addiction', *Journal of Psychopharmacology*, 3 (23), 2009

54. 'Drugs no worse than horse-riding? The folly of these 'experts' simply beggars belief', *Daily Mail*, M. Phillips, 09.02.09

55. 'Jacqui Smith slaps down drugs adviser for comparing ecstasy to horse riding', *The Guardian*, 09.02.09

56. Advisory Council on the Misuse of Drugs, *MDMA ('ecstasy'): A review of its harms and classification under the Misuse of Drugs Act 1971*, Home Office, February 2009 (Note: The document is incorrectly dated February 2008)

57. 'The cannabis conundrum', *The Guardian*, D. Nutt, 29.10.09

58. 'Gordon Brown backs sacking of chief drugs advisor Prof David Nutt', *The Telegraph*, 03.11.09

59. 'Lords must stop plan to reclassify cannabis' (letter), *The Guardian*, 25.11.08

60. Home Office, 'Drug Misuse Declared: Findings from the 2009/10 British Crime Survey'; p. 18 (Table 2.2: Proportion of 16-59 year olds reporting use of drugs in the last year, 1996 to 2009/10 BCS). Data come from the British Crime Survey. Comparable figure are not available pre-1996.

61. Pas, M., 'Mephedrone in Slovenia', DrogArt report, May 2010

62. 'Mephedrone: Overview of prevalence, use patterns, effect', EMCDDA, July 2010; p. 3

63. 'Mephedrone and the problem with "legal highs"', *The Guardian*, Emine Saner, 05.12.09

64. 'NRG-1 is 25p a hit and will kill many more than meow', *The Sun*, V. Wheeler, 31.03.10

65. 'Should miaow-miaow be banned?' *New Scientist*, N. Fleming, 18.03.10

66. 'Worthing drug-scare teen died of natural causes', *The Argus*, B. Parsons, 16.12.09

67. 'Parents of Amersham and Wycombe College student Ben Walters say he was "let down" by friends after morphine overdose', *Bucks Free Press*, 19.10.10

68. 'Legal but lethal: The drug snorted by school kids which is sweeping Britain', *Daily Mail*, C. Clark, 22.01.10

69. 'Scunthorpe parents call for mephedrone ban', BBC, 17.03.10
70. 'Meow meow sank its claws into my mind', *The Times*, G. Hattersley, 21.03.10
71. 'Review pledged over use of legal high drug mephedrone', BBC, 17.03.10
72. 'A collapse in integrity of scientific advice in the UK', *The Lancet*, Vol. 375 (9723), April 2010; p. 1319
73. *Ibid.*
74. 'New drug set to replace banned mephedrone as a 'legal high'', *The Guardian*, M. Townsend, 18.04.10
75. 'Is Carmen, 17, the latest victim of killer drug meow meow?', *Daily Mail*, 19.04.10
76. 'Young Cumbrian mum died from abusing drugs - inquest verdict', *Cumberland News*, 28.01.11
77. 'Scunthorpe community "awash with methadone"', BBC, 25.01.11
78. 'Teenage ketamine problems rising, drug charities warn', *The Guardian*, J. Doward, 01.05.11
79. Morris, H., 'Interview with a ketamine chemist', *Vice*, vol. 9 (2); p. 70
80. The Misuse of Drugs Act 1971 (Amendment) Order 2009
81. Ralph Metzner, 1983 Conference on Psychedelics and Spirituality. Cited in Eisner, 1989; pp. 33-4

Chapter Six: The Art of Suppression

1. Kerr; p. 226
2. Okrent; p. 355
3. Gemperlein, J., 'Full of Fury: Carry Nation', *Obit*, 07.06.2011
4. 'Prohibition worked', *Chicago Sun-Times*, 18.08.1988
5. *Ibid.*
6. Miron, J & Zweibel, J., 'Alcohol consumption during Prohibition', *American Economic Review*, vol. 81 (2), May 1991; pp. 242-247
7. 'Prohibition worked', *Chicago Sun-Times*, 18.08.88
8. Blocker, J. S., 'Did Prohibition really work?', *American Journal of Public Health*, vol. 96 (2), February 2006; pp. 237-238
9. 'Free to be slaves—the real point of the drugs debate', *Mail on Sunday*, Peter Hitchens, 02.11.09
10. *Ibid.*
11. Sinclair, U., *The Wet Parade*, T. Werner Laurie, 1931; p. 449
12. For example, Kerr (1985; p. 276) and Blocker (2006)
13. Miron, J. & Zweibel, J., 'Alcohol consumption during Prohibition', *American Economic Review*, vol. 81 (2), May 1991; pp. 242-7
14. Dills, A. and Miron, J., 'Alcohol Prohibition and Cirrhosis', *American Law and Economics Review*, vol. 6 (2), 2004
15. Dills, A. *et al.*, 'The effect of alcohol prohibition on alcohol consumption: evidence from drunkenness arrests', *Economics Letters*, 86, 2005; pp. 279-84
16. Blocker, J. S., 'Did Prohibition really work?', *American Journal of Public Health*, vol. 96 (2), February 2006; pp. 237-8

Notes

17. Data for 1850-2007 come from 'Apparent per capita ethanol consumption for the United States, 1850–2007 (Gallons of ethanol, based on population age 15 and older prior to 1970 and on population age 14 and other thereafter)', National Institute on Alcohol Abuse and Alcoholism. Data for 1790-1840 come from Lender, M. & Martin, J. K., *Drinking in America: A History*, Free Press; p. 184.

18. http://www.ias.org.uk/aboutus/who_we_are.html

19. Alliance House Foundation, *Financial statements for the year ended 31 March 2010*, Charity Commission ('Objectives and activities'); p. 3

20. Edwards, R. *et al.*, 'Daring to dream: reactions to tobacco endgame ideas among policy-makers, media and public health practitioners', *BMC Public Health,* vol. 11 (580), July 2011

21. Givel, M. S., 'History of Bhutan's prohibition of cigarettes: Implications for neo-prohibitionists and their critics', *International Journal of Drug Policy*, 22 (4), 2001; pp. 306-310

22. 'EU Tobacco Products Directive: Position Paper (09/11/10)', Pfizer

23. For example, see Di Castelnuovo, A. *et al.*, 'Alcohol dosing and total mortality in men and women', *Archives of Internal Medicine*, 166; pp. 2437-2445 and Holahan, C.J., 'Late-life alcohol consumption and 20-year mortality', *Alcoholism: Clinical and Experimental Research*, vol. 34 (11), Nov. 2010; pp. 1-11. For an overview of the protective effect of alcohol on the heart, see Ronksley, P., *et al.*, 'Association of alcohol consumption with selected cardiovascular disease outcomes: a systematic review and meta-analysis', *British Medical Journal*, 342, Feb. 2011

24. Goldacre, B., *Bad Science*, Fourth Estate, 2008; pp. 91-92

25. 'Cigs war won: Now cancer campaigners set their sights on beer', news.com.au, Malcolm Farr, 06.07.11

26. 'There is no such thing as a safe level of alcohol consumption', *The Guardian*, Nutt, D., 07.03.11

27. 'I am not a prohibitionist', *The Guardian*, Nutt, D., 05.11.10

28. 'Supermarkets urged to keep alcohol separate', BBC, 01.03.11. For Nutt's alcohol control strategy, see Nutt, D., 'Damming the flood: 21 principles to underpin a new approach to alcohol', http://profdavidnutt.wordpress.com/2010/08/

29. Courtwright; p. 4

30. Davenport-Hines; p. ix

31. Collin; p. 301

32. Davenport-Hines, 2001

33. 'Animals on drugs: 11 unlikely highs', *New Scientist*, R. Hooper, 25.06.09

34. Hart, C. *et al.*, 'Cause specific mortality, social position, and obesity among women who had never smoked: 28 year cohort study', *British Medical Journal*, 342, June 2011

35. Baum, D., *Smoke and Mirrors*, Little, Brown, 1996; p. 24

36. Stevenson, R., *Winning the War on Drugs*, Institute of Economic Affairs, 1997; p. 33

37. Musto; p. 5

38. Miron, J.A. & Zweibel, J., 'Alcohol consumption during Prohibition', *American Economic Review*, Vol. 81 (2), May 1991; p. 246

39. 'Making Sense of Drugs and Crime', Scottish Consortium on Crime & Criminal Justice; pp. 25-26

40. Joao Goulao, speaking at the International Harm Reduction Conference, Beirut, April 2011

41. 'Drugs in Portugal: Did decriminalization work?' *Time*, M. Szalavitz, 26.04.09 (See also Greenwald, G., *Drug decriminalisation in Portugal: Lessons for creating fair and successful drug policies*, Cato Institute, 2009)

42. Van den Brink, W., 'Forum: decriminalization of cannabis', *Current Opinion in Psychiatry* (2008), online at: http://www.encod.org/info/IMG/pdf/Brink_Decriminalization_Cannabis_2008.pdf

43. Advisory Council on the Misuse of Drugs, *Cannabis: Classification and Public Health*, Home Office, 2008; p. 18

44. 'The cannabis conundrum', *The Guardian*, D. Nutt, 29.10.09

45. 'Age standardised hospital episode rate for schizophrenia, people aged 15-74 years, 2005/06', London Health Observatory

46. Degenhardt, L., 'Testing hypotheses about the relationship between cannabis and psychosis', *Drug and Alcohol Dependence*, 71, 2003; pp. 37-48

47. Davenport-Hines; p. 182

48. 'Merry Xmas from Uncle Sam: poison rum', *Daily News*, J. Maeder, 28.03.00

49. 'Treatment of injecting drug users with HIV/AIDS: promoting access and optimizing service delivery', World Health Organisation, 2006; p. 1

50. http://www.avert.org/injecting.htm

51. Nelson *et al.*, 'Global epidemiology of hepatitis B and hepatitis C in people who inject drugs: results of systematic reviews', *The Lancet*, 28 July 2011

52. 'The price of Colombia's drug war', *Colombia Reports*, G. Cano, 25.01.10

53. Miron, J. & Zweibel, J., 'Alcohol consumption during Prohibition', *American Economic Review*, vol. 81 (2), May 1991; p. 246

54. Gamblers are able to place themselves on a register which bans them from all casinos worldwide. See www.bancop.net

55. *Howard Marks on Drugs* (film), Current UK, 2010

56. 'Professor David Nutt designs 'harm-free' alcohol', *The Times*, M. Chittenden, 14.03.10

57. Brown, R. H., *Forbidden Substances*, unpublished manuscript

58. Musto; p. 58

59. Thornton, M. & Bowmaker, S., 'Recreational drugs' in *Prohibitions* (ed. John Meadowcroft), Institute of Economic Affairs, 2008; p. 60

60. Mennell, S. J., 'Prohibition: a sociological view', *Journal of American Studies*, vol. 3 (2), Dec. 1969; p. 172

61. Cohen, S., *Folk Devils and Moral Panics*, Routledge, 2002; p. 38

Index